Guiltless Pleasures

Guiltless Pleasures

A DAVID STERRITT FILM READER

UNIVERSITY PRESS OF MISSISSIPPI / JACKSON

www.upress.state.ms.us

The University Press of Mississippi is a member of the Association of American University Presses.

Frontis: courtesy of the author

First Edition 2005

Library of Congress Cataloging-in-Publication Data

Sterritt, David.
    Guiltless pleasures : a David Sterritt film reader. — 1st ed.
        p. cm.
    Includes index.
    ISBN 1-57806-780-4 (cloth : alk. paper)
    ISBN 1-57806-818-5 (paper : alk. paper)
1. Motion pictures. I. Title.
    PN1994.S816 2005
    791.43—dc22   2004029419

British Library Cataloging-in-Publication Data available

FOR CRAIG, JEREMY, TANYA, AND MIKITA

CONTENTS

ACKNOWLEDGMENTS

"Fumbling in the Dark" is drawn from two *Christian Science Monitor* articles: "The Adventures of Movieman," 2 September 2000; and "Criticized," 21 January 2000. Copyright 2000 by The Christian Science Publishing Society; used with permission.

"Films, Fatigue, and Why a Critic's Opinion Is Just as Iffy as Yours" is a revised version of "How 'Festival Overload Syndrome' Affects Critics," published in *The Chronicle of Higher Education* 46:48 (4 August 2000).

"Cinephilia, Cinemania, Cinema" is drawn from "For Cinemaniacs, Moviegoing Is a 24/7 Way of Life," *The Christian Science Monitor* (23 April 2004); copyright 2004 by The Christian Science Publishing Society; used with permission; and "Essay 3" in Steve Erickson, ed., "Permanent Ghosts: Cinephilia in the Age of the Internet and Video," *Senses of Cinema* (www.sensesofcinema.com) 4 (March 2000) and 5 (April 2000); used with permission.

"Hollywood Players Who've Made a Difference" draws on four *Christian Science Monitor* articles: "Confessions of a John Cassavetes Fan," 11 September 1980; "Play 'Mystic' for Me," 10 October 2003; "Steve Martin Is No Fool—And Makes Films to Prove It," 15 November 1984; and "About Jack," 13 December 2002. Copyrights 1980, 2003, 1984, 2002 by The Christian Science Publishing Society; used with permission.

"Defining the Situation" is a revised version of an essay presented in the *Ventures in Research* journal and lecture series, Long Island University, 2001.

"Novelists and Their Movies" draws on three *Christian Science Monitor* articles: "Novelist Mailer Turns His Latest Book into a Movie," 4 September 1987; "E. L. Doctorow's Collaboration with the 'Enemy,'" 13 October 1983; and "First a Novelist, Now a Screenwriter," 4 February 2000. Copyrights 1987, 1983, 2000 by The Christian Science Publishing Society; used with permission.

"Allegory and Enigma" is a revised version of an essay written with Mikita Brottman and published in *The Chronicle of Higher Education* 48:17 (21 December 2001).

"Life Isn't Sweet" is an expanded version of essays published in *The Chronicle of High Education* (October 2004) and in *Fires Were Started: British Cinema Under Thatcher*, second edition, ed. Lester Friedman (London: Wallflower Press, 2005) as "Low Hopes: Mike Leigh Meets Margaret Thatcher"; used with permission.

"Monty Python" is a revised version of an essay written with Lucille Rhodes and published in *Cineaste* 26:4 (Fall 2001); used with permission.

"Creepies, Crawlies, Conundrums" is a revised version of an article written with Mikita Brottman and published in *The Chronicle of Higher Education* 49:21 (23 January 2003) as "*Spider* Reveals a More Nuanced Cronenberg."

"*Fargo*" is a slightly revised version of "*Fargo* in Context: The Middle of Nowhere?" in *The Coen Brothers'* Fargo, ed. William Luhr (London: Cambridge University Press, 2004). Copyright 2004 by Cambridge University Press; used with permission.

"Coppola, Vietnam, and the Ambivalent 1970s" is a revised version of an essay published in *The Chronicle of Higher Education* 47:47 (3 August 2001) as "Coppola, *Apocalypse Now*, and the Ambivalent 70s."

"Representing Atrocity" is a slightly different version of an essay published in *Film and Television After 9/11*, ed. Wheeler Winston Dixon (Carbondale: Southern Illinois University Press, 2004); used with permission. Earlier versions were given as the keynote address "Identity and Self-Representation: Cinematic Challenges and Opportunities" at the Conference of American Jewish Film Festivals presented by the National Foundation for Jewish Culture in Washington, D.C., 2001, and as an academic paper at the Society for Cinema and Media Studies in Minneapolis in 2003 in a panel on "Images of Suffering."

"Thanatos ex Machina" was published in *Car Crash Culture*, ed. Mikita Brottman (New York: Palgrave, 2002); used with permission. This essay was also published in *Senses of Cinema* (www.sensesofcinema.com) 14 (June 2001).

"Noé Stands Alone" is a revised version of "*Irréversible*," written with Mikita Brottman and published in *Film Quarterly* 57:2 (Winter 2003); used with permission.

"*Time Code*" was written at the request of *Scenario* magazine.

"Renaldo & Clara Meet John Cage" is a revised version of an essay published by *Senses of Cinema* (www.sensesofcinema.com) 5 (April 2000); used with permission. An earlier version was presented at the 2000 conference of the Society for Cinema Studies in Chicago in a panel on "Giving Hollywood the Slip (page): The Carnivalesque in Musical Movies," co-chaired by David Sterritt and Martha P. Nochimson.

"Challenging the Eye" is drawn from three *Christian Science Monitor* articles: "For Ken Jacobs, Moviemaking Is a Voyage of Discovery," 31 October 1989; "His Message: Film Is an Art," 30 April 1981; and "Robert Wilson," 12 March 1986. Copyright 1989, 1981, 1986 by The Christian Science Publishing Society; used with permission.

"Many Selves" was written on request for a forthcoming volume on the cinema of Willie Varela.

INTRODUCTION

Some years ago, *Film Comment* magazine introduced a feature called "Guilty Pleasures," in which invited filmmakers or other cinephiles list around a dozen movies they can't help loving even though they feel they really shouldn't—because the pictures are too silly, too offensive, too obscure, too lowbrow to praise in polite company, or perhaps too highbrow to suit a carefully cultivated "entertainment" image.

I've long enjoyed this feature, and for ages I never thought of questioning the premise behind it. Then a film-loving friend checked it out on my recommendation, and promptly asked me why any genuine pleasure should be considered guilty—especially where culture is concerned, since its manifestations are safely bounded by the screen, stage, or page.

I realized it in a flash: She's right. Pleasures are pleasures, and calling some of them "guilty" is usually a way of being cute or coy, not truly admitting to some kind of aesthetic misdemeanor. My friend's remark made me remember a conversation I'd had with playwright and occasional filmmaker Richard Foreman in his lower Manhattan loft, when he said he'd never been a drug taker, even in the sixties—his challenge was to rein in his teeming subconscious, not let it take over—but he sympathized with people who did, because they wanted to embrace the polymorphous perversity of their imaginations, just as he does by creating art.

For me, the inner journeys we take by artistic means (as either creators or consumers) are an enormously large part of what makes life worth living. Some people find this sense of liberation through *Casablanca* or *Gone With the Wind*, some through *Taxi Driver* or *Halloween*, some through *The Sin of Harold Diddlebock* or *Pretty Woman*, some through *Pink Flamingos* or *Flaming Creatures*, some through *The Wind Will Carry Us* or *Mysterious Object at Noon*, some through *Fahrenheit 9/11* or *The Passion of the Christ*, some through *Early Summer* or *Last Year at Marienbad*, which actually appeared on someone's "guilty pleasures" list. And so on, forever and ever, cinema without end. Which of these vehicles is less or more than admirable if it frees the mind and soul from what Foreman calls our "bloodless, dead, worker-bee-like society" for an hour and a half, a minute and a half, even a magical second or two along the way? This is the alchemy of art, and there's no reason to feel guilty about it.

This said, I'm the first to acknowledge that many pleasures don't come quickly or easily, but must be acquired and cultivated before they can be savored. Some of my favorite films of all time first piqued my curiosity because I found them amazingly hard to understand (*Hiroshima mon amour, Dog Star Man*) or to tolerate (*Faces, Numéro Deux*) despite their reputations, and I wanted to dig under their skins so I could understand what *other* people saw in them. This meant spending significant time with movies I didn't much like at the moment, learning to speak their language so I could make informed assessments of what (if anything) they had to say. If a film still struck me as glib, facile, or pretentious after I'd figured out its logic, lingo, and modus operandi, I'd at least have the satisfaction of hating it properly and thoroughly, to paraphrase Nam June Paik, the great video artist. But often I discovered layers, facets, and dimensions that I'd simply missed on first acquaintance, and that helped me toward ample artistic rewards once I tuned into their elusive wavelength.

These are the movies I've enjoyed most in my career as a critic, professor, and programmer, and they're the ones that lend this book its rationale. Some of the films, filmmakers, and subjects I write about are wildly far from the mainstream; others have undeniable roots in the money-driven systems of commercial cinema; others are somewhere in between. But each reflects a wish to challenge the norms and mores of our ever-more-constricted era, and for me that wish is the source of its interest and validity. What the movie world needs most is more imaginative artists, more adventurous commentators, and more intuitive, open-minded audiences. This book, comprising material written over many years for many publications, is an effort to support and encourage all of the above.

My fascination with movies that don't follow Hollywood's usual pathways—with films and videos that evade what's sometimes called the "excessively obvious" style of standard commercial fare—has played a strong role in shaping my career, and I'll give a brief account of this as a way of explaining the overall tone of the essays that follow. I went to Hollywood movies frequently as a child and teenager in a suburban Long Island town, but it never dawned on me that they might be taken as seriously as literature, drama, or music, about which I was far more excited. Or rather, it dawned on me exactly once, when I ran across Arthur Knight's book *The Liveliest Art* on the paperback rack in a local drugstore. Thrilled with the hitherto undreamed-of notion that film might be art, I bought the book and started reading it—only to find it was a hopelessly dull compendium of dates, names, and titles that made the liveliest art seem deader than a doornail.

My second epiphany was the one that stuck. During my college days at Boston University in the 1960s a friend suggested we take in a movie, and I suggested a double bill of *Hiroshima mon amour* and *Last Year at Marienbad*, which were playing for a few days at the Fine Arts, a nearby "art" theater. The main rationale for my choice was that two "art" films for a dollar was a bargain compared with the slightly higher ticket price at theaters showing more popular pictures. Both movies transfixed and exhilarated me, not because I understood them—in fact, they utterly baffled me—but because I'd never realized a movie could *be* baffling, challenging, and drastically different from anything I'd encountered in other forms of culture. Eager to plumb these mysteries, I discovered the end-lessly surprising range and variety of international art cinema via film-society and repertory-theater programs of Ingmar Bergman, the Italian neorealists, and the giants of the French New Wave, among others. Aware of the danger that such stuff might make me a cinema snob, I also kept watching as many worthwhile Holly-wood movies as I could, testing the newly formulated "auteur the-ory" embraced by some of my favorite critics and giving myself a de-facto course in film history at a time when cinema classes weren't remotely as ubiquitous in universities as they are today.

Shortly before graduating from college I took an entry-level job at *The Christian Science Monitor* for the sole reason that I had run out of money and needed to pay the rent. I expected to work there a few months and then move to some other field. (I had no idea what field, but I was sure it wouldn't involve journalism, which didn't interest me at all.) I wound up staying at the *Monitor* for decades, for three related reasons. One is that a longtime *Monitor* writer decided to retire, opening up a full-time critic job that the editors surprisingly offered to me. Another is that this period (the late '6os) is precisely when some thoughtful American publications started allowing themselves to take thoughtful views of popular culture—for instance, *The New Yorker* regularly printed Ellen Willis's writing on rock music. The third is that the very lowliness of my position struck me as one of its best assets. I was second or third stringer to all the older critics who wrote about film, theater, and music, which meant I was assigned to review the movies, plays, and concerts they didn't feel like bothering with—often the most excit-ing things around, precisely because they were low-profile events devised by people more interested in creativity than profits. I also liked writing about different cultural areas, since despite my love of film I was always content to skip a bad movie for a good music recital or theater piece. After a few years I moved to New York as the paper's first-string film critic and second-string everything else, seeing as many films as possible without missing stage works by Robert Wilson and Elizabeth LeCompte, concerts by Meredith Monk and the Philip Glass Ensemble, dance pieces by Merce Cunningham and Paul Taylor, and too much else to remember, much less mention here. These were very rewarding years, full of artistic experiences that often took me by surprise yet were subtly linked by the strong interest in visual expression that molded and propelled much of that period's experimental and avant-garde work in all sorts of media and disciplines.

During this period—from the late '6os through the early '8os, approximately—the *Monitor* largely allowed its critics to decide what was important, what deserved column inches in the paper's limited space, and what our comparatively intelligent readership would be interested in. Then things changed. The church that owns and publishes the paper tried to update its appeal by starting a TV branch called The Monitor Channel and a radio branch called Monitor Radio, both of which dramatically drained the newspaper's resources before eventually falling apart. New editors, struggling with scant success to rebuild the paper's drastically lowered circulation, decided the arts section should be "fun," thereby losing many of the readers that had remained loyal until then while gaining few replacements for them. This seemed woefully predictable to me, since the news side of the *Monitor* retained its commitment to serious reporting—especially of international affairs—resulting in a schizoid periodical whose front pages and back pages (news and features, roughly speaking) now reached out to different sensibilities (information-seeking and "fun"-seeking, roughly speaking) that had little in common. The bottom line for me was constantly shrinking space, sharply reduced discretion in what I wrote about, and continual combat with editors who resisted film-related subjects they didn't consider "fun" or "uplifting," and who took an attitude toward foreign film that (in a paper globally renowned for its overseas news coverage!) verged in some cases on outright hostility. There have been ups and downs, ebbs and flows, flashes of brightness and days of darkness in subsequent years, but at this writing the basic situation remains as I've described it.

My response to the newspaper's declining thoughtfulness and enterprise in cultural matters was not to seek a job at another publication—most of them are even worse—but to diversify, as popular parlance put it at the time. My friend Renée Shafransky was about to make her film-producing debut with *Variety*, a wonderfully transgressive movie written by Kathy Acker and directed by Bette Gordon, and she asked me if I would take over her adjunct professorship at Long Island University, teaching film history. I'd always imagined teaching as a healthy complement to writing—oral and interactive as opposed to textual and solitary—so I decided to give it a try. I enjoyed it enough to get a similar appointment in what was then the Graduate Film Division at Columbia University, but I also learned that without a PhD no full-time professor job (and no full-time professor salary) was likely to come my way. Since reading film history and theory had become my avocations anyway, it occurred to me that I could get some official credit for this by finally getting around to graduate school. I enrolled in the Department of Cinema Studies at New York University at the ripe old age of forty-five and emerged four years later with master's and doctoral degrees. During the last of those years LIU offered me a full-time professorship that had just opened up, and shortly afterward I increased my Columbia courses to three or four a year. All of which, combined with my ongoing *Monitor* career, has kept me from hanging around pool halls for the past few decades.

One reason for mentioning these things is to remind people it's never too late to go back to school, as the cliché has it, and in fact it can be downright pleasurable. Another reason is to point out the diversity of professions opened up by an interest in cinema. I think of this in a sort of Copernican way, with filmmaking at the center and an array of ancillary activities—criticism, teaching, programming, archiving, restoration work—orbiting around it as fully fledged fields in their own rights. I have accumulated many good years (and a few bad ones) in criticism, quite a few good years (with no really bad ones) in teaching, and several good years (the best of all) in programming, as a member of the New York Film Festival's selection committee, a five-member group that assembles the annual program for Lincoln Center's most prominent cinema event. The essays in this volume are inflected and inspired by all these professional experiences, plus countless personal ones that remain mostly between the lines because—unlike some critics—it's never been my habit to write "confessional columns," as my distinguished colleague Andrew Sarris once described his own writings.

This book comprises articles I've written over the past twenty-five years or so, all revised to some degree and in some cases combined with others to produce a more comprehensive look at a particular subject. Most of the essays were written in the more recent periods of my career, since the pieces I wrote before my heavy involvement with academia tend to be less substantial, more (literally) journalistic in approach. I can already hear the sound of some film-book critic typing the word "hodgepodge" in a lukewarm (or worse) review (that term is voguish in current reviewing) so I'll accept the description in advance. I myself have nothing against diversified essay collections, whose shifts of tone, style, and subject can keep both writers and readers on their intellectual toes as long as the varied components have solid underlying links—in this case my gravitation toward adventurous filmmaking and, more implicitly, my belief that worthwhile things can be conveyed in the (notably different) vocabularies of journalism and academic prose. Loosely speaking, the early pieces here are more casual and conversational, the later ones denser and more demanding.

The collection opens with three different takes on the questions I'm asked most about my work as a movie reviewer: What's it like to be one, how do I select what to see, and what makes me think my opinion is better than anyone else's, anyway? Cutting to the chase, the answer to the last question is that my opinion is no more

legitimate than yours at all, but it's probably more considered—
that is, I've probably spent more time thinking about it—and presumably it's lively to read, whether or not you agree with a word of
it. (If it's not at least a little successful on the latter level, you'd presumably toss this book out the window and we wouldn't be having
this discussion.)

The first of these essays, "Fumbling in the Dark, or, Sorrows of a
Film Critic," started with a *Monitor* editor's request for a behind-
the-scenes look at what I do for the paper. At about the same time
I wrote a *Monitor* article about a controversy that was brewing
around the year 2000, sparked by David Denby's much-discussed
New Yorker essay arguing that film criticism has entered a state of
decline and decadence, if not outright and irreversible exhaus-
tion. I have combined these pieces into a general overview of how
it feels to be a film critic at a time when some smart, savvy reviewers are starting to wonder if the state of the art might have become
moribund despite our own best efforts.

The second essay, "Films, Fatigue, and Why a Critic's Opinions
Are Just as Iffy as Yours," takes on related themes, using a droll
(and slightly unsettling) experience I had at Cannes as the starting
point for a look at how even sophisticated critics are affected by
context, environment, and mood while viewing the movies they
write about, at multiplexes and world-famed festivals alike.

The third, "Cinephilia, Cinemania, Cinema," was written in
response to a pair of documents, one written and one filmed, that
appeared a few years apart from each other: Susan Sontag's essay
"The Decay of Cinema," a eulogy for cinephilia published by the
New York Times in 1996, and the 2004 nonfiction film *Cinemania*, a
portrait of several obsessive New York movie buffs. Combining a
Monitor article about the *Cinemania* documentary with a 1999 essay
written for a series on cinephilia posted by New York critic Steve
Erickson on the admirable *Senses of Cinema* website, this piece pon-
ders the relationship among the three terms given in the title.
It also takes a position on the question of whether not just film

criticism but film itself may be about to die, if it isn't already dead. In each of these essays, the kind of cinema that's in the back or forefront of my mind—usually both—is the kind I've described earlier in this introduction: the adventurous, the audacious, the challenging. Ditto for the kind of criticism I care about. The rest is consumer-guide dross, of which I've written my fair share, and little of which (he said hopefully) you'll find in this collection.

The volume then shifts gears to deal more with specific film-makers and films. The people named in the title of "Hollywood Players Who've Made a Difference: Cassavetes, Eastwood, Martin, Nicholson" are all Hollywood figures—John Cassavetes, Clint Eastwood, Steve Martin, Jack Nicholson—yet each has shown a venturesome side at key moments of his career, directing and/or acting in movies that push the envelope of what Hollywood pictures usually see themselves as able to accomplish within the standard paradigms of box-office safety. Drawing on *Monitor* articles I wrote precisely because I was surprised by the boldness of particular movies they had made, this essay centers on such films as Eastwood's daring *Bird*, about jazz musician Charlie Parker; the respected *About Schmidt*, directed by Alexander Payne and a capstone of Nicholson's impressive oeuvre; the comedy *All of Me*, for which the New York Film Critics Circle gave Martin its award as best actor of the year; and Cassavetes's whole writing/directing career, which was always compelling even in its weaker moments. It was their clout as audience-pleasing stars that enabled these four to follow their own lights and take their own chances in such projects, two of which (the exceptions are *Bird* and most of Cassavetes's films, alas) provided the bonus of doing well commercially.

"Defining the Situation: Brando, Role-Playing, and the Western as Performance Art," first published in the LIU journal *Ventures in Research*, takes a more scholarly tack as it zeroes in on Marlon Brando—who died just a few weeks before this writing, at eighty-one years old—and *One-Eyed Jacks*, the only film he directed during his troubled, fitful career. Using ideas from sociology and performance studies, I explore Brando's strategy of foregrounding issues of acting itself as he directs his own portrayal of a western character who breaks many of the genre's molds, as does the film itself. I have not written a great deal on acting as such, so I am pleased to use this essay as a means of conveying some of my ideas on this endlessly rich subject.

"Novelists and Their Movies" discusses the American authors Norman Mailer, E. L. Doctorow, and John Irving, with reference to their participation in adaptations of their own work, incorporating discussions with the novelists and commentary on the films in question. Drawn from *Monitor* articles I wrote in 1983, 1987, and 2000, it uses diverse movies as its three-pronged focus: *Daniel*, the Sidney Lumet drama adapted from *The Book of Daniel*, a hotly debated Doctorow novel; *Tough Guys Don't Dance*, a largely forgotten Mailer melodrama based on a largely forgotten Mailer book; and *The Cider House Rules*, adapted from his own novel by Irving, who won an Academy Award for his efforts. I've had the opportunity to discuss the complex relationships between novels and films with a wide assortment of writers, including a memorable 2001 session at the Lake Placid Film Forum where I moderated a panel with Russell Banks and William Kennedy among its members. It is a subject I always find invigorating.

The next essay, "Allegory and Enigma: The Enduring Fascination of Fantasy," is an expanded version of a 2001 article I wrote for *The Chronicle of Higher Education* with Mikita Brottman, who has collaborated with me on many occasions. (Several of the pieces in this book are as much her work as mine, and I acknowledge every such collaboration with gratitude and love in this introduction.) This brief exploration of fantasy's enduring appeal was written in response to the huge anticipation (and, subsequently, the huge success) of Chris Columbus's screen adaptation of J. K. Rowling's novel *Harry Potter and the Sorcerer's Stone*, a phenomenal bestseller if ever there was one. Since the first installment of the *Lord of the Rings* film series was also barreling toward multiplexes around the world, it seemed a good moment to reflect on why fantasy is such an important genre in virtually all times, societies, and regions of the world. The insanely overrated *Rings* series became insanely popular, and remains so in "extended" versions (as if the movies weren't endlessly long to begin with!) on video-store shelves, and readers will imagine Harry Potter as a mainstay of the Hogwarts School of Witchcraft and Wizardry for the foreseeable future; so this essay remains relevant in its particulars as well as its more sweeping observations.

I wrote "Life Isn't Sweet: The Movies of Mike Leigh" in a different version ("Low Hopes: Mike Leigh Meets Margaret Thatcher") for an expanded edition of Lester D. Friedman's important book *British Cinema Under Thatcher: Fires Were Started* in 2004. The longer version in this volume takes on more of Leigh's career in more detail, exploring (among other things) the improvisational methods he uses to initiate and mold his works, the special resonance his movies have for American as well as British audiences, and the usefulness of ideas from Italian philosopher Giorgio Agamben in understanding the centrality of gesture (visual and verbal) to what I call Leigh's cinema of observation. The presence of a political dimension in Leigh's films is a key focal point here, as in the original version of the essay, not only because politics is at the heart of the book for which I first wrote it, but (more importantly) because this aspect of Leigh's cinematic sensibility has often been overlooked, undervalued, and misconstrued, and I want to do my bit in setting the record straight.

Staying on the English side of the Atlantic a little longer, I follow the Leigh essay with something, well, completely different. "Monty Python: Lust for Glory" is a critical overview of the British comedy troupe's career in film and video. And perhaps it's not so different after all, since I wrote it for the politically alert American film magazine *Cineaste*, and was therefore able to indulge my interest in the political currents that sometimes surge beneath the surface of what seem to be "merely" comical, satirical works. *Life of Brian* gets privileged treatment for that reason, but the Pythons' social and cultural critiques extend much further than that dazzling film, as might be expected from a troupe whose British members have roots in the cerebral halls of Oxbridge and whose single American member (Terry Gilliam) transplanted his life and career to Britain as a direct result of his raging disgust with the United States government in the 1960s era. Like the Pythons' other affiliates, he is often considered an "entertainer," and an uneven one at that. Look more deeply into their collected works, though, and you'll find more than meets the eye on first acquaintance. That deeper look is what I hope to encourage here, along with an enhanced appreciation of Python links with Dadaism, Surrealism, exquisitely honed contempt for the British Broadcasting Corporation, and a profound investment in the Holy Fool brand of visionary craziness.

Turning to Canadian film, I wrote "Creepies, Crawlies, Conundrums: David Cronenberg Comes of Age" with Mikita Brottman soon after we'd seen his 2003 psychodrama *Spider* at the Cannes festival. Published by the *Chronicle of Higher Education* in a slightly shorter version, the essay reflects our interest in a protean filmmaker whose most insightful works (including *Dead Ringers* and *Spider* itself) tend to be superficially hyped by cultists, praised with faint damns by critics, and usually both. Cronenberg has made many minor movies, but his growth as an artist has been as undeniable and unmistakable as it's been sporadic and patchy. At this writing, *Spider* shows him reaching new levels of thoughtfulness and maturity, and while it's hard to predict what he'll do in coming years, his status as a truly important filmmaker seems more strongly established than ever.

"*Fargo*: The Middle of Nowhere?" was written for *The Coen Brothers' Fargo*, a collection of essays edited by William Luhr, most of which were written by members and associates of the Columbia University Seminar on Cinema and Interdisciplinary Interpretation, a faculty seminar (one of about seventy-five sponsored by Columbia in sundry academic fields) that Bill and I have co-chaired for several years. Bill asked me for a wide-ranging article to open his anthology on this remarkable movie by director Joel Coen and producer Ethan Coen, and that's what I sat down to write. If nothing else, the film's importance justifies reprinting it here in a slightly revised version.

"Coppola, Vietnam, and the Ambivalent 1970s" also deals with a landmark American movie. I wrote it for the *Chronicle of Higher Education* in 2001 after seeing the long-delayed "director's cut" called *Apocalypse Now Redux* in Cannes, where it was received with deserved (if not unanimous) enthusiasm. Every critic in sight immediately started scribbling about the revised edition of the 1979 classic, but hardly anyone seemed very interested in the movie's reflections not only of the Vietnam war but also of a vast irresolution within American culture at large, encompassing issues ranging from the mass media's political impact to the nature and activities of the United States film industry, which Coppola seemed intent on subverting with his left hand and shoring up with his right. As my title indicates, this sociocultural ambivalence became my vantage point on *Apocalypse Now* and what it has implicitly represented for moviegoers of my generation.

"Representing Atrocity: From the Holocaust to September 11" has more complicated origins. I've been invited to participate in occasional activities by the National Foundation for Jewish Culture, and in early 2001 this worthy organization asked me to give the keynote address at its annual Conference of American Jewish Film Festivals, of which festivals there are quite a few in various locations. The conference was scheduled for November, and I was still working out my topic when the September 11 attacks on New York and Washington, D.C., took place. At that time I lived in a Broadway apartment building that was a one-minute walk from the Twin Towers of the World Trade Center, and one of my sons lived with his wife in another building equally close. I was in Canada at the Toronto film festival, slated to fly home that day, and when I heard the towers had gone down I was naturally frantic with worry until my family called to say they'd gotten out of Manhattan safely and were sitting out the remainder of the trauma at my other son's Brooklyn apartment. (All this was on my birthday, by the way.)

Back home and returning to work some days later, I knew my upcoming keynote speech would inevitably be inflected by the awful events that had just transpired. In fact, I felt, it shouldn't be merely inflected but actively shaped by the attacks, which reminded me in many ways of what I knew about the Holocaust and its horrors—its gratuitous cruelty, its largeness of scale, its mass killing in the names of faith and culture.

I've done a good deal of research on representations of the Holocaust in documentary film, and it struck me that reportage of the September 11 massacre—already flooding the media—at once recalled and contrasted with the many Holocaust histories brought to us by film and television over the years. On one hand, Holocaust accounts invariably contain little moving-image documentation, since little of that terror was captured by moving-picture cameras; on the other hand, events of 9/11 became internationally visible while they were still unfolding, thanks to omnipresent video cameras and instant TV coverage. Then again, Holocaust evils have been etched into our collective mind's eye for decades through images of atrocity filmed and photographed after the Nazi camps were liberated, whereas the physical containment of the damage inflicted on 9/11 rendered the death and destruction wrought there almost invisible to the eye.

These comparisons and contrasts seemed worthwhile to explore. So did my growing anger at the blitz of belligerent, increasingly vulgar 9/11 show biz that the American media started blasting almost immediately, hammering on aspects of the case that were readily turned into narrative (e.g., the hunt for Osama bin Laden) and grabbing hold of a nebulously defined "war on terror" to support commercially profitable "public affairs" journalism. I wrote my keynote talk with all this in mind, and delivered other versions at an LIU conference on "War and Peace: The Reality" and at the annual

Society for Cinema and Media Studies conclave in 2002, where my colleague Mikita Brottman gave a reciprocating paper that drew conclusions just the opposite from mine in at least one key respect—i.e., where I basically argue that less can be more where representations of real-life horror are concerned, she holds that a sort of knee-jerk denial makes us unwilling to face the very real atrocities we humans so frequently inflict on one another. She may well be correct. In any case, both of these essays are published in Wheeler Winston Dixon's smartly conceived collection *Film and Television After 9/11*, and mine is included here in a slightly modified version.

The essays I have introduced so far deal with diverse cinematic subjects and issues, linked (as noted earlier) by my fascination with modes of moving-image expression that challenge, redefine, or stretch the boundaries of the medium as it's conventionally thought of. That fundamental aspect of this book becomes more explicit in the pieces that follow, beginning with "Thanatos ex Machina: Godard Caresses the Dead," originally published in Dr. Brottman's anthology *Car Crash Culture*, comprising an extensive array of essays on the volume's eponymous subject. Jean-Luc Godard has been a pivotal figure for me since I saw *Breathless*, his first feature, during my college moviegoing years. I have written a book about his work (*The Films of Jean-Luc Godard: Seeing the Invisible*) and edited another (*Jean-Luc Godard: Interviews*) in addition to other reviews and articles I've devoted to him since my early days as a critic. Yet as of 2001 there was a Godard masterpiece I had never written about at length: *Contempt,* on which I was eager to expatiate, and which seemed a natural for the Brottman book since its indelible climax is a single, long-lasting shot of two main characters (played by Brigitte Bardot and Jack Palance, a perfect Godardian pair) lying dead in the aftermath of a fatal car collision that we've heard on the soundtrack while seeing a written "Adieu," the last word penned by Bardot's character before embarking on her fatal journey. *Contempt* is not an obscure film—critic

Colin MacCabe has called it postwar Europe's greatest work of art—but in today's parochial moviegoing climate it's known primarily to hardcore art-film buffs. I've finally written about it in order to remind readers of its excellence as well as to share a handful of my thoughts about it.

"Noé Stands Alone: An Experiment with Time" is a slightly revised version of an essay Dr. Brottman and I wrote for *Film Quarterly* after seeing the world premiere of *Irréversible* at the Cannes festival. It's a horrifying film in many ways—we didn't even make it out of the Palais des Festivals before Michel Ciment, the distinguished French critic and a longtime acquaintance of mine—was regaling us with a long list of instant arguments as to why no cineaste with a shred of moral fiber could tolerate it, much less defend it, for a moment. Well, *mon cher* Michel, we disagreed then and we disagree now. The case is made in this volume's essay, which begins with a Philip Larkin poem, one of Mikita's innumerable inspired ideas vis-à-vis Noé's film. (Somewhat later, she and John Waters introduced a screening of it at the Maryland Film Festival, where the inimitable John remarked that "only a straight filmmaker could think gay bars were so much fun," referring ironically to the early scene in the Rectum nightclub where a man's head is bashed to bits before our very eyes.) We aren't big admirers of Noé's previous feature, *Seul contre tous*, but we feel *Irréversible* is a truly important work that deserves far more serious attention than it has received.

I wrote "*Time Code*: Narrative Film and the Avant-Garde" on a commission for *Scenario* magazine, which then suspended publication just before my essay (illustrated by some of Mike Figgis's music-score-like screenplay) was due to appear. Figgis's film deepens for me each time I see it—it does the same for Figgis, he interestingly acknowledges—and I think it will emerge as a landmark work in the longer perspective of film history. My article is published here for the first time.

"Renaldo & Clara Meet John Cage: Aleatory Cinema and the Aesthetics of Incompetence" had its first incarnation as a paper I delivered at a Society for Cinema Studies conference in Chicago in 2000, on a panel called "Giving Hollywood the Slip(page): The Carnivalesque in Musical Movies," which I co-chaired. I prepared a somewhat different version—taking into account the feedback (some of it skeptical) that arose in the discussion portion of the panel session—when *Senses of Cinema* sent me an unexpected request to publish it. A final version, revised a tad more, appears here. The focus remains the same: how Bob Dylan and Frank Zappa, artists from the neighboring but different field of music, turn the disadvantage of inexperience into the advantage of experimentalism in their rare feature-filmmaking excursions.

Turning to avant-garde cinema in the most (metaphorically) hardcore sense, "Challenging the Eye: Three Avant-Garde Imagemakers" deals with the towering giant Stan Brakhage, the equally brilliant Ken Jacobs, and the utterly unique Robert Wilson, who is best known as a stage director but is also a gifted video artist. I could have added many other experimental filmmakers and video artists to this essay, such as my close friend Ernie Gehr, my late pal Warren Sonbert, or the infinitely inventive Bruce Conner, to name only three. Time and space are limited, though, and the three I've settled on nicely represent the broad spectrum of avant-garde imagemaking.

The collection ends with "Many Selves: Paradox and Poetry in the Cinema of Willie Varela," in ways the most specialized essay in the volume, since it zeroes in on a single moving-image artist who is not as well known as, say, the figures focused on in the previous article. I wrote this for a volume Varela hopes to publish in connection with his ongoing work as a filmmaker, videomaker, and professor, and I couldn't pass up this opportunity to afford him at least a little more recognition than he's received so far—not that he's an obscure figure within the circumscribed world of experimental film—and provide some guidance for any reader who might choose to seek out and attentively view his challenging, innovative work.

"I appropriate, therefore I am," is one of Varela's credos, and the same whimsical statement—construed more sweepingly—might be made by any good critic. We become experts on other people's work, which is a form of appropriation, but we try to formulate and convey our own perspectives on that work, which is a form of creativity, of originality, of having a publicly presented "I am" of our own. In discussing his artistry, the dauntingly intelligent Brakhage preferred the word "communion" to "communication," since it brought out the spiritual dimensions that implicitly informed his films and the urges that drove him to create them. I hope this book will serve, at least occasionally, as acts of communion between one critic and whatever readers are interested in exploring (if not necessarily agreeing with) a selected sample of his writing. That's the most I can hope for, and it's probably more than I *should* hope for, but a critic's lot is a modest one, so it'll have to do. Thanks for coming at least this far on the journey with me.

In the course of a career that's sometimes seemed more interminable than a *Lord of the Rings* movie even to me, one is helped in uncountable ways by uncountable people, which explains why I mention only a handful of them here. My gratitude goes to Seetha Srinivasan, director of the University Press of Mississippi, for proposing the idea of this collection some years ago, then waiting patiently for me to find the time to bring it together. I also thank Walter Biggins and the rest of Seetha's sterling staff. Thanks also to my Long Island University and Columbia University colleagues, two gracious and, well, collegial groups. I am grateful to the best *Monitor* writers and editors I've worked with over the years, and to the editors of various books and periodicals who have allowed me to reprint material here. I also want to single out such superior critical colleagues as Stuart Klawans of *The Nation*, Phillip Lopate of just about everywhere, and Andrew Sarris, easily the most influential of all critics (yes, Manny Farber and Pauline Kael included) on those of my generation. Affectionate thanks also to William Luhr, Sidney Gottlieb, Krin Gabbard, Cynthia Lucia, Christopher Sharrett, Pamela Grace, and all the members and associates of the

Columbia Seminar on cinema; and to my former colleagues on the New York Film Festival selection committee, especially Richard Peña, the world's most gifted programmer. Ditto to Wheeler Winston Dixon, Murray Pomerance, Ray Carney, Annette Insdorf, Susan Zeig, and . . .

And of course my son Craig Sterritt, my son Jeremy Sterritt and his unfailingly good-humored wife Tanya Van Sant, and the many friends we have in common.

And finally Mikita Brottman, who has given me more than she'll ever know—and this time I'm not referring to her collaboration on several of the essays in this volume, as mentioned above. Thank you. For everything.

Guiltless Pleasures

Fumbling in the Dark, or, Sorrows of a Film Critic

"How many movies do you see every week?"

That's one of the questions I'm most often asked about my work as a film critic. And it's one I can't accurately answer, for the excellent reason that I've never dared calculate the number.

I think of myself as averaging about a movie a day, and a little more if you count old pictures I revisit to research an article or prepare a class. But this doesn't count the film festivals I attend, where four-movie days aren't unusual. And when a festival is over, lots of releases have piled up while I was away. And if I speak at a cinema club, lecture at a museum, or do a guest shot on radio or television, more mandatory viewing may come with the job.

So naturally I tremble at the notion of adding this up. It probably comes to some ridiculously high number that would prompt some questions of my own: Is this a good life? Is it a life at all? Have we critics pulled the ultimate scam—getting paid for going to the movies—or have we hoodwinked ourselves by turning a refreshing pastime into a tiring, time-consuming chore?

Those are more things I don't want to contemplate, so let's move to the other question I'm most frequently asked: Where do critics see movies? In theaters or in cozy, crowd-free screening rooms like the one Roger Ebert inhabits on his TV show?

[3]

The answer is: both. Preview screenings come in two varieties, depending on the type of movie and the company that's releasing it.

Many films are previewed in screening rooms—small, comfortable auditoriums with a few rows of seats and a total absence of concession stands, which means nobody will be munching popcorn or crinkling wrappers during the picture. Critics like these minitheaters because they're clean, quiet, and dignified. You can almost feel like a grown-up watching the latest action yarn, gross-out comedy, or horror flick in such genteel surroundings.

Distributors aren't interested in making us feel like grown-ups, though, at least when they're peddling big-budget entertainment fare. Au contraire, they want critics to "ooh" and "aah" as uncritically as possible. So screening-room previews are usually reserved for intimate dramas, subtle comedies, and "art movies" from distant countries or little-known directors.

Expensive studio movies—or "audience pictures," as they're dubbed in the trade—are often unveiled in what I think of as "cattle-call screenings," craftily designed to encircle us critics with "regular people."

These previews take place in ordinary theaters with a few rows roped off for reviewers. The rest of the seats are filled with regular people who aren't regular at all, but invited guests who didn't pay for their seats any more than the critics did. They aren't chosen at random, either. Most are employees of the studio that's releasing the picture—in an extremely cheerful mood because they've gotten a freebie—or members of the movie's target audience, e.g., teenagers, if it's a youthful romance, or minority-group members, if it's an ethnic comedy. The theory behind these events is that the rollicking enjoyment of the regular people will induce the grumpy critics to lighten up and have a good time.

Most critics are less than fond of these crowded, sometimes noisy screenings. But they do have some legitimate value. As much as we like to think we're as normal as the next moviegoer, the fact is that no reviewer can anticipate all the tastes of the enormously diverse public that Hollywood movies aim for.

So watching a picture surrounded by members of its target audience can be helpful, revealing layers of entertainment value that the critic might not otherwise perceive. I vividly remember seeing the 1975 comedy *Let's Do It Again*, starring Bill Cosby and Sidney Poitier, at a jam-packed preview with a largely African-American audience. I would have enjoyed the movie under any circumstances—it's a funny if minor film—but the people around me were laughing at details of speech, gesture, and costume that I might not have noticed on my own. It was a valuable experience, reminding me that my personal responses aren't the only measure of a movie's worth.

Then again, those studios can be awfully cagey. A critic I know recalls a screening of *Top Gun* he attended in 1986—enjoying the calm and quiet of a studio-lot screening room until a few minutes before the lights went down, when a bus pulled up to the door and disgorged a mob of adolescent girls, clearly calculated to influence my colleague with their extroverted appreciation of Tom Cruise's manly charms. I suspect my colleague wouldn't have liked the picture anyway, but in this case the studio's machinations backfired.

So far I've been focusing on the movie-watching aspect of my job, but there's another part of the critic's life that people tend to forget: sitting at the keyboard and actually writing reviews. This is when the other activities of the profession—viewing films, talking with filmmakers, networking with other critics, and so on—must coalesce into an article that will convey not only my opinion of a film but also the competence of its craftsmanship, its relevance to our busy lives, the soundness of its ethical sense, and whether it's likely to appeal to the reader perusing today's paper, whose views on life may be very different from my own.

There's just so much you can squeeze into a six-hundred-word article, of course, but an ideal review accomplishes all of that and more. This brings to mind another question that's often just below the surface when people talk about movie critics. Are we real professionals with a useful trade? Or are we just wannabe directors, screenwriters, and stars, banging out reviews because we don't have the skill or savvy to make it in Hollywood ourselves?

It's likely that critics dream of showbiz success as frequently as other folks do—but no more frequently, and possibly even a tad less. One reason why it may be less is that we're in steady contact with Hollywood's products, so we don't have to work in Tinseltown to breathe its heady atmosphere.

Another reason is that we're not a gang of unemployable louts who've failed at filmmaking, but active writers whose line of work is a time-honored branch of journalism. I'm sure many of my colleagues would zip to Hollywood in a flash if they sold a screenplay, aced an audition, or persuaded a producer to part with a few million dollars. But just as many struggling filmmakers would happily zip into movie reviewing for its steady paychecks, interested readers, and freedom from the box-office blues.

I don't have a screenplay sitting in my drawer or a nifty "high concept" just waiting for the right producer. But with more than thirty years of reviewing behind me, I also have few illusions about the glitz and glamour of a critic's life. The day-to-day grind is full of mediocre movies that are little fun to watch or write about, and film festivals can be positively exhausting.

True, a masterpiece comes my way from time to time, and then I have the twin pleasures of discovering it and conveying the agreeable news to my readers. But to find those gems I have to sit through a daunting number of dull, disappointing, or downright terrible films. And sit through them I do, right through the closing credits. While other critics may walk out in a mid-screening huff, I prefer to let my disdain grow with every awful scene, anticipating the revenge I'll take when I get back to my keyboard.

Which brings me to one more question I'm occasionally asked: What keeps me going after all this time? The answer is simple, and I think many of my colleagues would say something similar. It's partly the pleasure of writing, and partly the pleasure of following an art and entertainment form that has a deeply rooted place in our society. But mostly it's a deep-down affection for the movies, coupled with a sort of idiot optimism that keeps me hoping for good cinema even after all the trash and gibberish I've been bombarded with over the years. Every time the lights go down there's a part of me that whispers, "Maybe it'll be good." I should know better by now, but I'm glad I don't.

So much for the assets and liabilities of being a professional critic. There's a larger issue that also needs addressing: Is movie reviewing itself in a state of acute crisis, decline, or decay?

Many film critics say yes. The first alarm was sounded in a widely read *New Yorker* article written in 1998 by David Denby, who became a staff reviewer for the magazine slightly later. Movie criticism is being dumbed down, he argued, as publications and broadcast outlets take an increasingly superficial view of film's artistic value and social role. Other pundits took up Denby's tone, lamenting a growing tendency for journalists to treat the art of cinema as nothing more meaningful than an excuse for munching popcorn at the multiplex.

Not every critic agrees, of course. Stuart Klawans, the exemplary film reviewer for *The Nation*, warns of a temptation to compare today's scene with a past that wasn't as rosy as nostalgic journalists like to imagine. When he was growing up in Chicago during the 1950s, he recalls, his family subscribed to the *Chicago Tribune*, which ran all its movie reviews under the byline Mae Tinee—a pun for "matinee," and a clear sign that the paper considered film coverage too frivolous to merit a real writer's name at the top of the column. So much for a Vanished Golden Age of Film Criticism.

This notwithstanding, a wide range of practicing critics do feel their profession is in decline. Moderating a panel on the subject at Colorado's respected Telluride Film Festival in 1998, film scholar Annette Insdorf cited the distinction drawn by legendary theater critic Walter Kerr between criticism and reviewing. The former aspires to in-depth discussion, Kerr argued, while the latter settles for quick opinions. Panelists acknowledged an escalating conflict between these approaches, and critics today often complain that reviewing is winning the battle.

Evidence for this includes the proliferation of "thumbs up or down" and "one to four stars" rating systems, which ignore the artistic and moral complexities of individual movies. (Several years ago the *Christian Science Monitor* started requiring me to use the "star-rating" system, and while I've had no choice but to comply, I've complained about it vehemently—and cogently, I think, since reasons for avoiding it are abundant—every chance I've gotten.) Also troubling is a divide between the reputations of talented critics and their ability to find mainstream outlets. In the same year as Denby's article and Insdorf's panel, the critical community was shaken when the New York *Daily News* fired Dave Kehr, long looked up to as one of the profession's most thoughtful members. Eyebrows raised again when the influential *New York Times* replaced chief film reviewer Janet Maslin with two new writers, one of whom had worked primarily as a book critic. As it happens, Kehr quickly found new affiliations, and while one of Maslin's replacements didn't last long, the other (A. O. Scott) has become an admired *Times* movie critic. At the time, however, skeptics asked a question of more than momentary interest: Would a paper as rich and resourceful as the *Times* hire a nonspecialist to be an art, music, or architecture critic?

I suspect the answer to that question is no. I also can't help remembering what happened when the *New Yorker* once found itself without a film critic when one of its staff reviewers "retired" after charges of unprofessional behavior and the other (Pauline Kael) hopped to Hollywood for what she hoped (wrongly, it turned out) would be a new, more exciting career. The magazine's response was to announce that no new film critic would be recruited, since existing staff writers could easily perform this easily done task, regardless of expertise or experience. So additional queries arise. Should film be treated as a second-class art form requiring less-rigorous commentary from less-experienced critics? And does this matter to readers—who may not care whether a movie column offers insightful analysis as long as it gives quick, practical information on what's playing and whether it's worth the price of a ticket?

Your view of these issues may hinge on whether you feel movies have a significant impact on individuals and societies, and whether this impact is as worthy of discussion as the entertainment value of the latest releases. After decades of writing about motion pictures, it's my strong impression that most critics become interested in film precisely because they consider it not only a diverting form of entertainment but also a social force, a cultural barometer, and a way of expanding our knowledge of the world.

In private conversations, though, critics often speak of the resistance they encounter within their publications when they move away from consumer-guide reviewing studded with celebrity names and snappy plot synopses. Ironically, a periodical may run editorials deploring Hollywood trends (too much violence, not enough family films) while filling its entertainment pages with articles and photos that serve as implicit advertisements for the Hollywood industry.

At the same time, movies that provide worthwhile alternatives to Hollywood product—such as overseas releases and films made outside commercial frameworks—are granted little or no space, on the theory that everyday readers aren't interested in them. This becomes a self-fulfilling prophecy: Readers aren't interested in alternative movies, so papers don't devote significant space to them, so readers don't get interested in them. If these films did receive more widespread coverage, distributors in search of audiences would carry them far beyond the large cities and university towns where they now primarily play.

Why are many publications so narrow in their view of film's variety and possibilities? Much evidence points to today's highly competitive media atmosphere. Newspapers and magazines compete not only with one another but also with a large array of cable-television channels and radio stations, plus the internet with its ever-growing list of venues and features.

In this environment, print publications are tempted to grab attention by any means necessary—and what's more attention-grabbing than the glitz and glamour of the Hollywood entertainment industry?

It's easy to fill pages with movie-star profiles and colorful photos from upcoming releases. "I knew an entertainment editor," recalls a film-critic friend of mine, "who said his job description was to find as many reasons as possible to run Sharon Stone's picture."

The first thing crowded out by such trivia is more-serious coverage, including in-depth articles and reviews of pictures that aren't on the distribution lists of the major studios. In addition to creating a misleading impression—that Hollywood products are all that matter—this blurs the line between journalism and advertising. Print pundits have rightly criticized TV networks for allowing news and entertainment to become part of the same media flow. Yet periodicals may think nothing of anchoring a page with publicity shots from a new Hollywood release, thus providing free promotion for a commercial product and allowing coverage to be dictated by graphic appeal (and studio publicity machines) rather than critical judgment.

Moviegoers may see little interest in these critical debates, finding them irrelevant to the day-to-day need for consumer advice. Few critics deny that consumer-guide reviewing has a valid place—capsule reviews and "critic's choice" features are a legitimate staple of film journalism—and just as few deny that Saturday-night fun is central to the role movies play in our lives. But this doesn't stop critics from worrying that insights and ideas are being literally crowded off the page by journalism's eagerness to jump on Hollywood's glamorous bandwagon.

To protest this trend is not to glorify a mythical "good old days" that never existed. Film criticism that's at once practical, entertaining, and thought-provoking has always been the exception rather than the rule, and the likes of Mae Tinee have wielded more than their share of influence during cinema's first century or so. Film culture has changed in recent years, though, and journalism is failing to encourage the most constructive aspects of that change. An ever-greater number of young people are taking courses in film appreciation, gaining more exposure to high-level cinema—and skills for understanding it—than earlier generations ever had. At the same time, the growth of home video has turned rental stores, websites, and movie channels into audiovisual libraries where *Citizen Kane* and *The Birth of a Nation* are only a phone call or a double-click away. Internet reviewers are also expanding discussion of film, and while they're still regarded by many observers as a cacophony rather than a choir, recent developments—such as the formation of online-film-critics associations to vet and organize their voices—point to increasingly helpful contributions from this quarter.

In this exciting climate, it's particularly ironic that experienced, knowledgeable print critics are finding their work overshadowed by an increasing emphasis on thumbnail evaluations and flashy photos. If their profession is to reverse its decline and realize its potential in the twenty-first century, film journalists must keep up with the growing sophistication of American moviegoers, and encourage the filmmaking community—as well as their own editors—to do the same.

Films, Fatigue, and Why a Critic's Opinions Are Just as Iffy as Yours

Place: the Cannes International Film Festival in May 2000.

Time: about two o'clock on the festival's next-to-last afternoon.

Event: a new movie by Béla Tarr, then and now the world's hottest Hungarian director.

Characters: assorted critics and scholars, arriving thirty minutes before the screening to beat the crowd.

Only there isn't any crowd. Perhaps the movie's title is to blame—somehow *Werckmeister Harmoniak* isn't quite as catchy as *Nurse Betty* or *Cecil B. DeMented,* hits of the 2000 festival that did have people lined up long before the show.

Or maybe it's the running time of nearly two and a half hours, although compared with Tarr's seven-and-a-half-hour *Sátántangó* this clocks in as a quickie. It certainly isn't the venue, since other attractions in the popular Director's Fortnight sidebar series have drawn large audiences.

Whatever the reason, the auditorium is only two-thirds filled when the film begins. The critics and scholars remain pleased with their cautious logistics, though. They've snagged the best seats in the house, and not one of the picture's hundred and forty-five minutes will escape their sharp-eyed scrutiny. Best of all, every half-empty row means fewer naïve moviegoers to rustle candy wrappers and complain about Tarr's avant-garde cinematics.

These prove as avant-garde as ever when the film commences. Based on a novel by László Krasznahorkai, whose work Tarr has adapted before, the story of this Hungarian-French-German coproduction starts with a young man named Valushka illustrating the structure of the solar system by choreographing his friends into a cosmic dance at a neighborhood saloon. Then an aging intellectual gives a spirited lecture on music theory, arguing that music has gone tragically astray ever since the baroque-era musicologist Andreas Werckmeister finished nailing down the system of equal temperament, whereby the octave is divided into twelve equal semitones—allowing for orderly modulations among a fixed number of scales—instead of following the series of naturally occurring overtones. This synthetic system has cut down music's infinite potential by confining it within arbitrarily imposed rules, the old pianist asserts, depriving humanity of the art's most glorious possibilities. So down with Werckmeister and all his works! (Presumably starting with Johann Sebastian Bach, the first great composer to carry his system to its full flowering.)

As the film proceeds we learn of schisms in the hero's family, political rivalries in his community, and tensions generated by a mysterious circus that's traveling through the region with two main attractions: a mysterious Prince, and a giant whale preserved for scrutiny on dry land. The whale has scored a hit with local citizens, including Valushka, who sees the creature as awesome evidence of God's creative power. But the Prince's edgy ideas have spurred consternation among people who fear his influence over a populace that has been suffering from unemployment, poverty, and hunger. Might he stir the masses to anger, violence, revolution? We'll never know, since dissension within the circus keeps him out of public view, and a large contingent of townspeople lurches into insurrection on its own, lashing out with implacable ferocity at whatever lies in its path.

All of this is passionately acted, rich with metaphorical implications, and photographed in the astonishingly long, fluid shots that have elevated Tarr to a high level of the auteurist pantheon. As for the film's fundamental theme, I see it as the ageless conundrum of how order relates to chaos—and just as important, how notions of stability and security relate to the simulations and simulacra that masquerade as order in our social, psychological, and political lives. Tarr engages with this in a spirit of radical ambiguity coupled with aesthetic and intellectual boldness, taking us beyond the limiting truisms of ideologically grounded art just as his visual style (and sound track, anchored in Mihàly Vig's pulsing score) takes us beyond the well-worn certainties of classical film style. If it were necessary to read an overriding Deeper Meaning into the picture, I'd suggest that Tarr is testing and probing (not positing or preaching) the notion that order is preferable to chaos even when the available kinds of order are inevitably flawed or circumscribing—such as the order of equal temperament in acoustics, which enhances some musical possibilities by excluding others; the order of domestic arrangements that promote emotional quietude by outlawing unruly passions; and the order of centralized political power (perhaps symbolized in the movie by the mummified whale, a relative of Thomas Hobbes's prototypical Leviathan figure) that allows everyday life to ramble through its habitual routines by stifling the disruptions of spontaneous rebellion and dissent. Tarr's hypotheses carry much dubious baggage once they leave the realm of abstract aesthetics for the realm of sociopolitical reality, which may explain why he has embedded his exploration in a narrative framework with such drastically uncertain elements. But this is the sort of thing that normally gets critics and scholars squirming with intellectual excitement.

If they're awake, that is. But such is not the case at this eagerly anticipated highlight of the world's greatest film festival. One cinephile conks out twenty-five minutes into the story, around the time of the musicology speech. Another falls asleep a little earlier, regains consciousness long enough to hear about the village's flirtation with fascism, then returns to slumberland. Another flees the theater at the half-hour mark, clambering over the legs and laps of other spectators (some conscious, some not) while mumbling that he's slept through the past twenty minutes and no longer has any idea what's going on.

Some members of the group (including this writer, well fortified with espresso before the lights went down) stay alert until the finale and applaud Tarr's visionary achievement at its conclusion. They also feel sympathy for their colleagues, who have missed one of the most brilliantly realized works in the entire Cannes program—and one that won't be easy to catch up with afterward, given the odds against something called *Werckmeister Harmoniak* arriving at anyone's local multiplex.

There's no mistaking the culprit in this situation: the dreaded Festival Overload Syndrome, which grows in power with every movie-crowded day and can conquer all but the most hopelessly obsessive viewer unless vigorous precautions (see "espresso" above) are taken.

Just about anyone is vulnerable to FOS, as the Tarr screening showed by taking such a toll on people who are ordinarily as sharp and savvy as anyone on the festival circuit. (In fact, Tarr's film isn't as esoteric as some of his previous work, as *Variety* indicated by giving it a glowing review under a headline that only this venerable trade newspaper could have come up with: "Magyar maverick's moving meditation.") I describe the scene not to belittle my colleagues, but to illustrate the differences between the way experts see many films and the way everyday moviegoers see them.

Becoming a responsible critic means cultivating a deep knowledge of film history and a broad awareness of ongoing international developments. While some go at this through book-reading and video-viewing, most feel a responsibility to see as many significant works as possible in the way their creators meant them to be experienced—as reels of thirty-five-millimeter celluloid projected onto a wall-sized screen in a public place. Since movies that won't sell many tickets aren't shown in many theaters, serious filmgoers are forced into courtship dances with FOS when festivals, museums, university programs, and other such venues make high concentrations of Important Cinema available on an all-too-fleeting basis.

Does this matter to civilian moviegoers who run no risk of overdosing, but just want to see a good picture on Saturday night? It certainly does, because critics and related professionals are more than tastemakers—they're program-shapers as well, exercising a strong influence over which unusually challenging films will move from festivals and arts centers to commercial screens where a wider range of viewers can discover them. Movies enthusiastically received at specialized events have the best chance of attracting bids from distributors and exhibitors. The technical term for this enthusiasm is "buzz," and it's as evanescent and indefinable as its name. All that's certain is that it rarely attaches itself to films that critics have slumbered through—even though a somnolent reception may be less the fault of the movie than of its unfortunate timeslot near the end of a fatiguing festival.

The uncertainties of professional film-watching don't end once a movie has crossed from the festival circuit to commercial release, moreover. They just take different forms, and a significant new factor enters the picture: conscious engineering by studio publicity departments, which do their best to ensure particular conditions that will induce particular responses, as I've discussed in this collection's previous essay.

It would be a boon if festival organizers could invent an escape hatch from Festival Overload Syndrome and the ills that travel in its wake. Critical opinions are not all that reliable under the best of circumstances, of course; pundits chronically disagree with one another, and occasionally with themselves upon different viewings of a single film. But along with their opinions good critics bring background knowledge, historical awareness, contextual information, and other intellectual benefits to their readers and students. These are generated most productively by experts who encounter the objects of their study—films—under conditions that encourage a full measure of sensory alertness and mental agility.

By and large, film critics and scholars are among the most responsible professionals I know, aware of and grateful for their privileged access to the most exciting art form of our time. Even when FOS overwhelms them for reasons beyond their control, most of the good ones are sure to see the movie again under better conditions, in which case the flawed first viewing becomes a bonus in the form of added familiarity with the film. This certainly happened with *Werckmeister Harmoniak*, aided by the swelling critical interest in filmmaker Tarr and the longtime critical fascination with Hanna Schygulla, the star of sundry Rainer Werner Fassbinder classics and still an imposing presence in European cinema. The film didn't play in a large number of American venues, but the more thoughtful American critics did their best to see it—including those who hadn't met its attention-span test at the Cannes screening—and its critical reputation became secure.

In sum, not even my annoyance with Festival Overload Syndrome reduces my respect for the best film critics I know, and *Werckmeister Harmoniak* helps explain why. Tarr's movie is a work of both spiritual adventure and philosophical analysis—more the former than the latter, in fact, which makes it even more challenging to write about—using a set of conspicuously modest raw materials (struggling people, awful environment, troubled epoch) to lift our minds and ultimately our souls beyond the encumbering confines of linear narrative and emotional habit that ordinary films trade in. *Werckmeister Harmoniak* was quickly nominated by the Film Critics International Federation (FIPRESCI) for the European Film Award as best European picture of the year, and my own review of it was published in the sophisticated Canadian magazine *Cinema Scope* and again, two years later, in the Minneapolis *City Paper* when the movie finally made it to that city under its American release title, *Werckmeister Harmonies*.

It remains true, however, that people who read and study critics' analyses should remember the trying conditions under which those critics do some of their most important work—conditions that may vary greatly from those everyday moviegoers are familiar with. Be the matter at hand *Werckmeister Harmoniak* or the latest *Harry Potter* epic, it's best illuminated by specialists whose motto isn't Eyes Wide Shut.

Cinephilia, Cinemania, Cinema

I recently found myself taking part in a mercifully brief debate on the *Film-Philosophy* website, a British internet salon for which I've written occasionally, on the true definitions of "cineaste," which another participant insisted can only mean "filmmaker," and "cinephile," which the same interlocutor said can only mean "film lover."

Trivial? You bet, and I soon logged out—partly from loyalty to *Cineaste* magazine, an American periodical for which I've also written, and about which I can say with certainty that it's more for people who love movies than for people who both love them and make them.

Two words with a closer connection, in my view, are "cinephilia" and "cinemania," both of which connote a profound affection for the movies. What divides them are differences of degree—a "philiac" is a tad more moderate than a "maniac" in most walks of life—and of practice. The average cinephile is content to see, ponder, and adore great films. The average cinemaniac is driven to see, see, and keep seeing everything in sight, with pondering often kept at a safe, tidy distance.

Specimens of these categories are far from rare, and may grow more common as new, improved varieties of home video make an increasingly wide range of films available for viewing alongside the theatrical fare exhibited in the large cities where most cinemaniacs, and many cinephiles, tend to reside. For this reason it's worth looking more closely at both breeds. This essay is drawn from material written for a series on cinephilia published by the *Senses of Cinema* website and an article I wrote for the *Christian Science Monitor* about the 2003 documentary *Cinemania*, itself available on DVD and surely a favorite of the species it wittily and sympathetically explores.

Cinephilia has become a fairly common term, used by and about moviegoers of very different tastes and generations. In an influential *New York Times* article of 1996, called "The Decay of Cinema," cultural critic Susan Sontag defined it as "the name of the very specific kind of love" inspired by cinema, which she describes as "both the book of art and the book of life," combining modernity and accessibility with poeticism, eroticism, mystery, and morality.

I have no real quarrel with the word cinephilia, especially when it's fleshed out in Sontag's elegant language, but I'm not sure it quite captures my own relationship to the world of film. Since cinephilia must be a personal thing by any definition, I'll get personal about it for a moment, and then make some observations about how it connects with my activities of film-related writing, lecturing, and teaching.

What has drawn me to the arts and humanities throughout my adult life has been the opportunity they afford for thinking and communicating about what may loosely be called the human condition. As a teenager, I was interested in novels, poetry, rock'n'roll—this was the '50s, after all—and especially the theater, which plugged directly into my fascination with role-playing and the deceptiveness of appearances, even though my experience with drama came more from reading plays than viewing them. I regarded my frequent moviegoing as a throwaway pastime, and found at least as much aesthetic excitement in some TV shows I watched (the visual experiments of Ernie Kovacs, the intellectual arguments on Sunday-afternoon "egghead" shows, the spontaneous poetics of Steve Allen's late-night program) as in the Hollywood pictures that paraded through the two movie theaters of my suburban town.

As mentioned in the introduction to this book, my lackadaisical attitude toward cinema was hardly altered by the lone film volume widely available at the time: *The Liveliest Art,* by Arthur Knight, whose recitations of studio history and plugs for Important Works struck me as the unliveliest thing imaginable. (This didn't stop me from scanning the TV listings for movies Knight mentions and checking them off in the book's index when I'd seen them—a practice shared by other fledgling cinephiles, I later learned.)

Everything changed in 1962 when I wandered into a double bill of Alain Resnais movies. What so excited me about these films, I later realized, was the experience of probing a set of existential puzzles through formal devices that seemed to have been specifically invented for the issues Resnais and his collaborators had chosen to explore. My future path was clear—from one revival house to another for as diverse an array of pictures as I could find. I had become, I suppose, a cinephile.

I'm fully aware that the story of My Life In Cinema is commonplace to the point of triteness, given the vast armies of '50s and '60s movie-lovers who followed the same basic route with minor variations of time, place, and titles. What makes my sensibility at least a little different from some others is that I always felt more skeptical of what lay around the next film-historical corner than many of my peers did. It seemed clear to me throughout the '60s, the '70s, and much of the '80s that cinema was the most fertile, inventive, and all-around exciting art form of our time. Yet it seemed equally clear that no art form could sustain such a vigorous pace forever, and that film did not have a monopoly on innovative and productive ideas even during this largely excellent era. From the beginning of my critical career in the mid-'60s, I joined my fellow cinephiles in probing the uncharted arcana of auteurism, genre analysis, and so forth; at the same time, though, I wrote as much on music and theater as I did about cinema. At issue here is not how I spent my professional and personal time, but my sense that the American cultural scene of the period offered aesthetic adventures of many different kinds, and no abstract commitment to cinephilia or anything else was going to stop me from plugging into as many of its pleasures as I could.

I don't raise the latter point to indicate that cinephilia is less than admirable and important, but to stress that at any given time cinema is less an aesthetic island unto itself than a component in a larger and more far-reaching cultural fabric. In the twentieth century film has probably been the most fertile and influential of all artistic media, but any cinephile with a sense of perspective will bear in mind the myriad ways in which it's been molded and contextualized by the large-scale aesthetic forces surrounding it. If cinema has lost a measure of its erstwhile glory, as many current critics contend, we must ask ourselves to what extent its energies have been inherited, extended, and perhaps even expanded by other art forms enjoying particularly rich productive periods that we can only limit and circumscribe ourselves by ignoring.

These considerations help explain why I evidently feel less of a jolt than some of my contemporaries at witnessing the sad decline—partly alleged, partly actual—of cinema art in the past decade or two. Also relevant are the temptations most of us feel to measure current pleasures against the nostalgic glow of an imperfectly remembered past. Of course there's far less excitement on the current American scene than there was in the Good Old Days of the '60s and '70s when a boisterous new gaggle of genuine giants (Martin Scorsese) and impertinent neoclassicists (Francis Ford Coppola) and nervy experimenters (Brian De Palma) and ambitious revisionists (Michael Cimino) and so forth were shaking up received ideas on what seemed like a monthly basis. But let's recall that bad movies were as plentiful then as they are today, and that mainstream audiences and critics undervalued many of that period's most innovative pictures (from *Who's That Knocking at My Door* to *Hi, Mom!* and beyond) just as they (we) are surely doing with similarly audacious work today.

That last notion is crucial, since major new steps are often misconstrued and underrated (or overrated) when they first arrive: *Citizen*

Kane and *Singin' in the Rain* and *It's a Wonderful Life* lost money in first-run theaters; *Vertigo* was dismissed by many as a self-indulgent bore; on the flip side, the George Lucas of *THX-1138* and the Steven Spielberg of *The Sugarland Express* were hailed as aesthetic hipsters by many a cinephile who failed to detect the seeds of commercialism and conformity lurking in these superficially offbeat attractions. Like others of my generation, I look smugly down on the philistines of 1960 who couldn't see the self-evident greatness of *Psycho,* now widely viewed as one of the most brilliant achievements of the American screen. At the same time, I recognize that the different sociocultural backgrounds and aesthetic priorities of younger critics may very well produce ingeniously argued books, essays, and articles demonstrating with persuasive vigor that *Hook* and *Always* and *1941* are as towering in their way as *Psycho* and *Imitation of Life* and *Shock Corridor* are in theirs. What will be at issue here is not some "goodness" or "badness" inherent in the films themselves, but the ability of cinephilia to generate artistically and intellectually sound modes of appreciation for works one loves enough to experience deeply, consider carefully, and share articulately with others. As long as film-oriented writers, talkers, and thinkers persist, cinephilia will remain alive and reasonably well. Mass audiences will continue to prefer *Patch Adams* over *Safe,* but it was ever thus, and the point and purpose of cinephilia are hardly diminished by the reluctance of Saturday-night moviegoers to cultivate exacting critical tastes.

This said, cinephiles—especially those who call themselves cinema critics—should feel a responsibility to reach beyond like-minded circles and encourage all moviegoers to broaden their tastes and proclivities. Existing for the consistently interested few rather than the usually uninterested many, cinephilia per se will endure on at least a modest scale as long as film-viewing is a cultural option. But film criticism (as opposed to film scholarship) exists for the many as well as the few, and I share the sense of insufficiency in this area that has led some of my critical colleagues to bemoan an incipient crisis in their profession. Critics for general-interest publications have usually mirrored the audiences they think they're writing for, albeit with less patience for the most patently awful pictures. The publications themselves have generally declined, though, in response to their own contemporary crises. Print is still the medium of choice for serious discussion of cultural and political issues, since broadcast outlets tend to privilege fast-moving glibness and the internet still lacks the time-tested cachet of paper-and-ink publications. Yet print outlets have lost an enormous amount of ground to cable TV, news radio, and other foes. (As the largest American city, New York had seven major dailies when I was growing up—my parents remembered when it had more—but today it has three, and two of these swim in red ink.) Faced with such pressures, many periodicals hope Hollywood's life-raft will carry them to sustainable circulations, if not the sort of journalistic attainments that intelligent publications used to aim for as a matter of course. So critics are asked to write long on the movie with the two-page ad in the latest issue, short (if at all) on everything else, undermining the responsibility to keep their craft above the lowest-common-denominator level of mere opinion-mongering.

Regularly employed writers have little choice about accommodating to such circumstances, if only because conscientious critics are easy for publishers to replace with facile hacks who'll embrace the most egregious policies for the sake of a position and a paycheck. Some publications have resisted all this, to be sure: There's high-quality reviewing in some periodicals with traditionally low circulations and free papers that don't rely on newsstand income, and some excellent critics manage to keep their jobs despite a steady stream of conflicts with the people who run their sections and departments. Still, the overall trend is a downward one, and this constitutes a deplorable waste for two related reasons. One is that good critics are in the best position to foster cinephilia, however one defines the meanings and limitations of that term. The other is that possibilities for the growth and refinement of cinephilia are greater than ever in an age when every well-stocked video outlet is a Library of World Cinema.

I know, I know, film-on-video is always already a degraded medium (low resolution, panning-and-scanning, etc., etc., etc.) that can never adequately substitute for the Real Thing in all its genuine glory. But the same purism (which has much to be said for it) applies to textbook reproductions of paintings, music performances on scratchy vinyl discs, and sundry other corrupted artifacts that have enriched people's lives throughout the age of mechanical reproduction, on the simple principle that having worthwhile cultural products in reduced form is better than not having them at all. While average Saturday-night audiences will continue to emphatically not care, the fact remains that video and the new digital media are making more great cinema available to a wider range of people than has been remotely possible in the past, opening the door to greater waves of cinematic literacy than we have ever known. If cinephiles fail to encourage and nurture this exciting prospect, cinephilia will certainly become the not-so-fabulous invalid that some already consider it to be.

Cinemania, as I said at the outset, is a somewhat different story. "Get some fun out of life," an old Hollywood catchphrase used to say. "Go to a movie!" But what if that's all you did? What if nothing on earth interested you except going to movies, and you had the leisure time to do it? That's a tantalizing question for anyone who likes film, and it's more tantalizing when you realize such people actually exist. They've even been profiled on film, most extensively in the documentary *Cinemania* by Angela Christlieb and Stephen Kijak.

The impassioned New Yorkers this movie portrays aren't filmmakers, film critics, or film professors. They're ordinary folks of various ages who have one thing in common—a notion that the good life means racing from one screen to another as many hours each day as possible. Think of the intricate schedules to be drawn up, the split-second travel routes to be plotted out!

As a constant moviegoer myself, I've gotten to know some of the *Cinemania* stars over the years. Jack Angstreich is a regular at museum and art-theater screenings, and I often chat with him as I head for my preferred seating location, far from the back-row outpost he favors. Roberta Hill shows up at venues of all kinds, and makes a point of hauling off as many flyers and programs as she can carry. And then there's Harvey Schwartz, who often asks me or another critic to smuggle him into a press screening if we arrive without a guest. Hearing a muttered "Couldja get me in?" from him is a way of knowing the show is about to start—although once we're inside I sit nowhere near the third-row-center position he loves, no matter how big the screen or booming the sound.

Haven't the friends of these folks ever suggested they get a life?

You might think so, but true cinemaniacs tend to have few friends except other cinemaniacs. "Film buffs do not socialize," says film buff Eric Chadbourne in the documentary. "Film buffs get together to see movies, [not] to have parties [or] to know each other."

Another figure in the movie, Bill Heidbreder, approaches the get-a-life issue even more bluntly. "Film is a substitute for life," he says. "Film is a form of living."

With this mindset, steady moviegoing—which means thirty-five-millimeter films on theatrical screens—is a must. The average cinemaniac (if there is an "average" cinemaniac) racks up an enormous number of viewing hours. "I see two or three films every day," says Angstreich, the movie-lover pictured on the documentary's DVD box. "Sometimes four or five."

And he's more picky than people like Hill and Schwartz, who are also *Cinemania* stars. "Roberta has probably seen over a thousand movies a year for over twenty years," said Angstreich when I asked him about the sheer quantity of films viewed by cinemaniacs. "I think I surpassed her at least one year, but I've gotten more fussy about how [correctly] movies are projected, so I see [fewer] than I used to. Harvey only has enough money to see films when they're free," continued the dark-eyed, raven-haired film fan, "which means museums and [press] screenings."

Moneyed or not, Schwartz manages to get his fill. On one day when *Cinemania* was being filmed, he calculated he'd seen five separate programs totaling nine hours and five minutes. Even he seems amazed to realize this. "Ewwwwwww," he says, smiling and grimacing at the same time.

As for video, cinemaniacs like Schwartz and Chadbourne use it to supplement their "real" moviegoing. That's not an option for a purist like Angstreich, though, who has told me he's run across only "six other people in the world" who share his refusal to watch movies on DVDs or cassettes. Ditto for Hill, who refuses to allow a TV set into her home. Angstreich acknowledges that every element of his life is structured around his moviegoing needs. If a person knows him well enough to expect him at a wedding or funeral, that person must also know him well enough to realize he won't show up if it conflicts with a film showing he just can't miss. All this results from conscious choices Angstreich has made about his life. These commenced in his last year of high school, when he decided to flesh out his frequent reading about cinema (he also loves literature and music) by seeing some international classics, which he instantly fell for.

Hill's constant viewing began when she was fourteen years old, and other cinemaniacs also started young. As adults, they have various ways of making ends meet despite their long hours in theaters. Heidbreder considers himself a philosopher and has a summa cum laude degree from the University of California at Berkeley, but he avoids a "real career" in favor of "boring work" so he'll have enough energy for after-hours viewing. Older cinemaniacs may receive social-security or disability payments. Angstreich, still on the young side, received a modest inheritance that supports his modest lifestyle. Some claiming to know him well make dark allegations about his mental stability, regarding which there is objective ground for question, given erratic behavior I've witnessed myself.

As content as he is with his habits, Angstreich admits cinemania isn't always a comfortable way of life, and his first-hand experience sheds revealing light on cinemania as a creed, a philosophy, a lifestyle. "I feel some frustration with living this way," he says. "I can feel sort of trapped. I can't go out of town, or even sleep late, if an important film series is going on. . . . If some film is coming to New York from a Russian archive for one or two screenings, you either see it that day or you never see it. DVD is supposed to make cinema culture more like book culture, but since I won't watch films that way, I'm still at the mercy of film culture. There's a sense of being on a treadmill. There's a Sisyphean aspect to it."

What makes all this worthwhile is the genuine affection felt by Angstreich and his fellow film fans toward the art form they love most. In this sense the smartest of them are cinephiles, not just movie nuts but solid partisans of serious film. "Each art breeds its fanatics," Sontag wrote, implying the overlap between the cinephilia she celebrates and cinemania, its stranger twin.

Angstreich doesn't like the insinuation of "pathology" carried by the "mania" part of the latter label. Yet he's even less comfortable with the cinephilia tag. "I agree with the critics who think 'cinephilia' is too clinical," he says. "Cinephilia basically means you make film into a fetish, which is different from taking a true aesthetic stance.

"I don't go to a film just to see Rita Hayworth," he continues, "or a particular person's camera work. I go to see a director's work, because the director is the one who holds all the film's elements in tension with each other. Nobody else is of intrinsic interest." Then again, he adds with a laugh, "I don't actually abide by this, since I *am* seduced by other elements." One such "element" happens to be Hayworth, whose charms Angstreich rhapsodizes about.

As strange as a cinemaniac's life might seem to most of us, it has supporters outside the fold. "They may be escaping from reality," says Mikita Brottman, a professor of literature at the Maryland Institute College of Art in Baltimore, "but everyone has ways of holding the world at a distance. Some people do this by making lots of money, or by having a large family. . . . Why must we believe that doing things with our bodies is real, while doing things in our minds is not? It might seem crazy to spend, say, six hours in a movie theater every day. But people think nothing of spending that much time in front of a TV set. The interesting thing is that television gives images that are closer to reality, and happen right in our living rooms. The people called cinemaniacs want something that's larger, grander than life. In a way, they have higher standards than the rest of us."

Angstreich wouldn't disagree. "There's no reason why 'reality' should be privileged," he says during a conversation with Heidbreder in the *Cinemania* movie. "It's just ideology to say, 'Oh, that [movie-going] is only escapism.' Who would *want* to live in this [social and political] reality?"

Looking at an experience through a motion-picture frame "intensifies" it, Angstreich argues. "When that frame is not there, it's just [everyday] experience, which is banal." He seems genuinely regretful that "there's no way to impose that frame on real life, to turn yourself into a [movie] shot."

That last phrase sums up a certain sadness behind cinemania: the always-unfulfilled wish that life could be as perfect as a great movie. This leads to a frustration that can show up in peculiar ways. "I don't think they're 'maniacs,' but they can be extreme," says David Schwartz, chief curator of New York's adventurously programmed American Museum of the Moving Image, a favorite hangout for cinemaniacs. "That can be off-putting for the rest of the audience—when one of them goes nuts because somebody's talking, or really yells at someone who's crinkling a food wrapper. With one of them, if the tiniest thing is 'off' with the projection, he can't take it, he just can't watch the film." None of which reduces Schwartz's affection for them. "I don't really think they're avoiding reality," he says. "For me, seeing a film is a real-life experience—in fact, it's a *heightened* real-life experience. . . . Most of [the cinemaniacs] are looking for that kind of [intense] aesthetic feeling. For other people, this is a small fraction of their lives, at best. For these people, it's a day-to-day activity. They don't see movies as a place where you check your brain at the door."

While cinemania may be for superserious movie buffs only, that doesn't mean their tastes are pretentious or their days are dull. "I basically like to be entertained," Chadbourne says. "Some of the foreign movies are deadly. They're called 'masterpieces' because you don't get any fun out of them." His favorite films? American comedies and musicals, especially when Ginger Rogers is in them. Hill goes for adventure movies and "a well-made historical film that doesn't send me running to the encyclopedia," while Heidbreder has "niched" himself with European movies produced after the World War II era. Angstreich favors French New Wave pictures of the '60s and Hollywood film-noir classics of the '40s and '50s. His enthusiasms range far beyond these areas, though. "In movies like *Once Upon a Time in the West* and *The Umbrellas of Cherbourg* and *Meet Me in St. Louis* and some avant-garde films," he tells me, "every element— music, stars, decors, colors—takes on a quality that makes me want to live in every frame."

Get a life? It sounds like a good life to me—although maybe I'm prejudiced, since talking with cinemaniacs has helped me face the fact that we professional movie critics are simply salary-earning cinemaniacs ourselves. In other words, we're all cinephiles in one way or another. And that's all right with us. "Film lovers are unique," says Heidbreder, adding, "We're also important, because we're the ones these great films are being made for."

Hollywood Players Who've Made a Difference

CASSAVETES, EASTWOOD, MARTIN, NICHOLSON

It's tempting for many critics, and irresistible for some, to claim that powerful Hollywood figures—especially those who count acting among their talents—must be cynically commercial by definition, or at least largely motivated by lusts for fame and riches. I think it's risky to posit much of anything by definition in the mercurial world of entertainment culture, and when this question is raised it's easy to point out people who elude the money-driven mold enough to be called exceptions that disprove the rule. This essay looks at three major on-screen players—using that word in both the general sense of "performer" and the Robert Altman sense of power broker—whose works, while indisputably uneven, are prime examples of star-driven creativity at work within the Hollywood system.

JOHN CASSAVETES

My first conversation with John Cassavetes took place in 1974, when his masterpiece *A Woman Under the Influence* had its

New York Film Festival debut. My last talk with him took place by phone immediately after the same festival's 1988 showing of *Opening Night*, a 1977 movie that was screened as a new work, since it had never managed to find its way to theatrical release. I was on the festival's selection committee and pushed hard to get *Opening Night* into the lineup, despite the strong fears expressed to me by a film-scholar friend that audiences would fail to "get" the film, thus ending the filmmaker's life—he was terminally ill with liver disease—on a sour note. Cassavetes was much too sick for a trip to New York, but his seat in a reserved box at the Lincoln Center auditorium wasn't empty: I sat in it myself, observing the audience from on high throughout the movie, which viewers "got" so obviously and completely that the film *did* then acquire a commercial release at last. I phoned John in southern California right after the screening to tell him how well his orphaned movie was received. That was the last of many chats over the years.

One of them took place when Cassavetes and his movie-star wife Gena Rowlands visited New York for the premiere of *Gloria*, one of his weakest films—weak partly because of studio interference with the project, and partly because John was always a bull-headed artist who followed his instincts even when *everyone* told him they were off target. In a *Christian Science Monitor* article on the film, I wrote that *Gloria* was, like many Cassavetes pictures, "a work of exhilarating highs and devastating lows," adding that even this flawed example of Cassavetes's art "never makes you wish you were somewhere else, watching some safer, less crazily impulsive movie." I think it's worth revisiting this particular afternoon with Cassavetes precisely because our attention wasn't centered on one of his greatest or most popular works; instead it was focused on his filmmaking philosophy in ways that didn't always emerge when we were discussing his career as a whole or a particular new movie that was clearly destined for critical and/or commercial acclaim.

I should add that while I no longer believe in concepts like "my favorite film," even for fun, at an earlier stage of my career I happily identified *A Woman Under the Influence* as just that, "despite a few hundred flaws that would have wrecked a lesser film," as I once wrote. "It's not easy being a Cassavetes fan," I continued, noting how bull-headed *I* had to be to remain "loyal to *The Killing of a Chinese Bookie*—a neglected masterpiece—against [its] onslaught of nearly unanimous bad reviews." But, my article went on, you have to admire a filmmaker who follows his own lights so relentlessly, with the faithful help of his actress wife and a long list of long-time associates. His films take dizzying risks, often teetering on the brink of disaster. Yet when they work, even in part, you know you've seen an aesthetic balancing act of the highest and most artistically rewarding kind.

Gloria had its beginnings after the 1977 crash-landing of *Opening Night*, which left Cassavetes with "a lot of debts," as he put it. (He provided much of the funding for the movies he wrote and directed, drawing on the money he earned by starring in movies, such as *Rosemary's Baby* and *The Dirty Dozen*, that *other* people wrote and directed.) To raise some capital, he penned the *Gloria* screenplay and peddled it to Hollywood studios. "Then my agent called," he said. "The good news was, Columbia would buy the script. The bad news was, they wanted me to direct it."

Cassavetes was joking when he called this "bad news," but it was a rueful joke, since his relations with the major studios were rocky. Happily, his marriage with Columbia went better than most, and he was able to explore the situation that fascinated him in the *Gloria* story: the forced partnership between a woman who's suspicious of kids and a threatened kid who has nowhere else to turn.

"There's a lot of pain connected with raising children in today's world," Cassavetes told me. "It's considered a big holdback. So a lot of women have developed a distrust of children. I wanted [in the film] to tell women that they don't have to like children—but [that] there's still something deep in them that relates to children, and this separates them from men in a good way. This inner understanding of kids is something very deep and instinctive. In a way, it's the other side of insanity. But we had to be careful how we evoked this in the movie. We avoided anything like a traditional mother-son relationship."

As a filmmaker, Cassavetes cared little about being fashionable. He addressed each of his films "to a certain audience—namely, people involved in the type of life style we're dealing with. *Gloria* is a movie for street people. I can't ask people who are comfortable in their lives, with no problems, to be spectacularly interested in this picture. That kind of person will criticize it and say we made up the story as we went along. I wish I had the ability to do that! Actually, we spend months and years working out the philosophical intent of each picture. And if that intent is strong enough, it will come across to people when we express it in human terms, and they will respond to it. Like all my films, *Gloria* wasn't made to please people. It's only a work, an expression. I just hope people will respond to it, and that's a lot different from trying to *please* them."

Besides being a busy writer and director, Cassavetes was a distinguished actor—and as a director he had a reputation for glorifying the performance aspects of his pictures, which separated him from filmmakers who concentrate on technical or visual elements. I asked him if he wielded a strong hand on the set—if he *directed* his movies a lot.

"I can't say I don't do it," he answered, "but I never do it well. I've never given one direction that's been good. Actors don't need direction, they need attention. I'll step in as a director—I'm laden with an ego, like everyone else—but whenever I have to open my mouth, I know I'm probably wrong. There's a unique warmth and camaraderie among actors. It's very uncomfortable to be the director. A good director is tough and unswayable. But I'm a sucker for actors—I have a soft spot, I like them. Years ago, I used actors to make a point. But, thank goodness, I learned not to do that."

One performer who never tired of working with Cassavetes was Rowlands, who found *Gloria* a particularly stimulating challenge. "It was a tremendously physical picture," she told me while sitting by her husband's side. "You never anticipate that aspect when you're reading the script—it just says, 'Then she jumps into the icy waters below,' and you thumb ahead to find your next dialogue. This role turned out to require enormous physical energy. And the emotional level took it out of me, too. But I loved doing it, partly because I've always wanted to work with a child on a one-to-one basis. Kids aren't brainwashed. You never know what they're going to do or say. It keeps you honest, in movies as in life. Also, it was a new experience having a leading man who doesn't read."

As many artistic chances as Cassavetes took in every one of his movies, he never saw a downside to making films about emotions rather than action and spectacle. "I don't think it's a risk," he told me. "It's one of the surest bets in town that people have feelings. If you don't believe that, you haven't experienced anything in life."

A colleague of Beat writer Jack Kerouac dubbed him "the great rememberer," and I'd dub Cassavetes, who had much in common with the Beat sensibility, "the great experiencer." He had to fight like crazy to get those experiences—those he'd had, those he'd witnessed, those he'd dreamed up in his raging imagination—on film, and lukewarm receptions given to many of his works were among the hardest of those experiences for him to swallow. But he managed, with flair and style. During our conversation about *Gloria* and its imminent release, I suggested that *Opening Night* may have failed to find distribution because it was a little ahead of its time, and since moviegoing habits had loosened up a bit in the interim, maybe he should put it on the market again. "Those fucking distributors," he said with a grim smile, "they had their chance. If any museum wants a copy of that film, I'll give it to 'em, for free. Any university that wants a copy, I'll give it to 'em, for free. But those distributors can offer me anything want, and 'fuck 'em' is what I say. They had their chance, and it's too God damn late."

It took a decade and a film festival to change his mind, and I'm a little surprised that happened even at the tail end of his life. He knew what he wanted, and on celluloid at least, he usually got it.

That's why I find so much of his cinema a thing of joy, a beauty forever, and an inspiration to me at the deepest levels of my life.

CLINT EASTWOOD

Go ahead, make his day—call Clint Eastwood the quintessential film-industry icon. He became a star playing The Man With No Name, and today his name is known around the globe.

Yet it's hard to slot him into a familiar Hollywood pigeonhole. "He's gotten a bad rap as an actor," says Richard Schickel, an Eastwood biographer and *Time* film critic, "because he likes to play taciturn parts. People say he can't or won't do more spacious roles, and he's just playing himself. But he isn't. He's a very serious actor."

Brian Helgeland, who wrote the screenplay for the 2003 drama *Mystic River*, one of Eastwood's most respected directorial efforts, has a similar view of his filmmaking. "As a director he likes to disappear," Helgeland says. "I admire that, because often 'style' is just manipulation, and . . . he doesn't want to [manipulate the audience or] tell you what to think."

That certainly goes for *Mystic River*, which deals with such disturbing issues as child abuse and vengeful violence, and contains notes of ambiguity that viewers have both cheered and criticized. Talking with Eastwood after its New York Film Festival screening in the coveted opening-night slot, I told him how much I enjoyed it. "Thank you very much," he laconically replied. Then he added, after a pause, "I'm not sure 'enjoy' is the right word. We wanted to say some [important] things in this movie. They're not on the surface, but they're there." Not many Hollywood luminaries would question the "enjoyment" value of their work—to a journalist, no less. It's another measure of Eastwood's willingness to defy conventional wisdom.

Eastwood has worked in a wide range of Hollywood arenas. He's done action, drama, and comedy, inhabiting every kind of character from hard-bitten cowboys to hard-boiled cops and laugh-producing goofballs. Not to mention age-defying romantic heroes. At this writing he's passed his seventy-fourth birthday, and it's only nine years since he romanced Meryl Streep in *The Bridges of Madison County*, only two since he wooed Wanda de Jesus in *Blood Work*.

Eastwood's success hasn't stemmed from some nebulous *je ne sais quois* based on an indefinable "gift" for acting. He thinks hard about his projects, and while his characters may be taciturn, that doesn't mean he is. "As a guy," Schickel tells me, "he's almost a motormouth. He's very shrewd, very funny, and we talk about all kinds of things. . . . He studied with real Method-type teachers in California, and if you get him on the subject of acting he's very voluble, and has well-defined tastes."

So why didn't Eastwood choose to appear on-screen in an important movie like *Mystic River*, occupying only the director's chair instead? "There was no role for [someone] my age in the story," he said when it premiered at the Cannes film festival. "It was much more pleasant for me to watch younger players at work."

Looking deeper, there may be another reason for Eastwood's absence from the casts of *Mystic River* and a handful of other films he's directed without acting in. The character type he plays most often—a thick-skinned, emotionally armored man—doesn't figure in the plot. Eastwood's fondness for that sort of role has caused skeptical viewers to scoff at his rigidity. The influential critic Pauline Kael famously described him as "a tall, cold cod."

But is it bad to be a cod? Rather than seeing Eastwood's screen persona as a circumscribed stereotype, some consider it a solid artistic creation in itself. Film critic Amy Taubin interprets the 1993 drama *In the Line of Fire* as a kind of acting duel between Eastwood, as a Secret Service agent, and John Malkovich, as an assassin who's a master of disguise. This format allows Eastwood to skillfully contrast his deliberately stiff, unyielding performance with Malkovich's ability to all but vanish into the part he's playing.

As a director, Eastwood lets actors follow their own ideas of how to create their characterizations—a habit his colleagues enjoy as much as he does. "I think most of us would read the phonebook for Clint," remarked *Mystic River* actress Laura Linney.

Kevin Bacon, who plays a cop in *Mystic River*, says he was struck by Eastwood's decision to give the last scene an open-ended quality that called for an unusual acting approach. "I asked the boss what I was supposed to be playing there," Bacon said over a lunch at Cannes arranged to launch the movie, "and he didn't give me an answer. He said, 'I think it's up to the audience.' That's one of the things that make him the only *independent* filmmaker working in the studio system. He can have an ending . . . that in a different set of circumstances [the studio] would say no, we've got to find out exactly what's going to happen. . . . I can't think of another director in the studio system who challenges those kinds of rules."

Eastwood's wish to cultivate an actively thinking audience—rather than a passively consuming one—dates back at least as far as *Bird*, his 1988 bio-pic about Charlie Parker, the legendary alto-sax player. "You don't necessarily say what's right or wrong," he told me when *Bird* debuted at the New York Film Festival, where I served on the programming committee that selected the movie. "You just give several points of view. I love the audience to work with you. Rather than be condescending or just give 'em a story with an ending, I love 'em to *think* about it."

Another of Eastwood's practices is to film only a few takes of each scene, unlike most directors, who want multiple versions they can consider for the final cut. "There's zero rehearsal," Bacon reports, "and maybe two or three takes. When people hear that [they think] it implies a hurried, rushed kind of atmosphere. But the truth is that it's very, very relaxed—the most relaxed I've ever been in, because it's so well prepared."

Tim Robbins, who plays a deeply troubled man in *Mystic River*, agrees. The part he played was "a dark place to go to," he told me, referring to the sexual abuse his character suffered as a child. But, he continued, "the good news is that the way Clint works is so confident and efficient [that] it became easier to go there than it would have been had I thought I was going to do twenty takes. You have to [hold some emotions back] when you're going to do it that often. When you know you're doing it once or twice, it's *all* out there every time."

Eastwood's career hasn't always played against the grain. He started as an actor in low-budget fifties quickies like *Tarantula*, about a giant sci-fi spider, and *Francis in the Navy*, about a talking mule who prefigured the orangutan Eastwood has featured in some of his own comedies. His breakthrough came as the aptly named Rowdy Yates in *Rawhide*, the television series where he honed his knowledge of the western genre. His career rocketed higher in the sixties with a series of Italian movies—derisively called "spaghetti westerns" when they were released—culminating in his third portrayal of The Man With No Name in *The Good, the Bad and the Ugly.*

Leaving aside the increasingly high reputations of those Sergio Leone westerns, these don't sound like auspicious origins for a Hollywood icon. Ditto for his starring roles in five movies about Harry Callaghan, a rogue cop who doesn't hesitate to take the law into his own hands. Beginning with *Dirty Harry* in 1971 and continuing through *The Dead Pool* in 1988—although Eastwood himself directed only *Sudden Impact* in 1983—this series was scorned by viewers who found a nasty, even cryptofascist tone in its cheerleading for vigilante justice.

A key to understanding Eastwood's career is to see how he's matured and mellowed since then. "At the time when *Dirty Harry* was made," Helgeland says, "it was thought of as a right-wing, reactionary [film that argued] the ends justify the means. *Mystic River* is the complete opposite. He's come full circle on that theme. . . . *Dirty Harry* ends when [Harry] throws his badge in the water, and I think that would be the *middle* of the film now. You'd see what happened to Harry from that point on. I don't think [Eastwood's] philosophy has changed so much, but it's the aftermath [of events] that he's interested in now."

Schickel sees a distinctively American mindset in Eastwood's philosophy. Pointing to *Mystic River* and the Oscar-winning 1992 western *Unforgiven* as two of his best and most characteristic films, Schickel says Eastwood is "drawn to themes that have to do with how the past impinges on the present. We [Americans] have a short history, and we worry a lot about it. Clint does that as well."

Eastwood's fascination with such themes has roots in his own life. "He started on TV and doing spaghetti westerns," Schickel says, "suffering enormous contempt from critics of the time. . . . But the great American story is remaking yourself into something that's more greatly appreciated, and that is Clint's trip. He's such an American guy, and such a California guy! He was born on the far end of the continent and suffered the disrespect that Eastern intellectuals feel for people who aren't all that well educated and swell. He wants to prove to those people that he's as thoughtful and intelligent as they are. His life has been a sort of trip toward thoughtful maturity."

Nothing is more American than jazz, and that's another central influence on Eastwood's life and work. His habit of filming most scenes in a small handful of takes reveals his wish to capture the spontaneous, mercurial moods of first-rate jazz. "He's very serious about it," agrees Schickel, "and he might rather have been a jazz [musician] than an actor. He's a wonderful pianist—at least it sounds good to me!" Jazz inflects Eastwood's themes as well as his directorial style. "To some degree he still thinks of himself as kind of an outsider," Schickel says, "and jazz guys are outsiders. . . . Clint identifies with that."

Not every Eastwood film is a major event, as even his supporters acknowledge. "Some are little entertainment and action pictures," biographer Schickel notes. "For a long time he had to make a movie a year . . . and he's never been someone who likes to develop [plot] ideas. He likes to have a finished script, and then maybe work on it a little with the writer. Sometimes they do well commercially, and sometimes they don't."

Still, the overall consistency of Eastwood's success speaks for itself, and the acclaim for a late film like *Mystic River* suggests that people are responding favorably to the increasing thoughtfulness of his work. "It's only lately that people are forgiving him for the spaghetti westerns," Schickel told me in 2003, "and for the allegedly fascist filmmaking in *Dirty Harry*. I think the spaghettis are among his best work as an actor, though—they're far better than most of the American films that were [being made] then. As far as I'm concerned, he has nothing to beg forgiveness for." I concur.

STEVE MARTIN

"I've always played an idiot," Steve Martin told me over lunch at a Manhattan hotel in the fall of 1984.

As if we didn't know. After all, this was *The Jerk* talking—the "wild and crazy guy" of *Saturday Night Live*, the star of *Dead Men Don't Wear Plaid*.

But he quickly let me know we shouldn't count on more of the same. Yes, farces were hot in those days—still are, for that matter—and the surest way to a fast buck was to peddle another *Bachelor Party* spinoff. Still, said the star, "I just can't bring myself to do that anymore. I'm the wrong age, and my emotions are completely somewhere else."

Don't get him wrong. He wasn't planning to audition for *Long Day's Journey into Night*, or even *Edge of Night*, its soap-opera alter ego. He was convinced, though, that his performance opposite Lily Tomlin in the comedy hit *All of Me* was a step in a new direction.

"This man is not an idiot!" he said, describing his *All of Me* character, a lawyer whose body is invaded by the transmigrating soul of a rich, daffy woman. In fact, said Martin, this character is "a contemporary person with some brains. The movie is wildly comic, but he's not naive or a victim of circumstances. He's an intelligent man who happens to get caught in a disaster. That's a big difference between this role and any other part I've played. And believe me, I really liked it. I liked not having to say, 'What's happening to me?' all the time. After a certain age you can't act adolescent anymore. I'd love to play James Bond!"

Bond would be a stretch, to put it mildly. But besides giving Martin a well-rounded role for a change, the pivotal *All of Me* showcased his talent in a less chaotic setting than had normally been his lot. "For the first time," he said, "I'm in a story with a beginning, middle, and end. It's old-fashioned and solid, like a drawing-room comedy. The hardest thing to do is tell a story straight. That's why I'm happy I made this little movie that works, not some extravaganza that overwhelms the senses. This movie was like going to school. I learned a lot about structure and character."

The results pleased moviegoers as well as Martin, judging from the box office. Some may have been drawn by the movie's raunchy moments and the bits of childish humor that Martin still hadn't completely escaped. But chatting before the film's premiere, Martin insisted that the solid story and characters were salable in their own right. "People wonder how it'll fare in a market where there's nothing but guys peering through peepholes at naked girls," he said. "Yes, those films do well, but other kinds also do well: *Tootsie* and *Heaven Can Wait.* I don't want to call this 'adult comedy,' because I think *All of Me* hangs in with the younger people, too. It has what Lily calls a naughtiness about it. But there are rebels even in the huge ten- to sixteen-year-old market—kids who like something a little older, more mature."

Even before his move to *All of Me* and "more mature" work, Martin had taken on a notable number of risky and interesting projects. The movie version of Dennis Potter's bittersweet TV drama *Pennies From Heaven* may have been an artistic failure in 1981, but it was among the most experimental pictures Hollywood had made until that time, mingling sober drama with bizarre comedy and surreal musical numbers. *Dead Men Don't Wear Plaid* was a commercial failure in 1982, but its format—new comedy scenes intercut with clips from old detective pictures—was one of a kind for a feature film. Since the transitional *All of Me* he has appeared in his share of stupid movies, such as the appalling comedy *Bringing Down the House* and the bland family film *Cheaper by the Dozen,* both released in 2003. But he has also stretched his talent in adventurous ways—writing and starring in the Cyrano de Bergerac spinoff *Roxanne* in 1987, acting in Mike Nichols's stage production of Samuel Beckett's classic *Waiting for Godot* in 1988, playing a mostly serious dramatic role in Lawrence Kasdan's rich *Grand Canyon* in 1991, and writing the successfully produced 1993 play *Picasso at the Lapin Agile,* which he has also turned into a screenplay. He has done a good deal of feature-film writing as well as some producing, bearing out his desire to generate his own ideas and mold his career into shapes that would be elusive if he left his fate in the hands of standard Hollywood producers and agents.

Why has Martin tested such uncertain waters instead of basking in the tried-and-true success of ordinary farce? "I did *Pennies From Heaven* because—in my mind—my career had sort of peaked with *The Jerk* and a concert tour I did," Martin told me. "I knew I couldn't go on being just a stand-up comedian, because there's a bell curve to this stuff. Pretty soon you aren't playing fifteen thousand seats anymore—you're playing ten, then three, then none. You're back in the clubs and doing TV commercials. Even though I was at the top of things with my act, I knew that was over. I was at the end of my rope emotionally."

So he made the "painful" decision to move fully into movie work. The big prize he wanted from Hollywood was "longevity," the ability to "make a movie, lay off for three years, then make another one." His model was "someone like Warren Beatty, who's always around even when he doesn't make a picture for four years."

Martin thought that would be paradise after his years of stand-up work. "Doing my act night after night was like always going up in smoke," he complained. "You do it—and it might be great, it might be lousy, but it's completely gone. I don't know if this is an ego thing, but you wish it would stay around. You work so hard on something that you'd like to be able to visit it again, instead of having it be a vague memory."

Since he had one successful film already behind him—*The Jerk*—he found he was "already a star" when he knocked on Hollywood's door. "It gave me an entree into the movies," he said, which felt good but had its disadvantages. "It wasn't like I had ten films to get my feet wet and understand how movies are made and what they're about," he recalled. With hindsight, he would have managed some things differently—such as making *Pennies From Heaven* after *Dead Men Don't Wear Plaid*, not before it. Coming at the peak of an "increasing bizarreness" trend, he said, the daring *Pennies* might have worked better commercially.

How does Martin choose his roles? He wasn't quite sure, even at the turning-point stage of his career. "All those questions are still being answered in my mind," he told me. "I still don't have a total grasp." He was certain about one aspect, though: He enjoys variety. "I liked doing *All of Me*, but to go out and repeat it isn't tempting," he said. "I'd be just as happy making a warm movie like *It's a Wonderful Life*. That's the business I'm in—try to make 'em laugh and cry. I'm not in the art business."

Martin entered the laugh-and-cry business as a southern California teenager, doing a magic act "in folk clubs where anyone could get up on Monday night." Later he got a TV writing job for which he was "really ill-equipped," worked on material for *The Smothers Brothers Show*, went back to stand-up work, and finally became a frequent *Saturday Night Live* performer, which, along with popular appearances on the *Tonight* show, launched him for good.

Although television was important to his early career, Martin soon decided that "TV is isolated—a place where you show off rather than learn." Accordingly, his transition to film was not smooth. "I had to learn how to calm down a little, because the screen's real big. You have to speak from your heart. When a character got mad in my act, I really exaggerated it. But when people in life get mad they sometimes get very quiet. There's a big process to learning these things." At the core of the process is figuring out how "to use your own personality," as a star like Jack Nicholson does. "He's a great actor whatever he plays. He's really an oddball, and that always makes him interesting. I'm not too much of an oddball in real life, but I *am* normal, and I think there's a place for normal people on the screen."

As of the moment when *All of Me* and its awards promised to give Martin's career more momentum and flexibility, he had a mixed self-assessment of his work. "There's not a great film in my background," he said with reasonable modesty, "but there's no clinker to be ashamed of. There are at least good moments or good intent in each one." This wasn't a bad track record, Martin thought, given the mediocrity of contemporary comedy. "A friend said recently that the old comedies, by [Charles] Chaplin and [Buster] Keaton, were really clever and funny and you really laughed," he mused. "I realized that was true. Those pictures didn't just skim along the surface with a funny situation every now and then. There's something we [later comedians] have forgotten, lost sight of."

JACK NICHOLSON

For a movie star, Jack Nicholson keeps a fairly modest profile. He doesn't do the talk-show circuit or grant many interviews to the press. If you see his face on a magazine, it's probably because the producers of his latest picture struck a publicity deal, not because he wants to sit in front of more cameras. This may stem partly from the fact that Nicholson—one of only two male actors to win three Oscars—is so famous that he just doesn't have to bother shilling for the studios anymore.

Or there may be another reason—one that stems from his desire to mine his psyche in a wide variety of roles, using his own selfhood to help bring alive everyone from the rebellious inmate of *One Flew Over the Cuckoo's Nest* to the obsessive-compulsive romance writer in *As Good as It Gets*, to mention two of many possible examples. "My secret craft—it's all autobiography," he told an interviewer in 1986, the period that produced hits as different as *Prizzi's Honor* and *Broadcast News*. So why would he spread that autobiography around in profligate ways that don't enrich a specific portrayal in a specific movie?

While this may be so, Nicholson is aware that his credibility as an actor depends on his ability to make viewers think he's a new person with every new picture. "That's always a hard job," he said at the Cannes film festival. "Anyone can act once or twice." But when audiences start to associate you with an off-screen persona, "you have to unconvince them of who you are" to make the character live and breathe on its own.

After working with Nicholson in the 2002 drama *About Schmidt*, director Alexander Payne says a key part of the actor's brilliance is his commitment to the role at hand, not triumphs he's had in the past or an image he's trying to build. "Any vanity he seems to have comes from wanting to be most truthful to the character he's playing," Payne said at Cannes, where *About Schmidt* premiered. Payne went on to give his impression of the actor's attitude: "I'm being Jack Nicholson inside this thing, my body, which is an instrument. . . . What is the most appropriate way for me to play this instrument for this character?"

While he may not be overly vain in the traditional sense, Nicholson can strut his stuff with the best of them. Take his appearance at the New York Film Festival when *About Schmidt* screened there on the opening night. First he waved to the Lincoln Center crowd with his patented impish smile. Then he swaggered across the stage for an amazingly long time, still grinning. And then he explained why he was making such a generous display of himself. "I just want to show you I'm still good-looking!" he called out to his applauding fans, without bothering to take the microphone. "Not like in the movie you're gonna see!"

His character in *About Schmidt* is a sixty-something suburbanite with a sagging face, a drooping spirit, and a paunch that's getting bulgier by the day. But then, Nicholson has never been handsome in the matinee-idol tradition of Cary Grant, Tom Cruise, and their ilk. His eyes are a tad squinty. His hairline started receding decades ago. His eyebrows—those eyebrows!—look like they're modeled on the flying buttresses of some ancient French cathedral.

But that ordinary-guy look is what makes him likable, and his ability to combine it with screen-grabbing charisma is what makes him unique. The first time I met him, in a Manhattan restaurant where we met to discuss *One Flew Over the Cuckoo's Nest* in 1975, I realized for the first time that he's close to funny-looking in ways. (Those eyebrows!) The next time we spoke was at Sardi's, where he picked up the New York Film Critics Circle's best-actor award for *Ironweed* in 1987, when I was chairman of the group. I was still struck by his appearance, but even more so by how unabashedly *thrilled* he was to receive a prize for what he'd thought of as a risky, offbeat performance in a risky, offbeat film. I also learned of a vulnerability I never knew he had. During his acceptance speech he'd mentioned his concern for a currently sick friend, and when a friend of mine happened to see him later in the restroom and muttered his hope that the ailing buddy would get better, Nicholson grabbed his arm and lengthily told the *whole story* of his friend's illness, getting more emotional as he went along and utterly oblivious of the fact that *my* friend wanted to get back to his table. In an alienated culture where few of us like to unburden our personal problems onto strangers, Nicholson seemed almost fragile in his need for attention and comfort at that moment.

This regular-guy quality is clearly a plus for Nicholson's purely professional side. "A basic reason why Nicholson has been a star for more than thirty years is that he's not a leading man," says Barbara Siegel, coauthor of *Jack Nicholson: The Unauthorized Biography*. "He's a character actor, and that's given him the opportunity—which he has wisely taken—to vary his roles," says Scott Siegel, her husband and coauthor. "He's always moved on to new opportunities, and as a consequence, he's never worn out his welcome." This wouldn't mean much if Nicholson didn't rise to the challenges he sets himself. But he does, and audiences have embraced him in every imaginable kind of part, even when the movies themselves weren't hits. His characters range from the laid-back lawyer of *Easy Rider* to the snoopy sleuth of *Chinatown*, from the military men of *The Last Detail* and *A Few Good Men* to the mentally troubled writers of *The Shining* and *As Good as It Gets*. Plus the moody astronaut of *Terms of Endearment*, turns as the Joker and the devil, and plenty more.

He has scored less resoundingly with the handful of pictures he's directed, including the 1971 basketball drama *Drive, He Said* and the 1990 detective movie *The Two Jakes*, an unofficial *Chinatown* sequel. But he's won the respect of his colleagues even when the final results were forgettable. "His enthusiasm is contagious ," said cinematographer Nestor Almendros after shooting *Goin' South* with Nicholson in the director's chair, adding that "it sweeps the crew along like a cyclone."

Nicholson sees variety as a key to his love of acting, and to his staying power in a profession that's quick to discard performers who grow stale. "I was a late-blooming success in a certain way," he says, "so I had a lot of ideas about how you establish some kind of longevity. I take a certain amount of pride in the fact that I don't [repeatedly] play the same thing. That's because you can get trapped in something— trapped by a success," he continued, speaking in a quiet drawl that sometimes sank almost to a murmur. "The tendency is to do it at least one more time. And then if you want to do a departure and it doesn't work, you're dead. I say that from watching other people do it. From the very beginning, I always tried to do a movie I felt was more accessible, and then do something very different, and create my own peaks and valleys. Because you can't dictate to audiences what they're going to like."

None of these were new Nicholson ideas in 2002, when he articulated them at the Cannes festival; his thoughts on such matters were already formed when I first met him in the 1970s. "Today longevity means more than it did twenty or thirty years ago," he said in the year of *One Flew Over the Cuckoo's Nest*, one of his most enduringly memorable movies. "Some actors' careers were enormous and involved a lot of work, but only lasted three or four years. I'm already past that, and I'm trying to do different stuff. . . . The trick for an actor is to give you the feeling that you're meeting a different person each time."

An important part of Nicholson's technique is to cultivate an all-important sense of spontaneity. "When you're working," he said with a smile, "you don't want to act if you don't have to. It can be interpreted a million ways by the people [who] see it, but ultimately the camera photographs exactly what's there. That goes for a vase or an emotion. . . . You should work in the interrogative mood all the time. You should be asking questions *of* the character, not making statements *as* the character. These are things which, experience seems to have shown us, dredge the subconscious."

Interestingly, none of this means Nicholson is one of the chameleon-like actors who change their appearances and personalities with every new role. "He isn't someone who strikes people as disappearing into a part, the way Robert De Niro and Dustin Hoffman do," says Mikita Brottman, who edited *Jack Nicholson: Movie Top Ten*, a collection of essays on the actor. "He turns every character into someone who's like Jack Nicholson, or like the way we *think* he is—a little sly, cynical, and selfish, but at the same time honest and sincere. He's the opposite of glib. He always seems genuine."

Of course, "seems" may be the operative word. "No one really knows the real Jack anyway," Nicholson said at Cannes, flashing his mischievous grin—and making you wonder if indeed it's "all autobiography," just as he says.

Defining the Situation

BRANDO, ROLE-PLAYING, AND THE WESTERN AS PERFORMANCE ART

Although the western once stood among Hollywood's most popular genres, those days are probably gone forever. *Au courant* directors like Quentin Tarantino and Richard Linklater show occasional sparks of interest, but nobody expects the "oater" to enter a new age of achievement or popularity. Conventional wisdom holds it to be a shadow of its former self, driven into obscurity by a variety of factors, including a decline in historical consciousness among postmodern American audiences and—catalyzing this particular aspect of the decline—the rise of science fiction in the late 1970s. That view is largely correct: The enduringly popular *Star Wars* series, for instance, is a thinly disguised western saga—the first installment borrowed heavily from John Ford's 1956 classic *The Searchers*—with spaceships and light sabers replacing horses and sixguns. Years later, science fiction still soars (from *Men in Black* to *I, Robot*) and westerns are still largely moribund despite occasional successes like Clint Eastwood's highly praised *Unforgiven* (1992).

This essay is therefore an exercise in historiography and nostalgia rather than current events and prognostication. It takes a close look at a classic yet unconventional western—the eccentric *One-Eyed Jacks*, directed by and starring Marlon Brando—that attracted much notice in the early 1960s, when westerns were still riding high in American cinema. It may attract more as critics reassess Brando's career following his death in 2004 at the age of eighty-one.

The popularity of westerns in the late '50s and early '60s does not mean that either producers or audiences took the genre's entertainment value or deeper significations entirely for granted. Indeed, by the late '50s, filmmakers and moviegoers alike had developed mixed and complicated feelings about the western. Film historian Philip French identifies a "sense of unease" surrounding the genre during this period. Even when westerns "began to attract the best acting talent, the most skilled writers and accomplished directors," French observes, "not just for occasional forays but regularly and with decreasing condescension," reviewers of the '50s still tended to admire or attack such films "less on their merits than according to the critics' view of what a Western should be." This tendency persisted even when particular westerns were clearly "marked by a manifest seriousness or an obvious contempt for the routine" (French, 15, 14).

Other factors made the situation still more complex. While television westerns of the early '50s were generally aimed at twelve-year-old minds—as was TV in general, according to many critics—the emotional cross-currents of "psychological westerns" by such filmmakers as Anthony Mann and John Sturges were not entirely overlooked, and the notion of the "adult" western was a significant theme in public discussions of cinema and TV during the later part of the decade. Although high-culture prejudices and lazy attitudes definitely lingered with regard to the genre, many thoughtful observers did recognize its potential as a vehicle for exploring substantial social, moral, and historical issues.

Brando, himself a complex and multifaceted figure during much of his film and stage career, appears to have occupied both the pro- and anti-western positions during the '50s, combining prejudice against the genre with awareness of its possibilities for serious expression. In a mid-'50s interview with Truman Capote, conducted for a *New Yorker* profile, Brando mumblingly revealed that the first project of his newly formed independent production company would be a western (French, 14). Thereupon he erupted into embarrassed laughter, according to Capote's account, wondering if he would "ever be able to look [his] friends in the face again," and then asserting more soberly that "the first picture *has* to make money. . . ." The implication here is that Brando had embarked on his western enterprise for purely economic reasons, seeing little connection between this project and the sort of lofty ambition he expressed elsewhere in the same interview when he noted the "great potential" of cinema for saying "important things to a lot of people," and when he claimed that he had established his production company "to make pictures that explore the themes current in the world today." Yet on the same occasion, Brando also asserted that his western would be about "hatred and discrimination" and the effects of these evils on a community—clearly a substantial theme worthy of exploration through any genre capable of dealing with it. What emerges from Capote's quotations is a profoundly mixed set of emotions toward the western, which is seen (simultaneously) as laughably frivolous, embarrassingly mercenary, *and* responsive and versatile enough to move beyond what Brando called "cowboys-and-Indians stuff" and deal with ideas as serious and significant as those found in other branches of cinema and, indeed, the arts in general. (Capote's interview, published as "The Duke in His Domain," was conducted about five years before *One-Eyed Jacks* was released; at that time the film's projected title was *A Burst of Vermilion*, and Brando refers to a "Mexican boy" as its primary focus.)

Revisited several decades after its initial 1961 release, *One-Eyed Jacks* proves to have been an accurate predictor of Brando's later involvement with such sociopolitical issues as racism and minority rights. True, critical response to the film has often focused on its classical revenge-oriented plot, with Brando as a magnetic bad guy just out of jail and thirsty for vengeance against the former partner who put him there—a fellow named "Dad" Longworth, whose very name trumpets the psychological subtext of the story. Pauline Kael describes it as a straightforward revenge tale "about a bandit whose only purpose in life is to kill his former partner" (Kael, 432). Many commentators have also noted its psychoanalytical angles: Kael calls it a "peculiarly masochistic revenge fantasy" (Kael, 432), French points out its "strong undertone of masochism" (French, 16), and Raymond Durgnat links the (oedipal) relationship between Brando's character and Karl Malden's evil Dad with an "underlying 'Freudian' pattern" (Durgnat, 269–70) to be found in numerous films of the period. Still and all, a viewer in later decades might be more likely to observe the drama's quiet commitment to the dignity of its Mexican secondary characters, written and portrayed as decent, forthright individuals who contrast vividly with many of the Anglos sharing the screen with them. Although the film does not announce its concern for equal dignity in an overt way, the respect accorded to its Mexican characters gives them impressive weight within the narrative. Indeed, several passages of dialogue are spoken in Spanish, and even the longest of these are left untranslated by subtitles, as if subtitling might appear to patronize or marginalize the Spanish-speaking characters, and perhaps the Spanish-speaking portion of the movie's audience.

Another aspect of *One-Eyed Jacks* that has been overlooked with surprising consistency is the importance in the film of performance and role-playing as major motifs. This is the only film ever to be directed by Brando, who (despite his claim of being "nearly broke" while developing the production) was able to use his earnings, fame, and general Hollywood clout to set up his own company and supervise whatever production he chose. It's always interesting to examine a genre film directed by an outsider to the genre itself—as when, for example, such master filmmakers as F. W. Murnau, Carl Dreyer, and Stanley Kubrick turned their hands to the horror film in *Nosferatu, Vampyr,* and *The Shining,* respectively. In such cases both the workings of the genre and the artistic proclivities of the director may stand in high and revealing relief. Interest is heightened further when the director is by profession an actor whose primary calling is on the performing side rather than the supervisory side of the camera. Charles Laughton's directing of *The Night of the Hunter* in 1955 is a classic case in point.

Such considerations certainly apply to *One-Eyed Jacks*, which benefited in at least three areas from the experience Brando had accrued during his acting career. For one, he brought to the production a strong commitment to cinematic expression. Such a commitment had been evident in his acting for years prior to this project, and was borne out by his shooting a million feet of film for *One-Eyed Jacks* and assembling an original cut of four hours and thirty-one minutes, shortened to two hours and twenty-one minutes for release (Wright, 62). For another, he brought to the project an obvious gift for guiding performances, honed and refined during his own work on stages and movie sets. For a third, he brought to the film a fascination with acting and role-playing itself—a fascination that clearly runs deep in his artistic personality, and serves as a key element in the narrative and construction of the film. So important is this interest to the effectiveness of *One-Eyed Jacks*, and so bold are some of Brando's means of developing it, that one might conceptualize some parts of this 1961 western as an extended exercise in "performance art" before that avant-garde term was ever devised.

Although the elements of role-playing and performativity have particular significance in *One-Eyed Jacks*, they are by no means unusual in the western genre as a whole. Looking at representative westerns from different periods of Hollywood history, one finds many examples of filmmakers using performance, theatricality, and role-playing as important motifs. As early as 1923, James Cruze's turgid yet ambitious *The Covered Wagon* stresses its own theatricality with the image of a curtain rising and falling over the beginning and ending of the film. Looking beyond such decorative elements to narrative action itself, one finds a vivid instance in the 1927 western *Red Raiders*, which shows a white cavalry soldier entering an Indian camp disguised as an Indian, his face covered by an Indian mask—a clear instance of "costuming" within the story, although the "costumer's" lack of professional skill is betrayed by his failure to cover the "white man's moccasins" that eventually reveal the truth behind his performance to his momentarily deceived "audience."

Moving beyond the silent-film era, *The Big Trail* of 1930 shows the villain flagrantly misrepresenting himself to the heroine; for us in the audience, his bad acting ironically underscores the artificiality of his pose. *Mystery Ranch*, a genre-bending 1932 release from Fox, is a low-budget production styled in many respects to resemble the highly theatrical horror-movie cycle then in vogue; it features an ostentatiously performing piano-player villain as well as a hero who poses as an ordinary person rather than the Texas Ranger he really is. Even more striking from a "performance" standpoint is the same year's somewhat higher-budgeted *Law and Order*, wherein the hero chases off a lynch mob while bad guys look on (like an audience) and "applaud" at the end; later Andy Devine's poignant character, Johnny Kinsman, treats his own execution by hanging as if it were a show, addressing the audience and admiring his own photo (publicity shot?) in the newspaper. Performance as a thematic element in *Law and Order* is also emphasized by much fuss over the character of Lotta, an actress—"America's Dramatic Queen"—whose arrival in a frontier town is eagerly anticipated.

Still in 1932, the pro-Indian western *End of the Trail* breaks the flow of its dramatic story with two impassioned speeches by star Tim McCoy on the mistreatment of Indians by whites. The first of these speeches (and the second, to a lesser degree) has a halting spontaneity that indicates the semi-improvised nature of the statements. This provides a moment of quasidocumentary realism—since we become aware of McCoy as performer rather than character—that throws into relief the fictional (albeit historically based) nature of the narrative as a whole. The film also contains a good example of performance as a dramatic motif when McCoy's character pretends to his little son that he is a soldier in good standing, even though he has been ejected from the military and is now a civilian. The film ironically rationalizes this masquerade by having the "performer" (McCoy) wear the true "uniform" of his new status—i.e., plain civilian clothing—which makes him appear to the world at large exactly as he should, even as he presents his special "audience" (the child) with a lie that addresses the boy on the same level of *make-believe* "reality" represented by the boy's own kid-size military uniform.

Other westerns capitalizing on role-playing and performance are not hard to find, and a few more examples will suffice. *Massacre*, produced in 1934, features an Indian hero who begins the story as a Wild West Show performer, and a black character—the hero's servant, played by Clarence Muse—who pays corrupt Indians to film him in a bogus ceremony. *Sutter's Gold*, released in 1936, has star Edward Arnold performatively tooting a recurrent musical motif. *The Texas Rangers*, directed by King Vidor in 1936, inverts the *Mystery Ranch* masquerade when characters played by Fred MacMurray and Jack Oakie pretend to become Rangers so their true bad-guy natures won't be discovered. *Union Pacific*, directed by Cecil B. DeMille in 1939, features a Barbara Stanwyck character who improvises and performatively "reads" a nonexistent letter to a dying man; there's also a Joel McCrea character who fools railroad workers out of a saloon and back to their jobs by staging the announcement of a nonexistent gold strike at the end of the track.

Not surprisingly, radio provides a vehicle for performance motifs in some westerns made before the television era. *The Last Outlaw*, directed by Christy Cabanne in 1936, shows the juvenile lead imitating the clothing and mannerisms of a singing cowboy whom his girlfriend has admired in a movie; later, during the siege of a cabin at the climax, he shoots a radio that's playing a song by a singing cowboy, venting frustration at the way his imitative performance has failed to help his romance, and incidentally letting the girlfriend know *he* is the one who has come to her rescue. In the forgettable *Call of the Canyon,* one of six movies Gene Autry released in 1942, the hero himself engages in western-movie heroics against a radio-show background. Of course, the entire "singing cowboy" phenomenon itself demonstrates the compatibility of the western with ostentatious performance—and incongruous performance, given the mismatch between sweet cowboy songs and the violent action that westerns normally trade in. Performance also pervades the monotonous pose of a character like the Lone Ranger, with his costume-ball mask and melodramatic name. More serious westerns continued to exploit performance motifs even as the genre reached the end of its Hollywood heyday. Examples from the '60s include Sam Peckinpah's moody *Ride the High Country* of 1962, where Randolph Scott enters the story in Wild West Show guise; John Ford's masterpiece *The Man Who Shot Liberty Valance,* also from 1962, with its elaborate play of reality and illusion; and Elliot Silverstein's comic *Cat Ballou* of 1965, with its flamboyant musical-ballad structure.

To be sure, a broad historical sampling of any genre will provide evidence of a broad range of recurring themes. Yet role-playing and performance crop up in westerns persistently enough to suggest some special link between these particular motifs and this particular genre. The connection may be rooted in a certain artificiality of the western itself—a genre that attempts to deal with a historical subject (the conquering and settling of the American frontier) in terms that preserve its historical atmosphere while keeping a sense of relevance and "identifiability" for contemporary moviegoers. That is, the western strives to be simultaneously historical and up-to-date, a difficult and in some ways contradictory project. Sometimes the contradictions of the genre lead filmmakers to strain against chronological limitations—as in a movie like *In Old Monterey,* which mingles the

Old West and World War II—or to portray Old West manners and morals in ways meant to flatter modern-day tastes and attitudes. The difficulty of merging old conventions with new sensibilities may make filmmakers acutely aware of the western genre as a construction, wherein historical material (whether factual, impressionistic, or downright mythical) must be rendered not only acceptable but actively appealing to spectators with "modern" tastes; in such an atmosphere, it is not surprising to find artifice of other sorts—performance, role-playing, imitation, masquerade, and so forth—operating with special vigor. Artifice, one might say, is on everyone's mind when a western is produced. This includes characters as well as filmmakers.

Even within the busy field of western-movie "performance," role-playing and "acting within the story" stand out with particular clarity in *One-Eyed Jacks*, reflecting Brando's preoccupations as an actor in addition to the preexisting traditions of the genre. The film's interest in theatricality becomes clear right after the opening credits, when a town is shown in an establishing shot framed through a large gate; this gives the image a stagelike effect—as if we were viewing it through a proscenium arch—that is hardly rare for a Hollywood film, but carries a definite suggestion of the theatrics to come. These theatrics lose no time in arriving, as we meet Brando's character (Rio) picturesquely posing on the margin of a bank robbery while his partners do the dirty work behind him.

The next scene finds Rio engaged in a different form of posing—namely, the seduction of a woman by means of an elaborate (and elaborately strung-out) lie. Falsehood piles upon falsehood in his blatantly manipulative speech: He tells her she has "something in [her] eye" in order to get close enough for a kiss; he apologizes for the kiss by lamenting his lack of "upbringing" with a show of utterly false sincerity; and—most outrageously—he insists she accept his gift of a ring allegedly bestowed on him by his mother, but actually stolen by him during the robbery that just happened. His pitch is interrupted on the brink of success by the arrival of his partners, warning of imminent danger from the law. Rio responds not only by abandoning his sexual pursuit but by retrieving the ring—that is, the "prop" in his lavish masquerade— from the very finger on which he has just placed it. Objects are always props in fiction films, of course, but in *One-Eyed Jacks* their nature *as props* will become apparent more than once, reflecting Brando's awareness of the expressive "role" that objects play not only in filmmaking but in life. (Indeed, we see isolated, prop-like objects as early as the opening credits, when the camera pans between a cowboy hat on the left and a rifle and saddlebags on the right—lingering in between on a blank stretch of brick wall, as if to emphasize their arbitrary, "floating" presence as the film begins to construct its meaning.)

Rio's care in retrieving the ring/prop signals the central importance of role-playing in his behavior and in his very nature as a human being. It is also the first of many elements in the film that suggest the importance of role-playing in Brando's vision of the world. Brando had built a strong reputation by the mid-'50s as an advocate of the "Method" acting developed by Konstantin Stanislavsky and his followers; audiences therefore associated him with "realism" and verisimilitude. Yet careful observers noted that these qualities were tempered with other elements—that the style he epitomized was a "*theatricalized* realism" and a "*near*-naturalism," as Oscar Brockett and Robert Findlay put it, that often appeared against *stylized* backgrounds and settings (Blum, 59). In short, Brando did not insist on some sort of "pure" realism. So it is not surprising to find a deliberately self-aware quality running through *One-Eyed Jacks*, in which his acting is often *visible as acting*. This is true on a double level, since (a) the character he plays is a *poseur*, pretender, and con artist, and (b) he *plays* this character with such evident gusto that his acting techniques are often plain to see.

An early example of this occurs in his first scene with Ben Johnson's character, where Brando plays Rio's coolness and taciturnity so broadly that they become self-proclaiming trademarks of Rio rather than the implicit, contingent behavioral traits they might have seemed in a more underplayed portrayal. Other examples are so numerous—Brando talking to Dad's family with his mouth full of food, Brando talking and drinking with a matchstick in his teeth, Brando cleaning his ear with a finger while romancing a woman—that critic James Naremore calls him a "nonconformist" actor who enjoyed "mocking" the "good manners" of traditional acting (Naremore, 201–2). Kael goes further, dubbing him "the Great Unpredictable" in a review of this very movie (Kael, 432). None of this is to say that Brando is "hamming it up" or even "over-acting" in the film; any tendency in this direction is offset by the sheer skillfulness and ingenuity of his work, which makes even the most obvious histrionic devices a pleasure to watch. Brando does seem intent on offering his audience three spectacles for the price of one, however: the sight of Rio's behavior; the sight of Rio's various "performances" for the benefit of other characters; and the sight of his own movie-acting performance, which calls attention to itself through the very forthrightness of its virtuosity.

Brando's artful self-awareness may have been underscored and enhanced by a technique he used to facilitate his dual function as director and star of this movie. "To help himself visualize his character in upcoming scenes," according to a biographer, "he had hired . . . a stage and film actor . . . to 'play' Rio not only by wearing his costume and standing in the right place, but by also delivering his lines and gestures" (Manso, 484). Watching this stand-in for himself surely encouraged Brando to think of his own performance in third-person terms more consistently than might otherwise have been the case.

The actorly dimension of *One-Eyed Jacks* takes on even more importance once the film enters its main phase, with Rio and his archenemy Dad Longworth working out their mutual distrust and animosity. It is apparent that both men employ role-playing as a devious tool in relating to other individuals and to society at large. Confronting each other for the first time since Rio's escape from prison, they both engage in masterly play-acting. Rio keeps his prison stretch a secret, expresses totally false affection for Dad, and professes only a vague idea of how long it has been since their last meeting, even though (as we learn much later) he knows to the day how long his jail term lasted. In turn, Dad lies about the circumstances of their last encounter and treats his long-dreaded expartner as a long-awaited prodigal son. Indeed, we discover that Dad is as much a master of role-playing as Rio is, having fooled the town into believing him a profoundly *reformed* sinner who is now devoted to family values and the public good. (During the opening of the town's fiesta, Dad seems perfectly at home as a public showman who introduces the festivities, literally dances in the street, and thanks the public for having rewarded his virtue by electing him sheriff.) The extended cat-and-mouse game between Rio and Dad takes place largely through deliberately assumed (and thoroughly false) attitudes, behaviors, and speeches. This is mirrored by the competition between Brando and Malden—also costars in the legendary *On the Waterfront* a few years earlier—as they *perform* these two "performers." The result is a story *and* a film that thrive on narrative performances *and* movie-acting performances.

Things become even more complex when Brando allows the "roles" within the story to contain bits of truthfulness along with the falsehoods that the characters are foisting on one another. For example, when Louisa tells Rio that she'd like to know him better, he responds with the ironically true statement that "you might wish you didn't"; and afterward he reveals to her—for his own tactical reasons—the fact that he has deceived her. Similarly, the town that shows such public confidence in Dad's publicly proclaimed goodness knows about his criminal past, as does his forgiving (and gullible) family. Yet deception remains at the core of both men's behavior, public and private. Rio claims to work in a "secret" government job (wrapping a "secret" within a lie) and shamelessly falls back on "dialogue" and "props" lifted almost literally from earlier "performances," as when he gives a necklace to Louisa—recalling the ring of the first seduction scene—while using a time-tested line ("You don't know how good you make me feel") to complete the effect. So pervasive is role-playing in the world of *One-Eyed Jacks* that even the virtuous women of the film engage in it when this suits their purpose—particularly when Louisa and her mother conspire to lie about her "purity" after her night with Rio, and later collude to hide her pregnancy.

Role-playing does not operate entirely through language and appearance, moreover. At times it bursts into bluntly effective action, enhancing the masochistic undertone noted in the film by some critics. Dad's punishment of Rio takes the form of a public whipping and maiming, for instance, conducted like a show in the town's public space; and Dad clearly relishes the spectacular aspect of this performance as much as Rio despises it. Rio later recuperates from his maiming in a Mexican fishing village where he rehabilitates his wounded hand (wrapped for the remainder of the film in a leather prosthetic device, now a permanent part of his costume) in scenes that might be called rehearsals for the gunfight that will take place at the climax.

The whipping scene provides the most vivid (and notorious) example of Brando's willingness to bring the dynamics of movie acting into the dynamics of the story he wanted to tell. Almost as heedless of cost overruns as Michael Cimino on the *Heaven's Gate* location, or James Cameron as *Titanic* doubled its original $100 million budget, he decided to use the hugely risky (because hugely expensive) technique of improvising while the cameras rolled in order to bring more reality and spontaneity into the film's performances. "As he worked with his actors," biographer Peter Manso later reported,

it was straight Method improv. For the sadistic whipping-post scene, which would become one of the movie's best-remembered episodes, Malden was positioned far enough back so he'd miss Brando by two feet, and was told to go at it until the sweat poured off his face. Given the risk of injury from the genuine twelve-foot bullwhip he was using, Malden started tentatively. With the line, "Have you had enough?," Brando was supposed to collapse, but once after several takes, Marlon wheeled and extemporaneously spat in Karl's face. "I mean, he put a real glob there," Malden recalled. "I wiped it off and ad-libbed, 'Guess you haven't had enough,' and went back to the whipping. Later he said he thought I was really going to let him have it. But he got the scene exactly as he wanted" (Manso, 484).

It is important to observe that Rio is *aware* of role-playing as a key element in his personality—not only when he tells deliberate lies (to Dad, to sexually attractive women, and so on) but also when he uses appearances to establish and maintain his presence as a self-assertive person who is determined to have his own way just about all the time. When one of his partners wants to ride into town and simply kill Dad Longworth outright, Rio's choice of words in vetoing the idea—"It's not my style"—indicates his deliberate cultivation of a *style* that incorporates real behaviors as well as outward displays. He consciously recognizes the effects not only of his lies but also of his true statements, as when he says, "Well, that's my sad tale," after telling Louisa of his time in prison. The very climax of the story, with its traditionally staged shootout and conventional triumph of hero (or antihero) over villain, is influenced by Rio's use of performance, as he pretends to have been mortally shot only to spring out from an unexpected new position and win the struggle.

In his influential study *The Presentation of Self in Everyday Life,* sociologist Erving Goffman writes that a

character staged in a theater is not in some ways real, nor does it have the same kind of real consequences as does the thoroughly contrived character performed by a confidence man; but the *successful* staging of either of these types of false figures involves use of *real* techniques—the same techniques by which everyday persons sustain their real social situations. Those who conduct face to face interaction on a theater's stage must meet the key requirement of real situations; they must expressively sustain a definition of the situation: but this they do in circumstances that have facilitated their developing an apt terminology for the interactional tasks that all of us share (Goffman, 254–55).

By the mid-'50s, Brando was deservedly recognized as a master of that "apt terminology" for face-to-face interaction in the public forums of theater and cinema; he was thus a master of sustaining the "definition of the situation" that Goffman identifies as an essential element in the presentation of a satisfactory self-image. *One-Eyed Jacks* finds Brando carrying his fascination with the activity of defining the situation (and, by extension, controlling the situation) beyond the level of professional craft, embedding it in the processes of meaning-creation within the fiction itself. Watching this film, one sees all of the interactional modes mentioned by Goffman in the sentences just cited—the (actual) staging of a not-in-some-ways-real character in a fictional work; the (fictional) activity of a confidence man (Rio) who induces real consequences in his world; and the employment by Brando of real acting techniques through which he defines the situation, that is, convinces us of the excellence of his performance and leads us to accept Rio as a convincing and involving character who *himself* is defining a situation within the narrative.

One-Eyed Jacks may thus be seen as an unusually multifaceted western that carries to surprising lengths the habitual concern of this artifice-conscious genre with role-playing and performance, at the same time reflecting a great actor's fascination with those same matters and carrying them into the fictional realm of narrative, action, and character development. "I work fourteen hours a day," Manso quotes Brando as saying during the film's production. "Directing by itself is hard enough. But I've found that there are no divisional lines between an actor becoming a director. Things are so subtly interlaced it is hard to know where one begins and the other ends" (Manso, 484). This complexity both enriches the film and underscores the affinities of its genre with issues of performativity and the presentation of self to others. In this sense, *One-Eyed Jacks*—and perhaps the western itself—is performance art, with a vengeance.

WORKS CITED

Brockett, Oscar and Robert Findlay. 1971. *Century of Innovation*, Englewood Cliffs: Prentice Hall, 573. Quoted in Richard A. Blum, *American Film Acting: The Stanislavski Heritage*, Ann Arbor: U.M.I. Research Press, 1977. Emphases added.

Naremore, James. 1988. *Acting in the Cinema.* Berkeley: University of California Press.

Capote, Truman. 1963. "The Duke in His Domain," in *Selected Writings of Truman Capote.* London: Hamish Hamilton, 1963, 417–18. Quoted in French, *Westerns: Aspects of a Movie Genre.* New York: The Viking Press, 1974.

Durgnat, Raymond. 1967. *Films and Feelings.* Cambridge: The M.I.T. Press.

French, Philip. 1974. *Westerns: Aspects of a Movie Genre.* New York: The Viking Press.

Goffman, Erving. 1959. *The Presentation of Self in Everyday Life.* New York: Doubleday. Emphases in original.

Kael, Pauline. 1982. *5001 Nights at the Movies: A Guide From A to Z.* New York: Holt, Rinehart and Winston.

Manso, Peter. 1994. *Brando: The Biography.* New York: Hyperion.

Wright, Will. 1975. *Sixguns and Society: A Structural Study of the Western.* Berkeley: University of California Press.

Novelists and Their Movies

MAILER, DOCTOROW, IRVING

The film industry has been drawing on novels and other forms of literary fiction since the early days of silent cinema. The results range from first rate to utter disaster, and responses by the original writers are just as varied—from "they've ruined my work" to "they did a splendid job" to "they gave me the money, so who cares?" Cross-disciplinary movies are especially interesting when the novelist is an important one and plays an active role in the shaping of the film. This essay is a trio of snapshots offering glimpses of such cases through a critic's eyes.

NORMAN MAILER

"I think a film should be as sinister and lively, as odd and riveting . . . as a dream," said Norman Mailer, novelist turned moviemaker. "A good powerful dream."

Mailer's own 1987 movie, *Tough Guys Don't Dance*, has the makings of a *bad* powerful dream. Based on his 1984 novel of the same (silly) title, it turns a murder-mystery plot into a melodramatic fandango so dark and delirious that it's hard to tell whether he wants us to laugh, cry, or cringe.

Actually, the answer is all three. *Tough Guys Don't Dance*, the only one of his novels Mailer himself has adapted for the screen, is the kind of movie that begs to be called controversial—a term some cultural commentators use as a reflexive form of praise, as if its meaning didn't imply a critical "con" as well as a promotional "pro." Mailer has benefited from that careless use of "controversial" as much as any writer in memory, using it to build a feisty media presence that has rivaled—many would say outstripped—his accomplishments on the printed page. His most respected works (such as his 1948 first novel, *The Naked and the Dead*, and some nonfiction writings) have made him a major figure whose influence couldn't be wished away by his worst aesthetic enemy. Yet it's hard to imagine a third-rate book like *Tough Guys Don't Dance* getting a fraction as much attention if it weren't the product of a self-aware celebrity with—in addition to a pair of Pulitzer Prizes and a literary ambition that has never seemed less than thoroughly genuine—a knack for turning the trashiest accomplishments into media-hyped gold.

The screen version of *Tough Guys*, written and directed by Mailer, serves up a string of weird variations on the book's sordid plot. It's about a lovelorn man (Ryan O'Neal) who finds two severed heads in his Cape Cod marijuana cache and can't figure out—his memory is too fogged by alcohol—wherher he's a villain or a victim. In a printed statement on the film, Mailer wrote that he wanted it to embody a "strange and sinister fever" that he suspects is rampant among "the pleasure-loving classes."

One suspects Mailer is a member of those selfsame classes, so one suspects he knows what he's talking about. I asked him for some detail on this in the attic studio of his Provincetown, Mass., summer home, near the locations where *Tough Guys* was filmed. Clearly in an affable and talkative mood, Mailer responded by saying that statement was "cooked up" as a promotional ploy—the kind of thing you write "to get people to read your script" and then forget about. Still, he didn't disavow it. "It is a picture about America," he said in the gruff but friendly voice that's one of his talk-show and interview trademarks. "It's not a realistic picture. These are not typical American citizens. But I do think there's been a kind of greed and irresponsibility loose in American life in the last four or five years. . . . This is a vision of some of the worst things that are going on in America now, and what could possibly happen to us if we keep going."

No amount of cautionary intent has gotten many moviegoers to swallow the grisly episodes of *Tough Guys Don't Dance* in the years since its initial (and brief) release, which may explain why Mailer has not done much further work in the feature-film vineyards. In any case, he said the tale's cautionary aspect is only marginal. For him as a once-aspiring auteur, the purpose of cinema is dark and dreamlike, not enlightening and instructive. "I think fiction can intensify the moral consciousness of a time," he told me. "I think theater can enlarge one's emotional appreciation of social situations. [But] film doesn't work on our minds. It works on all the places that have never been worked on by other art forms—all the synapses between our memory and our emotions and our nerves and our sense of time."

Hence the connection Mailer sees between cinema and dreams, which he calls "the interface, if you will, between life and eternity, between life and death. . . . Dreams, to me, are a dialogue between your soul and your self. It's a way for the soul to say, 'Look, you're not living in the proper fashion at all. These are some of the disasters, metaphorically speaking, that attend you.' "

Mailer sees a "dream logic" at work in every film, good or bad. "If someone throws up a hand like this," he said with an appropriate gesture, "and the next [shot] is some birds taking off like that . . . there's a connection. You might not be able to name the connection. But somewhere in that deep, mysterious world of signs, portents, images, and hints, there is a connection that makes sense to us."

E. L. DOCTOROW

"I resent the impact film has in this culture. As a writer, I find it's the enemy. All the rigorous and passionate moviegoing . . .

makes me very jealous. With its variations, like TV, it has probably done more than anything else to create a kind of profound illiteracy in the world today."

Such sentiments wouldn't be surprising from a man of words like E. L. Doctorow, except that he once collaborated with the "enemy," writing the screenplay for *Daniel*, based on *The Book of Daniel*, one of his most respected novels. This was in 1983, and he hasn't written another script—adapted or original—since.

Why not? Basically because he had "very mixed feelings" about the *Daniel* project, as he told me at the time. On one hand, he feared some viewers would feel there was now no need to read the novel, which treats the story—about the children of two radicals executed for espionage—in more depth and detail. It was also possible, he said, that his reputation as a serious writer would suffer.

On the other hand, he knew the film would reach a large audience that would never read the book anyway. And he made sure the movie reflected his own ideas. He insisted on having a say in all matters from casting to the final cut, and he worked closely with director Sidney Lumet.

When it opened, critics and audiences had mixed opinions about *Daniel*, which retains the novel's main themes while scaling down the plot and sanitizing some of the action. Doctorow told me he himself was pleased with it, preferring its condensed energy to the talkiness of *Ragtime*, which had been adapted from his novel by Michael Weller for director Milos Forman two years earlier.

What prompted Doctorow to tackle the movie world despite his doubts? Just an impulse. "When I have a choice between caution and recklessness," he told me at his modest Long Island summer home, "I'll choose recklessness. It was the more dangerous alternative—and therefore more interesting—to make the film rather than block it. All my life, I've done the most important things instinctively, without sufficient thought."

From the start, Doctorow wanted *Daniel* to echo his book closely, even though he felt "most movies are short stories rather than novels in their content and linearity." Once into it, he found screenwriting a snap. "It's another language," he said, "but you pick it up quickly if you deal in language. The principles of composition are the same, and you worry about the same things: Does it work? Are you repeating yourself? . . . Once you learn the tech-talk they use, you just move right in."

The only frustration, he said, was having to collaborate, an unfamiliar activity for most novelists. And even after the fact he seemed awed by the expense of filmmaking, although *Daniel* was a relatively cheap movie at $8 million, with many of the participants working for minimum pay. "I used to tease my friends about this," Doctorow remarked. "They said they brought in *Ragtime* for $32 million. I said I brought in my novel for $78—a few boxes of paper and some typewriter ribbons."

A controversial aspect of the *Daniel* film and book is the resemblance of two characters to Julius and Ethel Rosenberg, who were executed in 1953 after being convicted of stealing atomic secrets. Doctorow stressed that his characters are fictitious. "If I wanted to write about the Rosenbergs, I would have called them that. Anybody who knows me at all knows this," said the author, whose *Ragtime* put such people as Harry Houdini and Sigmund Freud into a fictional plot. "My interest was not in writing a documentary novel. I began not with the Rosenberg family, but with the extremity of their situation, and the law that was applied in their case. I used this for my own imaginative responses."

Doctorow expressed surprise at the flaps occasionally caused by his blending of fact and fiction. "Fiction and the imagination are another way of knowing," he told me, "as opposed to empirical investigation, legal discovery, journalism. I've never believed this is *life* over here and *art* over there. They mix up, and always have. I'm against precious and aseptic ideas of literature having nothing to do with life. So many of the great masters have jumped in with both feet: Dostoevsky, Dreiser, Tolstoy, Dickens. . . . They were steeped to the eyebrows in what was going on."

The themes of *Daniel* are diverse, including a child's fear of abandonment, capital punishment, and the effects of idealism on a family. Many are related to political ideas or circumstances. Yet the writer doesn't see the movie or novel as essentially political.

"What art does is to enlarge our own humanity," he said, "by allowing us to live vicariously the experiences of others—with whom we might not otherwise be in sympathy. We find ourselves living intimately with people we probably would not invite to dinner at our home, like Raskolnikov. A major function of all art is to keep us alive to each other. And that's not political at all. . . . At its best, in the great works, it's almost a religious function."

Since some of its key events are rooted in politics, however, is *Daniel* the kind of work that could prompt social change? "Once an Englishman called me the Balzac of the petrol pumps," remarked the writer, "because I want people who work at gas stations and wait on tables to read my books. . . . Of course, you want your work to have an impact. But I must admit my doubts about the efficacy of this."

These are the same doubts W. H. Auden had "when he said art didn't change anything," Doctorow continued, "and all the antifascist poets of the '30s did nothing to stop Hitler. . . . If a book or film can make any kind of change, it's usually quite slow. Art never quite catches up to outrageous reality. It's always lumbering behind history."

Sounds gloomy. Yet later, Doctorow agreed that culture includes "a process by which myth takes over from history. Today, a writer's function must partly be to investigate the myths of the past—the myths we've accumulated and live by—and contravene them with some kind of additional intelligence. Otherwise, they'll run rampant."

Here, then, is the social role of *Daniel* and other movies of its type. "This film probes some very uncomfortable things," Doctorow said. "But if people stop examining their national myths . . . something monstrous happens, and true totalitarianism sets in."

For me, this comment raises the question of whether movies themselves aren't just another set of steps in the mythmaking process. Doctorow listened to this suggestion, and admitted there is a built-in paradox. "But if enough people do this kind of work," he said, "things will be healthy and free-flowing, and no one vision will become entrenched. It's true, we add to the clutter, and use up some paper and trees in the bargain. But the alternative is silence. And I don't see how that's a more positive contribution."

JOHN IRVING

John Irving looks glum on the jacket of *My Movie Business*, his breezily written memoir about turning his novel *The Cider House Rules* into a film.

The photo is pure Hollywood illusion, though. Irving was dressed for a tiny part he played in the movie—"the disapproving stationmaster"—but behind his dour expression he felt "elated" when the snapshot was taken. Shooting of the film was about to wrap, ending what for Irving had been a thirteen-year effort to bring this story to the screen. So he was the opposite of glum as he strode into the lower Manhattan restaurant where we were meeting to talk about the project.

Two of Irving's nine novels had been translated into high-profile movies before: *The World According to Garp* and *The Hotel New Hampshire*. (*Simon Birch* and the later *The Door in the Floor* are only loose or partial adaptations of *A Prayer for Owen Meany* and *A Widow for One Year*, respectively.) Still, the decision to write his own screenplay for *The Cider House Rules* was a first. He embarked on it partly as an "experiment" and partly as an effort to "protect" the story's historical and scientific details, which he had painstakingly researched. In addition to penning his own screenplay, he struck a deal with Miramax Films guaranteeing that all "creative decisions" would be made by director Lasse Hallström, producer Richard Gladstein, and himself.

Like the novel, the movie has two main characters. One is Wilbur Larch, an aging physician (Michael Caine) who runs a rural Maine orphanage where women seek his help either to put their babies up for adoption or to terminate their pregnancies. He regards such decisions as entirely personal to the women who make them, and sees himself as a public servant who gives each patient "an orphan or an abortion," depending on her choice.

The other main character is Homer Wells, a young man (Tobey Maguire) who grows up in the orphanage and becomes Dr. Larch's protégé, until he makes his own decision not to perform abortions. He then leaves home for a very different kind of life among the African-American laborers on a New England apple farm. There, new experiences teach him lessons about life that prompt his eventual return to the orphanage and Dr. Larch's legacy.

Irving sees the novel and film as "political" works conveying a clear set of ideas. Yet he also wants them to be perceived as richly emotional tales in the spirit of Charles Dickens, whose books inspired him to become a writer when he was in his middle teens.

"It's didactic, but it's not a harangue," he said of the narrative. "I never imply that there's anything about the decision [to have an abortion] that is or should be easy. It seems to me this is among the most morally complicated and conflicted decisions that any woman or couple might need to make. But precisely for that reason, it's not a decision that should be legislated. It's not a decision that someone else should ever make for you."

Like many novelists who get involved in writing screenplays, Irving approached the task with mixed feelings about the movies. He rarely goes to theaters anymore—"It drives me crazy when people talk!"— but he enjoys videocassettes that allow him to indulge his favorite tastes. One reason he felt *The Cider House Rules* would make an effective film is that the plot reminded him of old-fashioned westerns.

"Homer is a young man trained to be a physician," Irving said by way of explaining this, "even though he doesn't want to be one. He's like the gunfighter who wants to hang up his gun, and he goes through three-quarters of the film saying, 'I'm not a doctor!' But there comes a time when he has to do what he's been trained to do.

There's a sense of [destiny] here that comes from my adolescent love of films like *Shane* and *High Noon*, where somebody's trying to quit something, but it's just the wrong time."

Another reason for trying the movie business was Irving's desire for a temporary break from the solitude of a novelist's life. "I'm not complaining," he said. "I've liked being alone since I was a kid . . . and I like my 'day job' better than writing screenplays. But when your working life is circumscribed by a four- or five-year cycle—which is what a novel represents to me—and in that working life you share what you're doing with no one, other than reading an occasional chapter to your wife, there's something very beckoning about the idea that you could have a successful collaboration. I just loved the friendship of it."

He also enjoyed sharing responsibility for the final outcome. "When you write a novel," he says, "the exactness of the detail is everything. . . . There is no such thing as too much specificity. That's what language [in a novel] is: With every door you open, you're responsible for closing it. But when you write a screenplay, you're not the guy who gets to close and open the doors. . . . The exactness of detail comes from the camera and the director, instead. In my [memoir] I liken this to merely putting up the scaffolding for a building someone else is going to build. You're not the builder, the director is."

Irving said he expected more screenplays to pepper his career—he had already written a film version of *A Son of the Circus*, although it remains unproduced as of this writing—but he'll always think of himself as a novelist first, and it's likely that Dickens will always remain his primary inspiration.

"A novel by Dickens never tries to persuade you intellectually," he said with admiration. "You are persuaded emotionally or not at all. . . . A piece on *Cider House* in *The New York Times* said, 'The film's tenderness occasionally verges on sentimentality.' I would say, 'The film doesn't verge. It is sentimental!' So get over it, and stop thinking that's a bad word."

Allegory and Enigma

THE ENDURING FASCINATION OF FANTASY

As of 2004, the Harry Potter phenomenon is still going strong on page and screen. The sixth and longest installment in J. K. Rowling's book series captured international headlines as readers (or at least buyers) clamored for copies before it had reached bookstore shelves. The first two features films based on Rowling's novels, *Harry Potter and the Sorcerer's Stone* and *Harry Potter and the Chamber of Secrets*, were walloping hits in 2001 and 2002, respectively—and predictions that director Chris Columbus's heavily literal adaptations would soon lose their novelty appeal were finessed when Warner Bros. cleverly hired Mexican-American filmmaker Alfonso Cuarón to helm the third entry in the franchise, pleasing critics and audiences with his darker view of Harry and his troubled past.

All that overshadowed these events in the cultural world was the overwhelming success of *The Lord of the Rings*, adapted for the screen from J. R. R. Tolkien's learned, literate trio of novels about a fabled "Middle-earth" and its long-gone inhabitants. The first installment of filmmaker Peter Jackson's trilogy, *The Fellowship of the Ring*, bored me silly but garnered many rave reviews and a gigantic box-office following. The second episode, *The Two Towers*, bored me again while pleasing fans as much as its predecessor had. The third movie, *The Return of the King*, irritated me a bit less—perhaps my expectations were sufficiently lowered by then—even as it drew critical raves (including a New York Film Critics Circle award for best picture) and ecstatic responses from moviegoers around the globe. The only fly in their elven ointment was that Tolkien only penned three such novels, plus a less ambitious prequel (*The Hobbit*) aimed primarily at children. After some murmurings about filming *The Hobbit* as a dazzling climax to his *LOTR* achievement, Jackson decided to move on with his illustrious career—at this writing he's helming a *King Kong* remake—leaving fans of the trilogy with nothing to anticipate but countless hours with the DVD editions, which proffer "extended" versions of movies that were far, far too long to begin with.

In the meanwhile, fantasy films have continued their triumphant march to the forefront of today's pop-culture scene. George Lucas has extended his *Star Wars* saga to six movies—so far—and Steven Spielberg, the other inventor of the modern blockbuster, has kept his hand in the genre with *A.I. Artificial Intelligence*, based on the Stanley Kubrick screenplay; *Minority Report*, a Tom Cruise vehicle; and plans for a *War of the Worlds* project. A wide range of other filmmakers dip into the field when its suits their fancies, yielding results as different as Tim Burton's artful oddities and Arnold Schwarzenegger's bruising box-office bonanzas.

Among the many lessons to be gleaned from all this, one is surely a reconfirmation of the enduring desire of both children and adults to immerse themselves in fantasy worlds—a desire that may have swelled further among Americans since the events of September 11, given the time-tested power of escapist art in troubled times. These fantasy realms of wizards, goblins, hobbits, androids, robots, and terminators have tremendous allure that consistently draws a wide and enthusiastic audience. In the age of the internet and MTV, why do fantasies—often more old-fashioned than new-fangled in their basic structures and concerns—still manage to pull in such eager crowds?

In an interview with *Newsweek* magazine's Malcolm Jones, author Rowling reported that she regularly gets letters from youngsters addressed to Professor Dumbledore—headmaster at the Hogwarts School of Witchcraft and Wizardry, her books' main setting—begging to be let into the school, which they're convinced really exists. Children of all ages are clearly entranced by Rowling's world of dragons, trolls, flying broomsticks, three-headed dog monsters named Fluffy, and a hippogriff or two. But if, as seems to be the case, the Harry Potter stories appeal to countless adults as well as children—adults who supposedly know truth from fiction—their spellbinding enchantment takes on more interest.

Part of the explanation has to do with the deep-seated human compulsion to immerse ourselves in the lives of others, especially when those others—like Harry Potter—are unlikely underdogs faced with the challenge of overcoming huge obstacles. If the unlikely underdog turns out to be gifted with special, supernatural powers, then all the better: At the heart of every dream, Sigmund Freud tells us, lies a wish. Also appealing is the escape such fantasies offer from the routine contemporary world and the often mind-numbing details of our everyday lives. Harry's battles on behalf of the noble house of Gryffindor against the dubious denizens of Slytherin seem a million miles from planning mortgage payments, keeping track of taxes, and the other mundane problems most of us have to deal with.

Equally compelling is the fact that fantasy worlds have their own ontological frameworks—their own histories, rules, and ways of life, baffling to outsiders but second nature to regular readers and viewers, who become self-taught cognoscenti of the mythological domain. Like avid followers of soap operas and sports teams, fantasy fans are special groups with their own sense of history, their own understandings of make-believe worlds, their own knowledge of characters' limitations and vocabularies, all of which inspire a disdainful clannishness at times. This elitism reinforces the arcane, hieratic character of fantasy domains whose idiosyncratic natures readily exclude unimaginative outsiders, casting them in the roles of worldly earthlings or stupid Muggles who can't tell an orc from a handsaw.

In short, magic must have rules, as fantasists from G. K. Chesterton to Tolkien have pointed out. But this is more easily preached than practiced. Many fantasy novels are weakened by internal tensions between the yearning for flights of fancy and the well-defined rule systems that authors impose on their imaginary realms. Most bookstores have a section full of third-rate sword-and-sorcery novels like L. Barker's *Quest for Earthlight* series and N. M. Browne's *Warriors of Alavna,* in which the characters' lives are so uninterestingly bound up with centaurs and unicorns that empathic engagement is precluded for most of us, making real narrative suspense or excitement almost impossible. It's hard to enter the lives of creatures who don't share human experiences or emotions.

In the best fantasies, however—the short stories of Ursula LeGuin, say, or magic-realist works like Carlos Fuentes's *Aura* and Angela Carter's *Nights at the Circus*—this tension is a primary source of power and surprise. One of the best things about the Harry Potter series is the way it locates "cracks" in the ordinary, everyday human world familiar to us all (a certain brick in a wall, a pillar between two train platforms) that provide secret portals to the fantasy otherworld. The most memorable of these "cracks," perhaps, is the piece of prosaic furniture that leads to Narnia in C. S. Lewis's classic *The Lion, the Witch and the Wardrobe.*

While every successful fantasy film and novel has cadres of devoted and sometimes competitive followers, all fantasies are not created equal. It's worthwhile to make distinctions between fantasy that's pertinent and instructive, on one hand, and the banality of unmitigated escapism, on the other. Critics may come to widely differing conclusions when assessing particular works, but it seems clear that the best fantasy novels function on multiple levels, often in subtle and intricate ways. Just as Thomas Mallory's *Morte d'Arthur* addresses painful issues related to personal loyalty, social conflict, and divine justice, Lewis's visionary works—whether child-centered fantasies like *The Chronicles of Narnia* or adult books like his space-fiction trilogy—explore sociological and theological issues including the nature of religious conversion, the challenges of moral struggle, and the rewards of spiritual growth. The most powerful fantasies operate at an allegorical as well as a literal level, exploring recognizably human conflicts and crises by recontextualizing them in imaginative frameworks that have resonated with readers since storytellers first elaborated them in ancient legends and myths.

Other fantasies are less thematically and aesthetically substantial. While the Harry Potter stories are full of captivating vignettes, Rowling's prose style has little of the fluid charm found in Lewis, the mythopoetic complexity conjured by Tolkien, or the magical depth found in George MacDonald's phantasmatic fairy tales. Anthony Holden, a judge of the Whitbread book awards for which *Harry Potter and the Prisoner of Azkaban* was a contender, drubbed Rowling for deploying a "pedestrian, ungrammatical prose style which has left me with a headache and a sense of a wasted opportunity." Equally important, the world of Harry Potter—like the realms of the weaker sword-and-sorcery novels—tends to be inoffensive and benevolent, if a tad more daring (references to death, occasional disobedience toward adults) than the most conservative children's literature. This innocuousness is appropriate insofar as the tales are aimed at youngsters presumed unready for the untrammeled complexities of adult life; but it precludes genuine insight into the daunting and haunting aspects of human experience—the very aspects that give weight and power to endlessly seductive fantasies like the *Morte D'Arthur* or the inexhaustibly suggestive tales of Norse, Greek, and Roman mythology. Compared with these earlier works, modern fantasies tend to be cleaner, more calculating, less impulsive and unpredictable.

This said, book publishers and movie studios have reaped huge rewards by recognizing that the most one-dimensional sword-and-sorcery saga may have surprisingly strong impact on a remarkably large audience. Scoff as we might at uninspired examples of the breed, it's clear that fantasy's age-old tradition is deeply anchored in the inescapable human proclivity for magical thinking, itself rooted in the mazes and mysteries of early-childhood experience. Whatever the limitations of Harry Potter and his companions, their stories share a primal significance with all deep-reaching flights of fancy, from fairy tales to *Star Wars* to *Dynasty*. Narrative elements like the family secret, the search for identity, the fear of abandonment, and the dread of defeat are as archetypal as characters like the wise old man, the powerful gatekeeper, and the evil stepmother, as explicated by Carl Jung and brilliantly applied by Bruno Bettelheim in *The Uses of Enchantment,* his classic study of fairy tales. However circumscribed their scope or clichéd their language, fantasies are meaningful in the way they relive the difficulties, limitations, and struggles of human understanding, especially as these are experienced by children. Imagine flipping a wall switch to light a lamp in the ceiling before the eyes of a baby who has no conception of electricity or wires. It's magic! The impressions we gather from an abundance of such mysteries every day persist long beyond infancy, affecting our ideas and inflecting our emotions throughout our grownup lives.

Fantasy, then, is not just the domain of childhood. The desire to escape the limited confines of our mental and physical routines and explore other dimensions of existence fuels much of human life, propelling a boundless range of activity and thought from the faux idealism of advertising scenarios to the transcendent hopefulness of spiritual quests. Even our language is rooted in the idea that the visible world is not "all there is" (think of a concept like "inner beauty"), and that to understand the world fully we must allow our imaginations to stretch beyond the things we ordinarily see, hear, and touch. Fantasy is appealing because it gives shape and form to our strong intuition that there's more to life than the reality that surrounds us every day.

Perhaps this explains the alarums sounded against such seemingly unobjectionable works as the Rowling tales and fantasy role-playing games like Dungeons and Dragons by finger-wagging Americans from the right (e.g., Christian conservatives) and left (e.g., defenders of rationality over religion). One might expect critics with theological or philosophical interests to embrace books and movies that lift thought beyond its lazy quotidian habits; yet many oppose such fantasies, asserting that claims of "expanding the imagination" are disguises for encouraging morbid inclinations toward paganism and the occult. The fascination with another, special realm—a realm attained only by a select few, with its own rules and rulers—is the same impulse that motivates religious and secular zealots, who naturally see alternative systems as competitors to be discredited and discarded. Fantasy and fundamentalism alike are driven by the narrative powers of allegory and enigma, and by the tantalizing hope that life-illuminating wisdom lies couched in cryptic lore. Fantasy regards these as mind-teasing entertainment. Fundamentalism sees them as gospel truth.

Life Isn't Sweet

THE MOVIES OF MIKE LEIGH

"The good that came from the Thatcher years was the fight against her."
—JEREMY HARDY in *The Guardian*

THE FIGHT

The policies and personality of Margaret Thatcher, hugely controversial during her period as Prime Minister from 1979 to 1990 and remaining so ever since, sparked a great many oppositional fights of a great many shapes, sizes, and degrees of effectiveness. Some of these played out on movie and television screens, where a striking range of filmmakers created works vastly more antagonistic than those usually found in earlier traditions of British cinema, such as the Griersonian documentary or even the so-called Angry Young Man cycle of the 1950s and '60s.

Mike Leigh was an important figure in this energetic skirmish. Albeit in a more oblique manner, his films of the Thatcher era join the best productions of such filmmakers as Derek Jarman and Stephen Frears by displaying an urgent "distrust with the current state of British life" and charting "the inexorably downward spiral of their homeland," in Lester D. Friedman's words; they remain strongly relevant today by virtue of Leigh's ability to see "far beyond the passing concerns of partisan politics" (Friedman, 10). Leigh is a gnomelike, bushy-bearded poster boy for those Thatcher-era artists who instinctively knew that their "alternative vision . . . need not . . . be overtly political" but could accomplish its mission by chronicling its milieu "with care and caution," raising crucial questions and dredging up discontents glossed over by the myths and mystifications of Thatcherite consensus and conservatism. Like the most gifted of his peers, Leigh thus "defined a turbulent era, revived the moribund British cinema, and froze a crucial moment in British culture" (Friedman, 11).

All this would surely have driven Thatcher crazy if she'd been paying attention—which she didn't do then and apparently hasn't done since, given Leigh's assertion in 1997 that "Margaret Thatcher is nothing but a philistine. Naturally, she doesn't communicate with artists of any kind. So I've got no letter saying she hates my movies.[1] But she's not sophisticated enough for that anyway" (Worth, 122).

THE FILMS

Leigh produced his first theatrical feature (*Bleak Moments*, 1971) and his first TV movie (*Hard Labour*, 1973) shortly before Thatcher won the leadership of the Conservative Party in 1975; his comedies *Nuts in May* and *The Kiss of Death* arrived in 1976 and 1977, respectively, and his masterly *Who's Who* had its BBC-TV premiere in the year (1979) when her Tory administration took power and 10 Downing Street became her official home. His subsequent films of the Thatcher decade range from the social satires *Grown-Ups* (1980) and *Home Sweet Home* (1982) to *High Hopes* (1988) and *Life Is Sweet* (1990), with the acerbic *Meantime* (1983) and the equally topical *Four Days in July* (1985) sandwiched in between. Leigh vented his ongoing sociopolitical anger in the brilliant 1992 short *A Sense of History*, written by and starring his actor friend Jim Broadbent, and the acerbic 1993 feature *Naked*, one of the most ferocious antiestablishment diatribes in memory.

He then turned to more intimate topics with the family drama *Secrets & Lies* in 1996, the comradely comedy *Career Girls* in 1997, and the brilliant (if uncharacteristic) Gilbert and Sullivan portrait *Topsy-Turvy* in 1999. While some critics saw these projects as retreats into a mellower mode by an aging and increasingly domesticated filmmaker, Leigh proved them wrong with *All or Nothing*, his compassionate 2002 drama about the miseries of working-class life, and the 2004 release *Vera Drake*, about a middle-aged woman of the 1950s who performs illegal abortions in her spare time— driven not by profit or ideology, but by an intuitive conviction that she is simply providing desperately needed care to desperately needy women who can't get it any other way.

My aim here is not merely to catalogue Leigh's films, but to show the ongoing concern with social, cultural, and political issues that courses through his career. The budgets (and hence the production values) of his movies have spiraled upward since *Naked* and *Secrets & Lies* gained international renown. Still, such subsequent works as *All or Nothing* and *Vera Drake* demonstrate his continued commitment to acute observation of British society and powerful criticism of its many shortcomings.

LEIGH'S LIFE

Leigh's insistence on confrontation has been consistent since he entered the public eye with his first major offering, the unsparing *Bleak Moments*, produced as a play in 1970 and a feature film in 1971. Confrontation is also detectable in his personal manner at times; he's been know to publicly insult an audience member for asking a poorly conceived question in a post-screening discussion, for instance. Psychologically speaking, this trait may partly stem from a subtly disorienting sense of belonging to more than one sociocultural world—or conversely, to no sociocultural world at all—in his early life. Born in 1943 in Salford, a Manchester suburb,

Leigh grew up in England's industrial north. His grandfather, Mayer Liebermann, had emigrated from Russia to England in 1902, and his father—a Jewish physician who abbreviated the family name—took pride in being an educated professional who chose to live and work among people in less fortunate circumstances. This exposed young Mike to an offbeat blend of well-schooled intellectual environs and steady interaction with the working class.

As for his own schooling, Leigh attended Salford Grammar School, where Albert Finney was one of his contemporaries, and by the beginning of his teens he was determined to be a stage or film director. What he later called "the most important, seminal experience" was his acquisition "by a fluke" of a scholarship to the Royal Academy of Dramatic Art, where beginning in 1960 he "trained as an actor in the most sterile atmosphere" and "spent two formative years questioning *everything* in that whole procedure." He moved in 1963 to the Camberwell School of Art in London, where he studied drawing and painting, and started night classes at the London School of Film Technique the following year. His first stage work, *The Box Play*, was produced in 1965. Subsequent biographical milestones include the appearance of *Bleak Moments* on stage and screen; his marriage to actress and frequent collaborator Alison Steadman in 1973; the stage production of *Abigail's Party* in 1977; the acceptance of his BBC-TV movie *Grown-Ups* by the London Film Festival in 1980; his formation of the production company Thin Man Films with Simon Channing-Williams in 1989; and a pair of Cannes festival triumphs: his best-director prize for *Naked* in 1993 (accompanied by David Thewlis's award for best actor) and the Palme d'Or given to *Secrets & Lies* as best film in 1996. The latter also garnered Leigh his only Academy Award nomination as best director.

It was at RADA in the early '60s that Leigh began to "sense other [cultural] things that were happening" and to start exploring some of these on his own terms. Influenced by adventurous theater artists like the Living Theater and Jerzy Grotowski, filmmakers like

John Cassavetes and the French New Wave directors, and avant-garde innovations like the Happenings of Allan Kaprow, he started articulating the notion that "writing, directing, designing, and filmmaking could all be combined on the floor rather than at the desk" (Bank, 115–16). From his newfound strategies and insights came his career-defining practice of developing his projects in tandem with his performers during long periods of improvisation and rehearsal before the camera rolls.[2] Leigh has described this process often, as in the concise account he gave critic Howie Movshovitz in a 1994 interview:

In broad terms, I gather a cast together and we go into rehearsal. . . . It's a question of creating characters and investigating their relationships, backgrounds and their ideas, and arriving at the premise for the film, and then working from a very simple structural outline.

   I then build the film up on location by rehearsing it from an improvisational state into a very tight, very highly disciplined condition, sequence by sequence, and shoot it. What goes to the cutting room is highly structured and disciplined. It's the kind of work that is obviously highly creative and collaborative for the actors. But the contributions of designers and cameramen are [also] greater than normal because everybody shares all aspects of the work. So you can get a rock-solid inner truth—textural, social accuracy—and a heightened, distilled cinematic, dramatic [and] even hopefully—although it sounds pretentious—poetic end product (Movshovitz, 52–53).

Standing at the helm, Leigh's own position is as undetermined and open-ended as anyone else's. "I know a lot and nothing at the start," he says. "I'm not an intellectual filmmaker; I'm an intuitive and emotional filmmaker. . . . I have feelings on the go and conceptions, which are more from the gut than the brain" (Movshovitz, 53). His function is not so much to craft polished results as to carve galvanizing moments from the living rock of living performances. "At its simplest," he says, "things happen in improvisation which I then structure, and that's the end product. But mostly that's not the case: Mostly what I do is to challenge what's happened and thus arrive at a more interesting dramatic essence" (Carney with Quart, 163).

Between the feature-film version of *Bleak Moments* in 1971 and the release of *High Hopes* some seventeen years later, Leigh's production funds came from TV rather than theatrical-film sources. Some critics therefore divide his career into TV and theatrical phases. I find such a division close to meaningless, given the consistency of Leigh's concerns and his organic growth as an artist, although of course the aesthetics of such larger-scale works as *Naked* and *Secrets & Lies* are affected by their expectation of big-screen distribution. In any case, while Leigh's definitive turn from TV films to theatrical films in the late '80s enabled him to broaden his visual scale, he was careful not to let the wide screen interfere with the sense of psychological intimacy and political pungency he had cultivated in his earlier work.

LEIGH'S LEANINGS

It is clear in retrospect that three key aspects of Leigh's work already mentioned—its collaborative technique, its psychological intensity, its political seriousness—produced some of their most imposing results during the 1980s. This is partly because they went against the grain of mainstream production in Britain and elsewhere, acquiring a distinctive aura that attracted attention from audiences and critics, whether pro or con. Even more important, they offered an implicit challenge to the self-satisfied set of individualist, materialist, and consumerist ideological positions that were Thatcher's regrettable gift to the nation that had elected her. Their politics were more often implied than overt, and film scholar Ray Carney has valid reasons for writing that Leigh's movies do not "offer [palpable] political alternatives or solutions in the Ken Loach mode" (Carney with Quart, 6). What needs to be added, though, is that Leigh's cooperative and communal methodology itself served as an implicit critique of the Thatcherist capitalism that Leigh so feared and loathed.

Along with Leigh's refusal to be a writer-director in the usual calling-all-the-shots mold goes a refusal to indulge many of the commonest practices in popular film, including—crucially, in my view—resolving stories with neatly tied-up conclusions, and ladling meanings or messages over the material like so much faux-nutritious sauce that's not nearly as good for you as the chef insists. Leigh has no particular qualms about being called a "political" artist as long as those according the label understand it the way he does. "I don't do films that are agenda-driven," he told me in a 1996 onstage conversation at the Telluride Film Festival during which we discussed his career as a whole. "I don't do work that is . . . propagandist," he continued. "But nevertheless, what I do is kind of political, in the sense that my characters are always identifiable, and I instinctively draw them in their social and economic contexts."

A phrase like "kind of" seems kind of evasive to critics skeptical of Leigh, of course, and he is very much aware that he's been attacked for not being more politically aggressive. Since his movies have always told straightforward stories with everyday characters, he recalls having an especially "bad time" during much of the 1970s because this approach was "unfashionable" in that period. "People said it was a bit decadent, old-fashioned, square. It didn't look avant-garde, it wasn't abstract or surreal enough. . . . I said I wasn't concerned with that. The art was there, and I didn't want to advertise it!"

The politics were there too, deeply embedded in his straightforward stories with their everyday characters. But this political dimension has often gone unrecognized, and the responsibility lies partly with Leigh himself, who is a subtle enough thinker not merely to pronounce but actually to believe that there is no dividing line between the personal and the political—or at most a dividing

line that's as shifting, permeable, and blurry as can be. Leigh's definition of "a political act" is

just to share with other people things that you feel, in a way that makes
them feel in some way. What I'm concerned with is the way we live our
lives, and what politics should be concerned with is the way we live our
lives, and what our lives are about. It's terribly important there are
filmmakers whose films have very direct, specific, political objectives,
and it's terribly important that those films work and cause changes to
happen . . . but I don't make films of that kind.

 I make films where I don't leave you clearly able to conclude what
I'm asking you to think or feel. I make films that ask a great number of
questions but . . . don't come up with too many answers. And I hope I
make films where you walk away from the [theater] with work to do,
arguments to have, things to worry about, things to care about.

"In that sense," he concludes, "I would regard what I do as political"
(Sterritt, 1996).

JOHNNY'S JEREMIAD

 Naked is arguably Leigh's most openly political film. It is
also among his most unabashedly angry works, showing the scars
he accumulated as an Englishman who clinically observed the results
of Thatcher's policies on the people he cares about most: other
Brits of the less-than-privileged classes, near whom he has chosen
to live and work throughout his career. *Naked* had its world premiere at Cannes in May of 1993, about two and a half years after
Thatcher resigned as Prime Minister upon losing her Conservative
Party leadership. Technically it is a post-Thatcher production. But
discursively it is a compendium of concepts and emotions stirred
up in Leigh by her rule and its aftermath. It is obvious that a phenomenon as powerful as Thatcherism could not have waned
overnight, even if she hadn't been succeeded in office by John
Major, her protégé. "The only caveat I would sound when people

remember the joy of her departure is that her legacy is still with us," wrote columnist and satirist Jeremy Hardy in *The Guardian*, "both in the privateering policies of New Labour and in the shape of all those cringing underlings of hers still in circulation" (Hardy).

Here is a passage (many others would serve equally well) that sums up aspects of England under Thatcher that Leigh and the film's main character, Johnny, find particularly galling. Asked if he was bored in Manchester before fleeing to London at the beginning of the film, Johnny replies,

No, I wasn't fuckin' bored. I'm never bored. That's the trouble with everybody—you're all so bored. You've 'ad nature explained to you and you're bored with it. You've 'ad the living body explained to you and you're bored with it. You've 'ad the universe explained to you and you're bored with it. So now you just want cheap thrills and like plenty of 'em, and it dun't matter 'ow tawdry or vacuous they are as long as it's new, as long as it's new, as long as it flashes and fuckin' bleeps in forty fuckin' different colours. Well, whatever else you can say about me, I'm not fuckin' bored! (Leigh, 21)

Johnny's jeremiad against boredom amounts to an impassioned indictment of what French critic Guy Debord calls the "society of the spectacle," wherein hitherto active tendencies toward meaningful thought and action—be they introspective in the manner of theory, or extroverted in the manner of practice—are diverted into cynically manipulated pathways at once *unproductive* for sociopolitical improvement and *productive* of profits for those who control means of production, distribution, and above all exhibition, not only of cultural products but of anything that can conceivably be publicized, sold, and bought. Which, in the era of high-tech "free market" ideology fostered by Thatcher and her ilk, has come to mean anything and everything there is.

Johnny's words struck a strong and disturbing chord among moviegoers, including American ones, among whom I count myself. As an American writing about a British filmmaker in a specific British period, I must stress at this point that nearly everything

Leigh explores and conveys in his best movies is as applicable to post-Vietnam culture in the United States as it is to British society in the Thatcher era. Thatcher inherited power from a Labour administration that had run out of steam, losing its ability to keep up even a credible appearance of progress toward a better country, a more empowered citizenry, a more humane world. She was succeeded by Major, a handpicked heir whose combination of working-class background and upper-class airs would be fine fodder for the barbs of a ferocious Leigh satire, if not a farcical Monty Python skit; he has been followed in turn by the Labour regime of Tony Blair, who speaks of George W. Bush in words as slavish as those accorded to Ronald Reagan by Thatcher, who called herself "his biggest fan." In a similar manner, Jimmy Carter's uncertain Democratic administration gave way to two (count 'em!) terms of Reagan's feckless rule, one (inexcusably) of George H. W. Bush's bloodthirsty administration, two (against all odds) of Bill Clinton's faux progressivism, and one (at this writing) of George W. Bush's escalating cryptofascism. Thatcher's reckless promotion of petty individualism, neo-Darwinian competitiveness, and repressive "morality" at least had the unintended consequence of fostering a cinema of outrage led by figures as various as Isaac Julien, Jarman, and Leigh, among others. We still await an equivalent opposition—or even a pale imitation thereof—on the American screen.

All of this helps account for Johnny's resonance with audiences despite the violent failings in his personality and behavior. Played by Thewlis in one of the most bravura film performances of recent decades, Johnny is an almost literal embodiment of intellectual and emotional anger at what Thatcher and her overseas counterparts have wrought. Thewlis was a key co-creator of *Naked*, of course, contributing not only the character details that Leigh always elicits from his performers, but also a great deal of the film's verbal and cerebral heft, generated via exhaustive research and exhausting rehearsal. The film's many moments of physical and psychological shock have been condemned by some critics as sensationalism, misogyny, misanthropy, or all three. Those charges can be debated on their own, but the point that counts is that Johnny's words and actions have a directly political intent, serving as comments "about the society we live in—the inequality between the sexes, the races, the classes," as Thewlis told me (Sterritt, 1993) a few months before the film's American debut, going straight to its cultural and political heart.

Leigh made the same point in slightly different words when I noted that the most powerful moments of *Naked* are frequently among its most abrasive ones, and asked the filmmaker if he feared a negative reaction to this from audiences. "*Life* is abrasive for a lot of people," he said, "and there's no getting round it. I think the function of art—and the cinema not least—is to confront these things. . . . I'm absolutely committed as a filmmaker to be entertaining and to amuse; but I am also concerned to confront . . ." (Sterritt, 1993, 43). In a 1999 interview he linked himself with ever-confrontational Johnny by calling the latter an "idealist who's so frustrated that he turns in on himself and becomes angry with the world [so that] everything he says and everything he expresses . . . is a lamentation on the terrible grip of materialism and the terrible lack of values in society." These resentments, Leigh pointedly noted, "are things which I share in essence" (Billington).

FAMILY VALUES

Brimming as he is with lamentations and resentments, Leigh has claimed no easy answers for the social, economic, and cultural problems faced by his characters. Nor has he used Thatcherism, or anything else, as a reason to treat those characters more gently than they deserve as individuals who are ultimately responsible for their own existential destinies. Critics who misunderstand this complain that Leigh aims sarcasm and derision at folks too personally addled or culturally deluded to live the proper lives he allegedly thinks they ought to be living. Quite the contrary, he belongs to a brave handful of filmmakers (e.g., Mexican director Arturo Ripstein and the late Luis Buñuel) who refuse to romanticize, patronize, or condescend to poor and disadvantaged people. His body of work amounts to a widely encompassing swell of sympathy and compassion for people who, beneath their motley exteriors, are no more nor less worthy than you, I, or Leigh himself of social conditions that encourage the abilities to love, work, feel a sense of inward dignity, and express the self as one sees fit.

He sees no need to convey this in sentimentalized terms, however. Few amiable personality traits are evident in *Meantime*, for instance, a 1983 movie seen as disseminating "a disturbing smog of defeatism" by even so strong a Leigh supporter as Michael Coveney, his biographer (Coveney, 171). But what this "smog" chiefly illustrates is Leigh's acute attunement to political realities, since for many people "defeatism" was a forced option in the Thatcher era. Leigh's aversion to proffering narrative palliatives of "hope" and "redemption" is exceeded only by his aversion to romanticizing—as opposed to accurately, dispassionately depicting—the awful conditions endured by the people he portrays. Indeed, the genesis of *Meantime* and its smog was simultaneously personal and political for Leigh, who told Coveney about it:

When I was shooting *Home Sweet Home*, I had this terrible flat . . . over a shop in the barren Bedfordshire countryside. . . . I was in the bath, listening to the radio very early in the morning, and this story came on about two unemployed kids in Warrington or St Helens or somewhere who had committed suicide. And I thought—I always go through something like this—what we're doing [as filmmakers] is irrelevant. *That's* what we should be doing. Something about unemployment. We were two or three years into Thatcher, it was already an issue, and it lingered at the back of my mind (Coveney, 171–72).

It clearly came to the front of his mind before long. In the same year Leigh told a *New Musical Express* interviewer that in *Meantime* he had "chosen, quite consciously, to say, this is that world where everybody's unemployed, which is the primary condition of what's going on" (Coveney, 172).

Meantime is a tragicomic commentary on that world, and also on an institution that runs into especially high hurdles therein: the family, in this case the working-class family, challenged at the best of times and positively besieged at the worst of them. Thatcher sounded off about "family values" with a rhetorical might and propagandistic main that such fellow demagogues as her contemporary Reagan and her spiritual heir George W. Bush could envy and applaud. She took office "attacking the permissive society and trumpeting traditional bourgeois values like respectability, family, and nation," as film historian Leonard Quart puts it. Yet despite her "ritualistic deference to the prime significance of the family," her aggressively promoted economic policies often "subverted many of those same values" (Quart, 21).

In an interesting critical twist, Leigh has been charged with echoing Thatcherite attitudes in portraying the English family. "In celebrating the virtues of the privatized family as a kind of escape route from political impotence and passivity," claims critic John Hill with regard to *High Hopes*, "the film, for all its apparent 'socialism', appears to end up reinforcing the very scepticism about more collective (or 'socialist') forms of political action that was already such a feature of this era" (Watson, 91). Noting that *High Hopes* culminates with the decision of a working-class couple to have a child, Hill writes that "while the film may, in this way, succeed in expressing values of care and responsibility which cut across the prevailing ethos of Thatcherism, it only does so by partly reproducing conservative (and, indeed, Thatcherite) values regarding the family and women" (Watson, 92).

Hill's argument, cited in Garry Watson's solid study of Leigh's work, should interest observers of both British and American society. This is because members of both have become adept at chirping platitudes about "family values" while using their own families as veritable wagon trains providing self-protective, xenophobic, fiercely intolerant circles of defense against whatever may threaten them, challenge them, or simply call their complacency into question. I have witnessed this phenomenon in Dwight D. Eisenhower's traditionalist era, Reagan's reactionary time, and George W. Bush's neoconservative one, and it is obviously not limited to those periods.

This said, and without joining the needless Watson-Hill debate as to whether Leigh neurotically "has it in" for childless women, I agree with Watson that Leigh does not see "the privatized family" as an "escape route" from the imperative of collective action for social change. For one thing, Leigh's movies (of the '80s and other decades) reveal an intricately complex attitude toward the family, which he celebrates as haven, home base, and familiar terrain—all compatible with the "escape route" hypothesis, to be sure—but which he also calls radically into question as *huis clos*, inflictor of physical and spiritual claustrophobia, and site of oppressions, rebellions, and competitions that inscribe a fiercely critical near-microcosm of Thatcher's nation as a whole.

For another thing, Leigh has had a streak of socialism (without Hill's quotation marks) in his political personality since early life, along with a complementary streak of anarchism and an ingrained skepticism toward all things capitalistic. As noted, he grew up during the 1940s and '50s in the northern working-class zone of Manchester and Salford, where he attended local schools. "There was a Labour government which started a national health service," he said in 1991 to a journalist interested in his Jewish roots, "that is now being destroyed by the Tories. The first thing my [physician] father did was to dispose of his private patients as soon as he could. . . . We weren't Orthodox, but there were a lot of Zionists in the family that went back an unusually long way." He recalled that in the 1950s he and fellow members of Zionist youth groups "shared our money and learned about socialism. . . . It liberated us from the bourgeois, provincial Jewish constraints. We were actually rather anarchic, but we also worked by getting people together in groups and working creatively." He said these experiences "contributed to [his] ability to be sympathetic to everybody and at the same time be tragic and comic" in his outlook (Stone, 28–29).

For still another thing, Leigh sees steely links between English society's increasingly materialistic, acquisitive strain and the fate of the English family. This is illustrated even by *Naked*, which appears on the surface to have only the faintest connection with family life, yet which Leigh says is about "the waste and the unpredictable nature of things" bequeathed to England by Thatcher and her political heirs. While he says he "didn't want to make a documentary about homelessness" he adds that "everybody in it, in a manner of speaking, is rootless, or at least displaced. . . . So the discussion about family continues, but here by default rather than directly" (Carr, 56). Even though family operates in *Naked* as a submerged issue rather than a conspicuous theme, therefore, the film emerges as an affecting sidelong glance at an institution Leigh sees as anything but a ready escape route. If it *were* one, surely the movie's desperate characters would make a stab at escaping through it!

LOST IN SPACE

Leigh elaborated further on his political views in 1994, as *Naked* started to reach a wide public. "The fabric of society is crumbling in England," he said, "there are people all around the streets. And while *High Hopes* was on one level a lamentation for socialism being something that maybe has gotten lost somehow, [*Naked*], if I come out of the closet about it, takes more of an anarchist view. I despair that society really will be able to organize itself, ever. . . . In the end, what [*Naked*] is about is this guy, like a kind of lost communication satellite, floating around the atmosphere, wasted. . . . I wanted to do a millennium film, and the peculiar thing I felt about a possible pending apocalypse is that it doesn't seem incredibly unfeasible now" (Carr, 56).

Thus did Leigh, who started his career a few years before the Thatcher era with the dark social satire of *Bleak Moments*, evolve by the immediate post-Thatcher years into a chronicler of socioeconomic waste and prophet of apocalyptic disaster. And of course the energy driving this evolution came somewhat from Thatcher herself, since her belligerently conservative reign ignited the conflicts with the cultural left in which Leigh played such a fascinating role.

Leigh's millennial fears point to another set of perspectives useful in grasping the political import of even his homiest, homeliest films. It is revealing that Thatcher's father—who "shaped her political personality," as Quart writes—was a "petty bourgeois Methodist grocer and self-made man" who "lived by such values as self-help, moral virtue, and public duty" (Quart, 17). Mutatis mutandis, a wide array of Leigh characters can be described in similar terms.

WHAT'S WHAT

Alan Dixon in the masterly *Who's Who*, made in 1979 on the very eve of Thatcher's heyday, is a perfect example. Played by Richard Kane, he's as petty a bourgeois as one can imagine, shuttling between his job as midlevel clerk in a London brokerage firm and his home life as self-satisfied householder and husband to a cat fancier (Joolia Cappleman) who clearly cares more about her felines than about her spouse. Perhaps as compensation for his domestic tedium, Dixon indulges a sincerely felt investment in "moral virtue and public duty" by giving over a substantial portion of their house (and his brain) to a secular shrine celebrating English values of the most conspicuously reactionary kind. His collection comprises royal portraits, impeccably maintained charts of aristocrats and their families, autographs from the rich and famous—or, when a member of the rich and famous refuses to provide one, a form letter refusing his request—and other such curios.

Among the many oddities here is that Dixon's slavish collecting of lore and mementos hasn't given him much real knowledge of the aristocratic scene. A cheeky coworker demonstrates this near the end of the film, feeding Dixon a line of bogus information that Dixon responds to not with an honest "I didn't know that," but with the sorts of clichés and platitudes that he feels his type of patriotic chap *should* say in these circumstances. On hearing that an (ersatz) earl lost his fortune, for instance, Dixon knowingly responds, "The thirties were a difficult time for everyone," only to find that the nobleman in question lived in the nineteenth century—and moments later, that the nobleman is a made-up fiction who never lived at all.

While this aspect of *Who's Who* casts a sardonic light on the petty end of the middle class, another aspect does the same for the *hautes bourgeoises* on the other end. Much of the film chronicles a dinner party (a phrase that makes Dixon sigh with vicarious pleasure, even though he doesn't get to attend them) given by two upper-level employees of the same brokerage firm. These scenes are a tour de force of satirical analysis, portraying what's essentially a piddling little get-together at which the drinkers and diners work ferociously hard to convince themselves they're having an absolutely fabulous time enjoying the privileges that (in their eyes) people like them automatically deserve. The appearance of the main course—an utterly ordinary hunk of meat—is greeted with great gasps of pleasure; anticipation of a commonplace apple crumble is equally keen; yet at the end of the evening the reveling quintet is bored, tired, and literally fed up in stomach and soul, although nobody present would dream of admitting this. One of Leigh's most perfectly titled films, *Who's Who* is a superb summary of the fixation on *breeding* that Thatcherism eagerly inherited from a class-obsessed past and turned to its own power-driven purposes. In this movie as in life, manipulative notions of "moral virtue and public duty" shore up the Thatcherite cultural cluster of neo-Darwinian ideas, "mythic meritocracy," and prostration before "traditional bourgeois values like respectability, family, and nation" (Quart, 18, 20).

It is not so much these values that Leigh attacks—although attack them he does, when necessary—as their uncritical embrace by a citizenry that uses them to stave off any temptation to think scrupulously about their society and (dare one say it?) to change that society in ways that could make it better for people just like them, not to mention folks even less well off. Once again, Leigh deploys seemingly humdrum materials to provoke his audience into recognizing the dread liabilities of self-deluding lifestyles and ideas.

Also important is Leigh's insistence on addressing political and ideological issues not in theoretical terms (even those of "against the grain" popular cinema) but rather in terms of social and cultural constructions, which is to say, the routines and rituals of the way real, everyday people conduct their real, everyday lives. Film scholar Ray Carney puts this well when he observes that Leigh's movies explore networks of "intertwined imaginative issues on which the individual characters and scenes [can be seen as] variations" in an "echo-chamber" sort of way. Carney argues that each of Leigh's figures "is seized up in an emotional and intellectual 'cramp,' which manifests itself as a mechanical routine or pattern of thought and feeling" that allows Leigh to play out verbal and visual realizations of his two deepest commitments: "a rejection of all idealized, abstracted, intellectualized understandings; and a belief in the centrality of social connection and involvement" (Carney with Quart, 148–49).

TWITCHES AND CRAMPS

Such talk of mental cramps and social connectivity helps focus attention on the deeper, darker dimensions of Leigh's more "entertaining" works, which have often been mistakenly assessed as snobbish lampoons of English mannerisms to which Leigh and his collaborators feel smugly superior. It is hard to write about Leigh without citing Dennis Potter's famously dismissive *Sunday Times* review of *Abigail's Party*, produced on the London stage in 1977, recorded on film in the same year, and aired by the BBC on the popular *Play for Today* program. Potter's brilliance as a dramatist is forcefully borne out by such indelible works as *Pennies From Heaven* (1978) and *The Singing Detective* (1986), two of the most psychologically trenchant miniseries in television history, British or otherwise. By contrast, his abilities as a critic come into serious question when one ponders his response toward Leigh's play—which offers a single-minded critique not of derisory individuals but rather of the materialism, conformity, and unexamined mental "cramps" into which they've been educated, indoctrinated, and funneled by the tenor of British sociocultural thought as the Thatcher era started cranking into high gear. *Abigail's Party*, wrote Potter of its TV version, is an exercise in "rancid disdain" that amounts to

a prolonged jeer, twitching with genuine hatred, about the dreadful suburban tastes of the dreadful lower middle classes . . . [that sinks] under its own immense condescension. The force of the yelping derision [becomes] a single note of contempt, amplified into a relentless screech. As so often in the minefields of English class-consciousness, more [is] revealed of the snobbery of the observers rather than [sic] the observed (Coveney, 120).

Nor do particular performances escape Potter's eagle eyes, as when he condemns Alison Steadman's allegedly "nasty" portrayal "of the dreadful, blue-lidded Beverly," whose "every gesture [is] honed into such lethal caricature that it would not [be] too surprising if she . . . suddenly changed shape in the manner of the fat, thin or elongated reflections in a fairground mirror" (Watson, 12).

Leigh biographer Michael Coveney finds Potter's review a "broken-backed polemic . . . unsupported by detail or example" (120) and Leigh commentator Garry Watson, seeing Potter's extremely "visceral . . . mixture of revulsion and accusation" in terms of Jacques Lacan's psychoanalytic theories,[3] submits that for Potter the play functioned "as the kind of site that . . . marks the intrusion of the Lacanian Real," characterized by a breakdown of the symbolic order (i.e., principles of language and logic) and an extreme, objectively disproportionate sense of existential anxiety (Watson, 12).

How could a dramatist as generally smart, sensitive, and savvy as Potter react to Leigh's dramatic comedy with such an extraordinary blend of misjudgment and hostility? Aesthetically speaking, I find *Abigail's Party* a stimulating and provocative play that has had the bad fortune of finding its widest audience via a third-rate movie version that falls far short of Leigh's usually high cinematic level.[4] Cinematic shortcomings are not what set Potter off, however, and I think illumination of his tirade can be found in the extreme fretfulness it expresses over the instability of Steadman's performance, with its constant risk of shape-changing grotesquerie and (one presumes) its threat of psychological disintegration too fractured and disorienting for a defenseless viewer to bear.

POLI/TICS

The key word here is "gesture," every one of which in Steadman's portrayal (according to Potter's review) is honed into "lethal caricature" of angst-producing volatility. Italian philosopher Giorgio Agamben argues that by the end of the nineteenth century the Western world had largely lost the interest in body language that had earlier fascinated an array of observers, from clinicians Gilles de la Tourette and Jean-Martin Charcot to cinematographic pioneers Eadweard Muybridge and the Lumière brothers. Along with this "obliteration and loss of gestures" came an inability to understand the "transfiguration [of gestures] into fate," that is, a profound misapprehension of what the symbolism of gestures can express and reveal[5] about distinctions between "power and act, naturalness and manner, contingency and necessity" (Agamben, 1992, 48, 50–51, 52).

In this climate, the main compensatory mechanism found by artists was "theater," by which Agamben means a "precipitous attempt to recover the lost gestures in extremis" via whatever forms of aesthetic articulation (modern dance, Proustian prose, and so on) lent themselves to so radical and compulsive an enterprise (52–53). Chief among such articulations were those of silent cinema, then a fledgling art. Invoking and extending Gilles Deleuze's argument that cinema transcends the traditional notion of the image as either *pose éternelle* or *coup immobile*, producing instead the dynamic *coup-mobile* or movement-image, Agamben asserts that modernists need to break the "paralyzing power" of images as "immovable and eternal forms" and liberate them into fragments of mobility and gesture—just as philosophy must claim the *idea* not as "an immobile archetype . . . but rather a constellation in which phenomena arrange themselves in a gesture." If there is truth in Samuel Beckett's suggestion that cinema is "the dream of a gesture," then the filmmaker's task is "to introduce into this dream the element of awakening." All of which leads to the conclusion that "cinema has its center in the gesture and not in the image," which means that "it belongs essentially to the realm of ethics and politics," not merely to that of aesthetics (Agamben, 54–55).

Leigh's movies are emphatically not silent. Their characters are forever rattling on about one thing or another, eloquently or (far more often) the opposite. Johnny's elocutionary torrents are exceptional in Leigh's films, serving an exceptional purpose—to wit, revealing oral energies and verbal gifts as doppelgängers of emotional rage and sexual dysfunction crying vainly for release and redress in a socially stifling era. The great majority of other Leigh characters are vastly less skilled in using words as tools, instruments, and weapons; but this doesn't mean there is no deep signification in the small talk—nay, infinitesimal talk—that shapes and inflects their interactions. Linking the tenor of Leigh's dialogue to the improvisatory methods that produce it, critic David Thomson observes that conversations in Leigh's works offer "flights of talk that are hilarious, poignant, and so wordy that . . . we can [at especially brilliant moments] suddenly see how close this inspired spontaneity has come to Oscar Wilde, Harold Pinter, and Joe Orton." Thomson adds that Leigh has an "obsessive ear" for the "rhythms" of everyday speech, that he is "very good at getting a certain kind of monotone English humor," and that he "loves the strange lilt of it," sometimes (literally) to a fault (Thomson, 510).

This is helpful as far as it goes, but Johnny's rants aside, the fact is that in most Leigh films the "flights of talk" are almost empty of content that might be called informative or interesting, even to the characters themselves; indeed, many of the most wordy passages are so devoid of appealing content that they're less reminiscent of Wilde's spot-on pithiness than of the anything-but-empty silences in a typical Pinter play. Leigh's major characters speak mainly in clichés, platitudes, and truisms so trite that we barely need listen to intuit what they're meant to convey—namely, a ritual recognition that somebody else is in one's company and etiquette requires one to acknowledge this by making vocal noises. The speech that ensues may have utilitarian value, as when an employer offers well-meaning advice (e.g., *The Kiss of Death*) or asks a guest (e.g., *Who's Who*) how she's planning to get home; or it may carry overtones of caring and affection, as when couples struggle with the question of having a baby (e.g., *High Hopes*) or siblings suddenly open up to each other (e.g., *Life Is Sweet*) in unprecedented ways. Most of the time, though, speech among Leigh's characters is more a matter of reflex sound-making (the sort of thing called "grooming talk" by some sociologists) than of anything like communication on a truly human scale. Recognizing and valuing this, the late American critic Pauline Kael observed that in *High Hopes* some "scenes that our instincts tell us shouldn't work . . . are the bedrock of the movie" (Kael, 88).

KAEL'S CRAW

It is pleasant to observe that a critic as picky as Kael found a "bedrock" in *High Hopes,* and it's intriguing to wonder why, then, "our instincts" (read: Kael's instincts) might give the impression that some scenes "shouldn't work" even though they do. The most obvious answer is that Kael's famous approach to criticism—see the movie once and bat out the review over a keyboard and a bottle of wine—gave her only an intuitive grasp, not a thought-through understanding, of how Leigh and company are using (inarticulate) speech and (ungraceful) movement not as actorly devices to tell and teach us things, but rather as *gestures* meant to be felt and fathomed in purely *expressive* terms. Like others skeptical of Leigh's work, Kael doesn't get beyond the straight psychological levels on which most films and plays operate. She's able to concede that the scruffy *High Hopes* couple of bike-messenger Cyril and squirmy Shirley are "believable mates," because believability is something most movies want and her eyes are peeled for it; but look for her to embrace paradoxes of plot or contradictions of character, and you'll come up disappointed almost every time.

Kael's great (and ongoing) influence makes her a good example of the many critics who have fallen prey to this limitation. Look at another statement in her *High Hopes* review, for instance, where she complains, "the irony that the only true marriage is that of the unmarried pair can stick in your craw." This is not the place for an archeological dig into Kael's craw, which also harbored (from this film alone) the working-class couple's "spontaneity . . . unforced smiles . . . open eyes turned to the future, and the pot smoking that marks them as good people" (Kael, 89). But the hard time she had swallowing these characteristics isn't hard to figure out. One cause is her inability to realize that Leigh's project is not to champion dubious underdogs—by almost any measure, Cyril and Shirley are more indecisive and confused than simply "good" and "open-eyed" people—but rather to record their vocal and physical gestures (via those of observant actors under his rigorous guidance) and thereby unveil the messages they convey about life in an inhibiting, often suffocating culture.

And they convey so much! Once again, Agamben cuts to the quick of modern physicality when he asserts that the meaningfulness of gesture started to regain its lost recognition when neurologist Oliver Sacks, MD, was struck by three apparent cases of Tourette syndrome during a brief stroll down a New York City sidewalk in 1971—exactly when Leigh was embarking on his major phase with *Bleak Moments*, tellingly enough. Agamben hypothesizes that observers lost their sensitivity to this (intrusive!) phenomenon for some one hundred years precisely because it is ubiquitous in the modern (and, Frederic Jameson would surely add, the postmodern) epoch—that "ataxia, tics, and dystonia [have] become the norm and . . . at some point everybody [has] lost control of their gestures and [is] walking and gesticulating frantically" (Agamben, 51). Leigh's characters aren't always frantic, outwardly at least. But something deeply dysfunctional appears to be going on within them, and Leigh's self-appointed task is to recover its reality and significance, not just aesthetically but socially, culturally, and always already politically.

For too many critics, Leigh's cinema of observation is not an enduring exercise in courageous analysis but a lazy indulgence in that old bugaboo of cutting-edge cinema, bad acting, here abetted by bad improvising and bad directing, as well. Since space doesn't permit a thoroughgoing look at this contentious topic, I will make only two observations here. One is that bad acting unquestionably exists—take it from me, a movie reviewer for almost forty years—and often in films that instantly, lastingly capture the public imagination. The other is that some of modern cinema's most gifted directors have been outrageously dismissed for eliciting performances taken as "bad acting" for the sole reason that they signal authentic *human* truths rather than the manufactured *Hollywood* truths we have been educated (or conditioned) (or brainwashed) to regard as realistic. These directors are a diverse lot—the indefatigable Cassavetes and the endlessly inventive Andy Warhol are textbook specimens at very different points on the cinematic scale—and while Leigh has certainly made mistakes and miscalculations like those others, he is their equal in terms of tenacious vision, radical methodology, and unstoppable integrity.

Leigh's mission has been to pinpoint the ineffable realities that our all-too-effable exteriors do such a lamentably good job of concealing in historical periods when what Herbert Marcuse calls "excess-repression," a phrase that distills the essence of modernity, has become a social given that almost nobody dares question or explore. Leigh's is a cinema where talk isn't small, it's microscopic; gesture isn't grand, it's ungainly; and almost everything sticks in the craw, not by accident but by the filmmaker's poignant, precisely calibrated purpose.

Above all, it is a cinema of noises, bodies, and (to invoke the title of a seminal Cassavetes film) of faces, whose tics, ataxia, and dystonia have endless things to reveal if we can overcome our post-Thatcher brands of Thatcherism enough to realize that attention *must* be paid. This brings us back to Agamben, who exquisitely describes goals that Leigh's best artistry invariably strives to manifest:

All living beings are in the open: they manifest themselves and shine in their appearance. But only human beings want to take possession of this opening, to seize hold of their own appearance and of their own being-manifest. Language is this appropriation, which transforms nature into *face*. This is why appearance becomes a problem for human beings: it becomes the location of a struggle for truth. . . . We may call tragicomedy of appearance the fact that the face uncovers only and precisely inasmuch as it hides, and hides to the extent to which it uncovers. . . . Be only your face. Go to the threshold. Do not remain the subjects of your properties or faculties, do not stay beneath them: rather, go with them, in them, beyond them (Agamben, 1995, 90, 93, 99).

Going with faces, in faces, and beyond faces is precisely what Leigh so often manages to do. He and his characters are the anti-authoritarian, the anti-culture-industrialist, the anti-Thatcher itself made cinematic flesh. They are rough beasts, to be sure. But the world has been a subtly better place since they started slouching into Leigh's studios to be born.

NOTES

1. One can't help thinking how much Alan Dixon in *Who's Who* would have treasured such a letter, as a bolster for his self-esteem rather than (far more appropriately) the opposite. This character and movie are discussed later in this essay.
2. The credits of Leigh's earlier films say "devised and directed by Mike Leigh," while the later ones say "written and directed by Mike Leigh," indicating the importance he places on his own role as guiding figure during the improvisation/rehearsal process and collector/collator of the results into a finished screenplay that may then be published under his name. The term "devised by" has always seemed a bit more accurate and honest to me in Leigh's case than "written by," but he rarely loses an opportunity to remind moviegoers of how centrally important he regards the contributions of his casts and crews to his finished films. He is not the only director to require primary contributions (narrative ideas, character traits, dialogue) from his performers, of course; the French auteur Jacques Rivette and the American filmmaker Robert Altman are among the others who regularly do so.
3. Like many cultural critics using Lacanian theory, Watson deploys the notion of the Real far too loosely, as if this "order" referred to the material actualities of the physical and psychological world rather than a kernel of unmediated, unmodulated perception that is experienced in infancy and can never be captured or conceptualized in terms of the thought processes we inevitably acquire in subsequent life.
4. Supporting my low assessment of the film *qua* film is Leigh himself, who has called it "really quite a mess" with "patchy, inconsistent lighting" and occasional glimpses of a carelessly handled microphone swinging into frame (Coveney, 114).
5. Agamben takes the appearance of Friedrich Nietzsche's writing as the moment representing the "climax" of this erasure, calling *Also Sprach Zarathustra* the "ballet of a humankind that has lost its gestures" (52).

WORKS CITED

Agamben, Giorgio. 1995. "The Face." In *Means Without Ends: Notes on Politics*, 90–99. Minneapolis: University of Minnesota Press, 2000.

Agamben, Giorgio. 1992. "Notes on Gesture." In *Means Without Ends: Notes on Politics*, 48–59. Minneapolis: University of Minnesota Press, 2000.

Bank, Mirra. 1997. "Mike Leigh." *Films in Review* 48:1/2 (January/February); reprinted in *Mike Leigh: Interviews*, edited by Howie Movshovitz, 113–21. Jackson: University Press of Mississippi, 2000.

Billington, Michael. 1999. "Mike Leigh Interviewed: II—Mike Leigh's Filmic Style." In "Mike Leigh Interviewed." *Guardian Unlimited* (11 November

1999): <<http://film.guardian.co.uk/Guardian_NFT/interview/0,4479,1
10594,00.html>>

Carney, Ray, with Leonard Quart. 2000. *The Films of Mike Leigh: Embracing
the World.* Cambridge: Cambridge University Press.

Carr, Jay. 1994. *"Naked:* English Director Mike Leigh Turns His Uncompromising
Vision on the Way Things Are." *The Boston Globe* (27 February); reprinted in
Mike Leigh: Interviews, edited by Howie Movshovitz, 55–58. Jackson: University
Press of Mississippi, 2000.

Coveney, Michael. 1996. *The World According to Mike Leigh.* London:
HarperCollins.

Friedman, Lester D. 1993. "The Empire Strikes Out." In *British Cinema and
Thatcherism: Fires Were Started,* edited by Lester Friedman, 1–11. London:
UCL Press.

Hardy, Jeremy. 2000. "The Bitter End." *The Guardian* (25 November): <<http://
www.guardian.co.uk/Thatcher'Story/0,2763,402708,00.html>>

Kael, Pauline. 1991. *"High Hopes."* In *Movie Love: Complete Reviews 1988–1991,*
87–89. New York: Plume. Also quoted in Watson, *Cinema of Mike Leigh,* 95.

Leigh, Mike. 1995. *"Naked."* In *Naked and Other Screenplays,* 1–95. London: Faber
and Faber.

Movshovitz, Howie. 1994. "Mike Leigh's Grim Optimism." *The Denver Post*
(22 February 1994); reprinted in *Mike Leigh: Interviews,* edited by Howie
Movshovitz, 51–54. Jackson: University Press of Mississippi, 2000.

Quart, Leonard. 1993. "The Religion of the Market: Thatcherite Politics and the
British Film of the 1980s." In *British Cinema and Thatcherism: Fires Were Started,*
edited by Lester Friedman, 15–34. London: UCL Press.

Sterritt, David. 1993. "Mike Leigh Calls It as He Sees It." *The Christian Science
Monitor* (7 September): 12; reprinted in *Mike Leigh: Interviews,* edited by Howie
Movshovitz, 42–44. Jackson: University Press of Mississippi, 2000.

Sterritt, David. 1996. "Sensitive 'Secrets & Lies' Reflects Creative Journey."
The Christian Science Monitor (27 September): 13.

Stone, Judy. 1991. "Mike Leigh." *San Francisco Chronicle* (21 November);
reprinted in *Mike Leigh: Interviews,* edited by Howie Movshovitz, 26–29.
Jackson: University Press of Mississippi, 2000.

Thomson, David. 2002. "Mike Leigh." In *The New Biographical Dictionary of Film,*
509–10. New York: Alfred A. Knopf.

Watson, Garry. 2004. *The Cinema of Mike Leigh: A Sense of the Real.* London: Wallflower Press.

Worth, Larry. 1997. *"Lies* Director Shows True Colors." *New York Post* (5 August);
reprinted in *Mike Leigh: Interviews,* edited by Howie Movshovitz, 122–23.
Jackson: University Press of Mississippi, 2000.

Monty Python

LUST FOR GLORY

And now for something completely identical! More than twenty-five years after *Monty Python's Flying Circus* wrapped its final season, and seventeen years after the troupe capped its cinematic career with *The Meaning of Life*, all of its major works—the full Monty, so to speak—returned in 2000 on DVD and VHS, accompanied by supplementary materials that fans, scholars, and other obsessive-compulsives will be poring over for decades to come.

At once a mainstream comedy team, a performance-art troupe with boldly original ideas, and an object of near-cultish veneration by admirers around the world, Monty Python remains a touchstone of modernist humor even though its members long ago abandoned their tightly knit group identity. Revisiting the company's history and accomplishments has become easier and easier, thanks to video releases and Python-related books. A walk through their career has much to reveal about the evolution of contemporary British comedy as well as their own achievements in the realms of satire, absurdity, and silliness.

Although their output as a group is plentiful enough to fill (literally) a dozen DVDs, the Pythons have a fairly brief history of steady association. The legendary TV show that started it all, *Monty Python's Flying Circus*, premiered in October 1969 via the British Broadcasting Corporation, had a hiatus in 1971, then continued its run until early 1973. This period produced three series of thirteen episodes apiece, all written by and starring the full Python contingent: John Cleese,

Eric Idle, Terry Jones, Michael Palin, Graham Chapman—the only member now deceased—and Terry Gilliam, the non-British member who created the animated sequences. A fourth series of only six installments appeared in late 1974, but Cleese was absent from the screen, although he helped write some of the sketches. David Morgan's interview book *Monty Python Speaks!* reveals that the remaining Pythons found this truncated season uneven in quality and tone. But their disappointment over the show's dwindling momentum was counterbalanced by the American debut of the first series on a handful of PBS stations, in venues ranging from the unsurprising (New York, Chicago) to the surprising (Dallas, Buffalo) to the very, very surprising (Scranton, Erie, and little Watertown, N.Y.).

Five theatrical films are the other main pillar of the Python oeuvre. Chief among them are *Monty Python and the Holy Grail* (directed by Gilliam and Jones in 1975) and *Life of Brian* (directed by Jones in 1979), both razor-sharp historical comedies, and the episodic *Meaning of Life* (Jones, 1983), the last major project to involve all six members. The other films are *And Now for Something Completely Different* (Ian MacNaughton, 1971), which recycles earlier Python material, and *Monty Python Live at the Hollywood Bowl* (Terry Hughes, 1982), which provides the most extensive record of the troupe's onstage performing style. As of this writing, endeavors in other media include fourteen recordings and seven books, including three volumes based on their movies.

While this is not an enormous body of work, it has exerted enormous influence on large- and small-screen comedy, thanks partly to its high laugh content and partly to its innovations in comic writing and performance. An early sign of the group's originality was its decision to work as a consort of equals, never elevating a single member to star status—even though temptations tantalizingly arose, as when Cleese began to develop a large personal following and a set of escalating ambitions to go with it.

Another mark of the troupe's inventiveness is its rejection of familiar TV formulas, from standup joke-telling to sitcom-style narrative. In place of standard formats the troupe cultivated a stream-of-consciousness sensibility calling for mercurial change from one moment to the next. Even when a loosely strung story does unify an installment of the show, as happens in some of the later programs—the adventures of a muddled chap (Palin) on a cycling tour, for instance—its verbal and visual action follows the same free-association (il)logic that characterizes the installments containing multiple sketches.

This emphasis on outlandish juxtaposition is encapsulated in Gilliam's animations, which join the segments of a given show by contributing yet another level of *dis*junction. What might have served as a smokescreen for continuity gaps becomes the mightiest continuity gap of them all—and a hugely effective one, since, as Gilliam has acknowledged, the ability to insert an animation at any given moment allows the Pythons to end a routine as soon as it reaches its comic climax. This eliminates the need for follow-through and denouement that they saw as built-in structural flaws of conventional TV-sketch humor.

Ironically, the BBC gave the Pythons unwitting help by its diffident manner of launching the series. Uncertain what audience the program would appeal to—and worried that it might appeal to very few indeed—the network slipped it into a late-night timeslot that made it somewhat inconvenient to watch (in the pre-video era) and thereby lent it a tinge of the exotic and esoteric. After honing their skills on widely watched programs like *The Frost Report* and *Do Not Adjust Your Set*, the Pythons found themselves playing to what Palin later described as an audience of insomniacs and intellectuals. This isn't what they would have chosen, but it boosted the reputation for offbeat eccentricity that would become their calling card—and continued to serve them well when the Public Broadcasting Service put them on American airwaves after commercial networks showed little interest.

This aura of far-out originality paid particularly high dividends when it merged with the group's penchant for self-reflexive approaches to TV itself, going far beyond the dollops of mannerly lampoon being offered to English viewers by David Frost and company. In his hefty *Monty Python Encyclopedia*, critic Robert Ross points to the troupe's throwaway use of guest stars (Ringo Starr, Lulu) as evidence of their subversive attitude toward celebrity culture. He also cites a guest appearance by a newsreader from the rival ITV network as a near-revolutionary moment in British television, since it took an unprecedented shot at the sharply drawn boundary between ITV populism and BBC gentility. In our current age of niche markets and fragmented audiences, Ross observes, it's almost impossible to imagine the "massive war-lines" that existed in the fifties and sixties "between the cheap and cheerful entertainment of commercialism and the booming, experienced, educational voice of the Beeb."

Monty Python made the Beeb one of its favorite adversaries, bringing TV self-satire to levels hitherto unknown on either side of the Atlantic—even in smugly impertinent shows like *Saturday Night Live*, which the Pythons saw as a commercially minded, celebrity-centered vehicle given to cutting its own throat by inducing its stars to abandon ship for solo careers. Just as important, the Pythons wielded their satirical scalpels with enough canny wit to keep their best shows fresh and funny long after these specific culture wars faded from the screen.

Although video now puts the group's near-complete history at every fan's fingertips, a grasp of the full Python picture requires a more extensive look into the past. The strongest single influence on its style was Spike Milligan, the writer-director-comedian who anarchized British radio in the fifties with *The Goon Show*, did the same for TV with *A Show Called Fred* and *Q*, and made a handful of classic theatrical shorts including *The Case of the Mukkinese Battlehorn* (1956) and *The Running, Jumping, and Standing Still Film* (1960). Watch the beginning of the *Battlehorn* movie—a gloved hand smashing a museum showcase with a brick, then plunging into the wreckage and *stealing the brick*—and you have proto-Python zaniness in its purest form. Milligan later called the Pythons his "nephews," and they lionized his unflinching looniness from their formative years through their last major projects—even giving him a poignant cameo role in *Life of Brian*, where he plays a bearded old man who can't quite keep up with the Messianic fervor erupting around him.

While every member of the group was influenced by Milligan's mixture of surrealistic lampoon and button-pushing subtext, the deepest elements of the Python pedigree can be traced a lot farther back than the fifties. Ian MacNaughton, longtime director of the *Flying Circus* program, recognized this when he rhetorically asked whether *The Goon Show* could have found its distinctive personality if the Marx Brothers hadn't paved the way; whether the Marx Brothers would have emerged if not for the inspiration they drew from burlesque; and whether burlesque would have existed without the British music-hall scene before it. As college-trained comedians with copious amounts of book-learning to supplement their well-tuned instincts, the Pythons were well aware of their forebears and the lessons to be learned from them—as their taste for historical satire and media-referential pastiche clearly shows.

Not surprisingly, college is where Python's five British constituents first came into contact with one another. Cleese and Chapman studied law and medicine (respectively) at Cambridge University, where an interest in performing led them both to the Footlights Club, a Cambridge institution for almost a century. Each year the club produced a show called the *Footlights Revue*, reaching a high point when the 1960 edition—*Beyond the Fringe*—struck international box-office gold and made writer-performers Dudley Moore, Peter Cook, Alan Bennett, and Jonathan Miller the "four most famous Englishmen until the Beatles came along," as the *Monty Python Encyclopedia* puts it. Riding this wave, Cleese and Chapman created the club's 1962 presentation, *Double Take*, which got engagements in the United States and New Zealand over the next couple of years and helped Cleese land a writing gig with Frost's fledgling TV hit, *That Was the Week That Was*. Idle entered the Footlights in 1963, completing what would become the Python troupe's Cambridge contingent.

Over at Oxford University, meanwhile, history majors Jones and Palin teamed up in 1963 to write revue sketches and slapstick routines. Later they moved to television with *The Frost Report* and sketches for Marty Feldman, then a rising comedian. Eventually they joined Idle on script work for *Do Not Adjust Your Set*, a children's TV show that they saw as an apt vehicle for the childlike (i.e, crazy and anarchic) humor they wanted to cultivate. Palin and Jones also wrote and acted in *The Complete and Utter History of Britain*, which Jones— a disciple of Buster Keaton, insisting that beauty and integrity are indispensable ingredients of worthwhile comedy—later called the most Python-like of these early television efforts.

Gilliam, a former advertising artist and aspiring cartoonist, came to London after fleeing the United States in disgust at American arrogance and hypocrisy during the Vietnam era. He was creating collage-like animations for *Do Not Adjust Your Set* by 1969, but he'd first encountered a Python-to-be four years earlier at Harvey Kurtzman's influential American humor magazine *Help!*, where he succeeded future feminist leader Gloria Steinem as assistant editor— just in time to supervise a photo shoot of Cleese for a *fumetto*-type story about a man who becomes sexually obsessed with his little girl's doll. ("Mommy, my Barbie's hair is all mussed up! And her clothes are all over the place!") Increasingly well versed in one another's styles and ideas, and increasingly well known for their stage and media credits, the five Brits and one Yank formally coalesced into Monty Python in spring of 1969, motivated partly by mutual respect and partly by awareness of the freedom offered to comedy writers by the BBC, which tended to be more interested in keeping costs down than in supervising script content.

These matters of Python prehistory are significant since they illuminate details of personality and predilection that would shape the troupe's work for years to come. With some justification, the British members are often lumped together as middle-class Oxbridge types, and they did share certain outlooks on the world. All came originally from the provinces, for instance, and tended to see London as "slightly the enemy," in Palin's words. All grew up in bourgeois surroundings, as well, inheriting a slight degree of awe and suspicion toward professions like law and education, which they parodied so relentlessly in their shows.

One shouldn't generalize about them too freely, however, since they didn't drop their diverse approaches to life and work any more than they overcame the friendly rivalries induced by their Oxford and Cambridge backgrounds. Cleese and Chapman usually wrote together, specializing in carefully structured, verbally elaborate sketches that often start with a confrontation between two contrasting characters. (This reflected their own contrasts: Cleese focused and methodical, Chapman scattered and intuitive.) Jones and Palin formed another team, gravitating toward more visually oriented and eccentrically paced material. Idle preferred writing alone, spinning some of the group's most flamboyant wordplay, and Gilliam devised his free-form animations in comparative isolation.

These patterns persisted for years, as did the troupe's overall working habits—writing their scripts on carefully timed schedules, reading their sketches aloud for comment (and sometimes rejection) by the other members, and making group decisions about who would play which role in which sketch, regardless of who wrote the material in the first place. Tensions arose, as when Chapman's alcoholism complicated the shooting of *Monty Python and the Holy Grail*, but in general these highly idiosyncratic talents worked together smoothly and efficiently.

Still, no troupe lasts forever. While some commentators feel Python disbanded primarily because individual members were eager for solo flights—Cleese as a comic star in *Fawlty Towers* and elsewhere, Gilliam as the director of increasingly ambitious feature films, Idle as an author and songwriter, and so on—the group's comic energy was manifestly on the wane by 1974. Cleese gives what may be the most bluntly candid assessment in *The Life of Python*, a BBC documentary subsequently released on home video. "We were repeating ourselves," he recalls. "I felt [Chapman] and I only wrote two genuinely original things in the whole of the last series [and] I felt that everyone else's material was also repetitive, and that if anyone did a sketch I could say, 'It's that sketch from the first series combined with that sketch from the second series. . . . ' Once you could begin to identify sketches like that, I thought, why are we doing it?"

The wonder is not that Monty Python ultimately fell apart, of course, but that it succeeded so brilliantly when it was together. Its slumps will be recalled by anyone who ever dozed during a *Flying Circus* segment, and Cleese's critique is borne out by an intermittent sense of been-there-done-that even in the show's third season, when its energy was still basically intact. The troupe's overall inventiveness quotient is remarkably high, however, and its video releases constitute an extensive library of comic know-how.

Python admirers will find an unlimited number of entry points into this material, but certain characteristics stand out in particularly high relief when the movies and TV shows are consumed in the concentrated sessions that video allows. Among the most striking is the political dimension of the Pythons' comic world. There is little evidence that any Python thought of himself as a political comedian, much less a political commentator. Still, these were educated entertainers with ideas and opinions, and while intelligence and intellectuality needn't go together—Chapman, for example, was both a trained physician and the troupe's most notoriously scatter-brained member—it isn't surprising that coherent social, cultural, and political views made their way into the Python mix.

This is nowhere more evident than in *Life of Brian*, accurately held by most critics to be the group's most successful large-scale work on sociopolitical as well as comic, narrative, and aesthetic grounds. Chapman plays the title character, a part-Jewish-part-Roman man who's mistaken for the Messiah by a motley band of all-too-eager followers, even as Jesus himself sermonizes and allegorizes off-screen at the same moment Brian's increasingly absurd life is unfolding. Brian's adventures take many forms, from his efforts to escape the adulation of his acolytes to the kidnapping of Pontius Pilate's wife by a Jewish liberation group he joins. The tragedy of his ultimate fate—crucifixion with other transgressors—is counterpointed by the comedy of its treatment, as a fellow sufferer admonishes the whole cross-hanging gang to smile, whistle, and look on the bright side of life. Rarely have the sins of the Roman Empire and the conventions of the Hollywood cinema been so scathingly skewered in a single stroke of truly inspired sarcasm.

Underpinning this film's overall success as a political satire is its success as a sustained story with three-dimensional characters, a vividly etched historical setting, and a neatly integrated set of carefully developed subtexts. Four of these subtexts stand out as the most important: the conformity and mindlessness of conventional religious belief; the arbitrary nature of personal and political power; the complexity of nationalism and colonialism in world history; and the ease with which legitimate political discourse shades into self-serving ideological cant.

Far from being subtly embedded in the film's comedy-driven narrative, these points of interest leap to attention with a force and clarity that Bertolt Brecht would have applauded. The commentary on religious tradition starts at the very beginning, as the Magi pay their respects to the infant Messiah, then grab back their gold, frankincense, and myrrh when they realize they've gone into the wrong house and kowtowed to an ordinary baby named Brian instead of the Jesus they're looking for. In commentaries on the DVD edition, various Pythons take the line that they never wanted to parody Jesus' actual life and message—the original title, *Jesus Christ: Lust for Glory,* was quickly scuttled—and that their targets were religious *institutions* rather than religious *ideas.* Yet the movie is supercharged with the notion that orthodox religious ideas are often (if not always) based on heedless self-delusion, a reflexive need to find and follow authority figures, and the proneness of humanity to misapprehend and misunderstand the world.

These categories overlap, moreover: All three come into play when Brian and other characters hear Jesus give his Sermon on the Mount, eager to be in the presence of a putative Messiah but getting the words wrong ("Blessed are the cheesemakers?") and adding bad hermeneutics for good measure ("It clearly refers to *any* manufacturer of dairy products"). Later scenes bring out a more particularized target of the movie: the division of Judaism and Christianity into sects and cults that often war with one another. Members of the People's Front of Judea despise the Judean People's Front and the Judea Popular People's Front more than they despise the Romans themselves; and Brian's new followers split almost instantly into factions that debate whether the master's sandal (which slipped off his foot as he ran from them) or his gourd (a meaningless object he acquired haphazardly) is the holy relic they should worship.

Foolish arguments play a part in the film's lampooning of political discourse, as well. In a richly parodic scene aimed at both revolutionary rhetoric and identity politics, a character played by Idle interrupts talk about overthrowing the Romans with calls for female power, finally revealing his personal desire for a life more self-determined than nature is prepared to give him. The dialogue here is mercilessly sharp:

Palin: Why are you always [going] on about women, Stan?
Idle: I want to be one. . . . From now on, I want you all to call me Loretta.
Cleese: What?!
Idle: It's my right as a man. . . . I want to have babies. . . .
Cleese: But you can't have babies.
Idle: Don't you oppress me!

Eventually admitting that he has no womb or other child-bearing equipment, he decides that recognition of his "right to have babies" is enough to satisfy him. What's the point of his victory? "It's symbolic of our struggle against oppression," says Palin's character, frantically rationalizing the situation. "It's symbolic of his struggle against reality," retorts an exasperated Cleese.

Equally eloquent is the scene wherein the People's Front of Judea shore up their commitment to their cause—and the strength of their egos—by rehashing how harsh the Romans' domination has been. "What have the Romans ever done for us?!" asks PFJ leader Cleese with great indignation. But there are answers to this question, and one by one the members blurt out responses, causing Cleese to modify his position one increment at a time. "Apart from the sanitation," he finally thunders at the end of the sequence, "medicine, education, wine, public order, irrigation, roads, the fresh-water system, and public health—*what have the Romans ever done for us?*" Structurally, this scene resembles the great Spanish Inquisition sketch on the *Flying Circus* show, where a dramatic statement is also ludicrously modified until its effect is lost; but politically, it's a sophisticated take on the multifaceted nature of colonial experience, which is far less monolithic than political polemicists often acknowledge.

The prevalence of sociopolitical satire in *Life of Brian* doesn't mean the Pythons can't pull their punches—or make outright compromises—to attract as wide an audience as they feel the traffic will bear. Among the deleted scenes included on the DVD edition is a punchy episode about a character called Otto, the leader of a Semitic suicide squad whose insignia combines the Star of David with the swastika. He arrives near the end of the movie, searching for the Messiah who will, he's convinced, "save Israel by ridding it of the scum of non-Jewish people, making it pure—no foreigners, no riffraff, no gypsies!" In their DVD commentary, Idle and Gilliam claim the scene was eliminated because it slowed the movie's comic pace and confused preview audiences by introducing a new character. But it's hard to see how Otto is any more a "new character" than, say, the beard salesman who interferes with Brian's flight to safety a bit earlier. And sure enough, Idle finally admits that the question of this scene finally boiled down to whether its comic value was enough to justify the potential offensiveness of portraying a pro-Semitic fascist with stridently Hitlerian ideas.

Mainstream comedians though they ultimately are, the Pythons have nonetheless shown a commendable proclivity for performances, images, and concepts that seem outrageously—or refreshingly—out of sync with today's notions of sociopolitical good taste. This is partly a function of the period during which they reached their peak, from the *Flying Circus* premiere in 1969 through *Life of Brian* in 1979, since at that time the entertainment scene was somewhat more relaxed about possibly offensive nuances than it has become in more recent decades.

Still, the main motivation for this calculated indulgence in tastelessness—what theorist Mikhail Bakhtin would call the carnival spirit of strategically inverted values—was the Python sensibility itself, so sweeping in its satirical scope that it rarely took time to notice whether some demographic group might feel affronted or antagonized. The hugely popular "pepperpot" characters aren't just women with shrill voices and monotonous minds, for instance; they're men *playing* women with shrill voices and monotonous minds—and when a female character *is* portrayed by a female Python partner (usually Carol Cleveland, good sport par excellence) you can count on her personality being defined more by her hair and breasts than by her words and thoughts. Such stuff is less an attack on correct feminist thinking than on correct thinking period, and if it scuttles all sanctioned ideas of decency, propriety, and refinement, that's pretty much what the Pythons intend.

Ditto for enormous amounts of outlandish gay parody (sometimes led by Chapman, the group's gay member) and various kinds of race-based humor; see Episode 33 for a dose of the former, with Chapman himself as homophobe in chief, and Episode 29 for a good example of the latter, with Palin and Jones in blackface roles that make Spike Lee's movie *Bamboozled* look almost tame. If there's any excuse for all this, it's that (a) other Python sketches are full of straight white males who also act like idiots, and (b) let's face it, it's funny. But carnival theorists in general and Python loyalists in particular will contend that no excuses are necessary.

A different sort of Python trait is the group's aforementioned fondness for media satire. This sometimes hits targets close to home, as in the parody of a BBC instructional documentary called "How Not to Be Seen," wherein characters who don't manage "not to be seen" are promptly blown up by the film's officious narrator, unsubtly suggesting that the BBC has the power to annihilate anyone who doesn't meet its preposterous standards. Cinema takes many satirical hits, as well, and their variety is impressive: an existential drama improvised in a junkyard; parodies of Art Cinemah à la Luchino Visconti and Michelangelo Antonioni; a Sam Peckinpah version of *Salad Days*; a *Garden Club* show replete with Ken Russell-type tits and ass; and so on. At times the *Flying Circus* program itself provides a starting point for social or political humor. One episode begins with an announcement that Her Majesty the Queen is scheduled to tune in, and then presents two of the most flagrant grossout skits in *Circus* history—a report on cannibalism in the British Navy and the notorious undertaker sketch, which ends with the studio audience rising up in protest. God save the Pythons?

Two of the group's strongest affinities are with the Dada and Surrealist traditions. The first of these nourishes an anti-art stance (or at least an anti-pretension stance) that underlies Python's quasipolitical eagerness to debunk the pompous and the pontifical. The second reveals—perhaps paradoxically—an artistic sophistication that enhances the Pythons' appeal for savvy spectators like the intellectuals and insomniacs who constituted their early audience. Examples abound, but one particularly uproarious instance appears in Episode 32, where a sketch about a naval expedition is populated by *sailors* who are also *hippies* with the names of *female Hollywood stars* interviewed by a *journalist* who turns into a *pirate*, all of which leads to a *Yellow Submarine* lampoon and a visit to a *lake*

inside a London *house*. The satirical tactics here are richly hetero-
geneous, unified (if that's the word) only by a dreamish irrational-
ity as bold as it is unflinching. Surrealism undergirds much of
Python's output, but in offerings like this it reaches an oneiric
intensity that spills over the boundaries of conventional comedy
with extraordinary abandon.

True to form, the DVD edition of *Month Python's Flying Circus* contains various extras. Some are useful, as when a click of the remote
switches you from a TV sketch to an in-concert remake of the same
bit—allowing comparisons between the troupe's live and on-camera
styles, and between renditions of similar material in different time
periods. Other supplements will interest only Python buffs, and
even hard-core fans may soon stop bothering with "dictionary" definitions of Python neologisms, Gilliam animations out of context,
and random sketches from other discs in the series. Such materials
recall the inspired title of a CD-ROM released by the Pythons a few
years ago: *Monty Python's Complete Waste of Time.*
   The feature-film DVDs are largely free of such frivolities. This is
good insofar as it cuts down prices a little, but it's disappointing
that a film as ingenious as *Monty Python and the Holy Grail* has no
extras to offer but some trailers. (*Grail* is another parody with a
political edge, incidentally, debunking a central Western power
myth and playing Brechtian havoc with traditionalist ideas ranging
from benevolent despotism to chivalric masculinity.) It's a pleasure to report that the excellent *Life of Brian* fares very well in the
supplement department, however, with rich commentaries, an
informative "making of" documentary, and remarkable deleted
scenes. Among the latter are the Otto episode described earlier
and, more briefly, an exquisite shot of Cleese doing a silly-walk-
style dance on a distant hilltop.
   There are various reasons why such memorable moments
landed on the cutting-room floor, and these can be as engrossing
as the material itself. Some have to do with political content, as

with the Otto scene, while others are based on artistic judgments related to pace, timing, and rhythm. Sometimes different Pythons have different accounts of what was decided and why. It's fascinating to hear Idle explain a trim by referring to three-act narrative structure and proper story development—and then hear Gilliam argue that lively moment-by-moment bits are much more important than correct plot construction.

Such comments offer revealing insights into the thinking of individual Pythons, especially when they go beyond creative methods to aesthetic and even philosophical matters. Remember the bearded prisoner chained to the wall in the *Life of Brian* dungeon? Palin analyzes him in psychological terms, saying he's an inherently funny character because he insists on behaving in such a curmudgeonly manner toward his new cellmate, the only person who could possibly become his friend and companion. By contrast, Gilliam discusses him in political terms, saying the poor creep is funny because he insists on being a raging right-winger with a "law and order" fixation even though he's a pathetic victim of exactly that ideology. Both are right, and both offer much Pythonic food for thought.

Life of Brian is the best Python movie, but all of their good material holds up well on video. In visual terms, the troupe usually thought small, which helps explain why the epic-prone Gilliam really needed to strike off on his own. (His commentary on the *Brian* disc reveals how irked he was when Jones's camera positions failed to capture the grandeur of the sets he'd designed.) Mixed and matched or watched straight through, the Python oeuvre has yet to be surpassed. It's hard to imagine a time when creators and consumers of comedy won't be watching it for ideas, inspiration, and fun.

Creepies, Crawlies, Conundrums

DAVID CRONENBERG COMES OF AGE

David Cronenberg's admirers were surprised when his promisingly titled *Spider* debuted at the Cannes International Film Festival in 2002 and proved a near-anomaly among his works: no mutated insects, grotesque creepy-crawlies, demented entomologists, or hypnotic special effects. Nor is it a sequel to *The Fly*, the 1986 remake that became one of his biggest hits.

Cronenberg has strayed from his primary horror-film obsessions in the past, as in *M. Butterfly*, a melodrama of gender ambiguity and sexual deception based on David Henry Hwang's popular play, and *Dead Ringers*, an essay in abnormal psychology rather than the supranormal per se. Still and all, *Spider* is something of a departure for him—a restrained, almost austere portrait of psychosis, delusion, and dysfunction where his ever-present tropes of disfigurement and trauma are always already internal, visible to us only through the mind's eye of a psychologically tormented protagonist. While fans of *Naked Lunch* and *Crash* may find it too moody and unspectacular, its sympathetic portrayal of a deeply troubled soul finds Cronenberg moving toward a more mature and introspective stage in his eclectic, often controversial career.

Cronenberg has been sparking interest and debate since the 1970s, when he gained a cult following with luridly titled thrillers like *Shivers* (1975), *Rabid* (1976), and *The Brood* (1979), all dealing with ordinary people besieged by malign, infectious pests. The moviegoers most drawn to him were aficionados of horror and science fiction—genres of dubious respectability that led skeptics to regard him as a minor purveyor of sensational shocks. It didn't help that his budgets were low, his technical resources limited, his actors less than stellar.

Or that he hailed from Canada, which has never managed to establish a distinctive cinematic voice in the way some European and Asian countries have, partly because of the three-way geographical split among its Ontario, Quebec, and British Columbia branches. Cronenberg is a mainstay of the Ontario group, along with Atom Egoyan and Don McKellar, who make different sorts of movies but share his penchant for unconventional structures and sociocultural critique. Some consider him a national asset worth every penny of the Canadian government's filmmaking subsidies. Others take the dimmer view expressed in a widely quoted post-*Shivers* article written for *Saturday Night* magazine by Canadian critic Robert Fulford, called "You Should Know How Bad This Film Is. After All, You Paid for It."

Cronenberg graduated from the exploitation-film ghetto in 1980 with the slightly higher-budget *Scanners*, about a cult of people with destructive telepathic powers. He then scored enough box-office success with the 1982 techno-thriller *Videodrome*, about a malignant TV show designed to invade the minds and bodies of its viewers, to get the job of filming Stephen King's novel *The Dead Zone* (with Christopher Walken as a man who awakens from a coma with powers to see the future) a year later—an assignment that put him on his best behavior, resulting in a movie that's both impeccably crafted and surprisingly tame. His book-based movies since then include William S. Burroughs's *Naked Lunch* (1991) and J. G. Ballard's *Crash* (1996), both thought unfilmable by Hollywood studios. He has also developed original projects like the gynecological horror-drama *Dead Ringers* (1988) and the sci-fi fantasy *eXistenZ* (1999).

Cronenberg has never been a dependable hit-maker or a favorite with consumer-guide reviewers, but thoughtful critics have taken him seriously, with mixed results. Some find him a deeply personal filmmaker who has taken familiar formulas of the horror, science-fiction, and psychological-drama genres and put them through highly original transmutations and recombinations, arriving at apocalyptic visions of rare forcefulness.

Others agree with the influential academic critic Robin Wood, who finds him a conservative, even reactionary allegorist of contemporary culture. According to this view, summed up in Wood's essay "An Introduction to the American Horror Film," the best horror fantasies serve to liberate their audiences by unleashing anarchic monsters that embody the unquenchable spirit and inevitable return of libidinal urges. This puts us in momentary touch with truths about nature—human and otherwise—that we normally repress and deny, to our psychological and spiritual peril. This interpretation puts Cronenberg's movies in opposition to "progressive" films that use horrors as metaphors for bourgeois institutions like marriage and family, which Wood considers oppressive. Wood deplores Cronenberg's conception of the so-called monstrous as physically disgusting and metaphysically obscene, manifesting a paranoid view of the body in general and sexuality in particular.

Feminists have an extra bone to pick with him, asserting that women's bodies find especially dark fates in his stories. It's more accurate to see Cronenberg as a misanthropist than a misogynist—he's an equal-opportunity cynic, if he's a cynic at all—but there is something grimly characteristic in the *Videodrome* image of Deborah Harry snuffing a cigarette on her breast, the *Naked Lunch* shot of Judy Davis injecting dope into hers, and so on, stretching at least as far back as *Rabid*, when the vampiric Rose ends up dead on a garbage heap.

Many a Cronenberg man meets a similarly harsh end, of course, such as the twin gynecologists played by Jeremy Irons in *Dead Ringers*. Then again, they aren't your everyday gynecologists, and Cronenberg's camera seems awfully fascinated by the bizarre instruments they invent for their nightmarish examinations of female anatomy.

Sexual politics aside, Cronenberg has received more analysis than any filmmaker this side of Oliver Stone from critics who think theatrical movies are outgrowing their modernist roots and entering a new postmodernist era. Evidence is easy to come by in the disjunctive structures, self-reflexive overtones, and genre-bending scenarios of movies as diverse as *Videodrome, Naked Lunch, Crash,* and *eXistenZ.* Cronenberg's rejection of traditional lenses for viewing human experience—including all manner of philosophical and ideological schemes—produces an apocalyptic, often doom-laden spirit that's eminently suited to the postmodernist idea of contemporary culture being severed from the myths of a shared past. The literal meaning of "apocalypse" is "an unveiling," usually in the sense of an unveiling of a state of affairs that has been present all along. Often in apocalyptic narratives, what is unveiled is the future, which turns out to have its roots in the present moment. Many of Cronenberg's films are steeped in this spirit, using scenes of violence and dysfunction as metaphors for tendencies toward anomie, disorientation, lawlessness, and chaos. In this sense, they can be regarded as paradigms of postmodern thought, which is characterized by the breakdown of previous meaning systems and subsequent feelings of disillusionment, anxiety, and apathy.

Here again, though, Cronenberg proves difficult to pin down. Postmodernists champion the end of master narratives and all-embracing worldviews; hence their affection for fragmented films like, say, the David Lynch dramas *Lost Highway* and *Mulholland Drive.* Cronenberg has busied himself positing an intricate network of new mythologies and unifying themes, however, suited to the still-emerging conditions of the postindustrial landscape. The dangers of science and medicine, the implacable grasp of contemporary media, and the feral enticements of uncontainable sexuality loom large in his vision, which combines a pessimistic philosophical outlook with a sense of existential excitement conveyed by the relentless audacity of his style. Sex loses its allure as intimate fun in *Crash*, offering murky new pleasures in the fusion of sensual gratification with technological disaster. Science forfeits its status as a civilizing force in *eXiztenZ* and *The Fly*, taking on alchemical powers that bend biological nature into unheard-of configurations. Mass media unveil their innate incoherence in *Videodrome*, revealing themselves as invasive parasites capable of hard-wiring humanity into their perverse domains. Such films present a vision of society on the cusp of a future that's bewildering and barbaric from a humanistic perspective, yet alluring and perhaps liberating for those who plunge adventurously into its intimidating depths.

Given the radically strange contours of Cronenberg's fictional world, it isn't surprising that his characters are often as disoriented as we'd be if we found ourselves wandering through it. His long-time fascination with mental aberration, prominent in such signature movies as *Videodrome* and *Dead Ringers*, surfaces again in *Spider*, which gains much of its eerie power from a refusal to separate the protagonist's delusion-riddled thoughts from the everyday surroundings in which he's adrift.

Set in the nineteen-sixties, the film begins when the title character (Ralph Fiennes) is released to a halfway home in London after years in a psychiatric institution. Disturbed and inarticulate, he shuffles through the grimy streets of the neighborhood where he grew up, jotting notes in a small journal he keeps inside a knotted sock. Harrowing memories start to recur, inducing him to relive his former days. We experience them too, shuttling through the skein of past and present that constitutes Spider's tumultuously jumbled mind. As a boy, we learn, his name was Dennis and he had a close relationship with a loving and protective mother (Miranda Richardson), who gave him his nickname after witnessing his curious habit of making little webs from strands of thread. Later in his childhood he was traumatized when his abusive father (Gabriel Byrne) apparently murdered his mother after she caught him having sex with a local prostitute (also played by Richardson, this time with snaggly teeth). When he remembers this woman moving into the family home, Spider's thoughts become increasingly distraught, leaving us unclear as to what actually happened to his mother, and what role he may have played in her death.

Spider is based on a novel by Patrick McGrath, who grew up on the grounds of the Broadmoor hospital—England's most famous institution for the criminally insane—where his father was medical superintendent. McGrath also collaborated with Cronenberg on the screenplay, and his hand is evident in the finished film, which is more compelling as a finely wrought portrait of mental illness than as the psychological horror film it appears to be on the surface. *Spider* grimly evokes the nightmarish world of the protagonist's mind, encompassing him with an atmosphere of dingy suffering, faded wallpaper, dirt, filth, and grime that echo and reflect his turbulent inner state. The streets he shuffles down are shadowed by the looming tower of an enormous gasworks; the dark alleys and bridges he skulks across suggest a subconscious landscape full of psychosexual tensions. Spider himself, with his layers of shirts, obsessive scribbling, and stringing up of threads, is a frightening example of a man trapped in a self-spun web of anguished visions.

Spider's tortured thought processes and tenuous relationship with reality recall the novels of Samuel Beckett, whose craggy appearance was an influence on Fiennes's concept of the character, as the actor noted at the Toronto International Film Festival, where the film had its North American premiere. This literary touchstone notwithstanding, Cronenberg captures Spider's inner life in largely nonverbal terms, relying less on dialogue and action than on details of lighting and decor. "Patrick's first draft had voiceover narration and insects," Cronenberg said at the Cannes festival. "I really felt this was a different kind of movie, and I'd rather use damp, moldy wallpaper . . . to give you the interior of Spider's mind."

Spider provides a subtler evocation of key Cronenberg concerns—psychological disorder, agonies of abjection, violence of body and mind—than many of his earlier films. It is very much a Cronenberg movie, though, continuing his exploration of yet another ongoing theme: irresistible transformations in which the boundaries of self fracture and disintegrate. These transformations take different forms in different films—an abandonment of self to a collective impulse or gestalt (*Shivers, Rabid*), a merging between two beings (*The Fly, Dead Ringers, M. Butterfly*), a surrender of independence in order to serve incomprehensible conspiracies (*Scanners, Videodrome, Naked Lunch*). What's unusual in *Spider* is that the transformation is entirely internalized, as the markers of the protagonist's selfhood collapse, wish-fulfillment fantasies merge with self-punishing delusions, and the very nature of human identity is called into question. *Spider* includes few of Cronenberg's patented twists and turns of plot, and unlike such movies as *eXistenZ* and *Crash*, it presents no harrowing fusion of flesh and technology. Instead we come face to face with something at least equally disturbing: a terminally disordered mind, with no hope of improvement.

The minimalist aspects of *Spider* may prove a momentary departure for Cronenberg, who said at Cannes that he'll cheerfully return to "effects and violence and gore" if they're called for by a story that catches his eye. It's also possible, however, that his interests are taking a more pensive, inner-directed turn. He suggests as much when he acknowledges that *Spider* was a particularly personal project for him.

As he put it at the Toronto festival, "Flaubert said, 'Madame Bovary, *c'est moi.*' I say, 'Spider, *c'est moi.*' I think I'm just *that* far away from being Spider at any given moment, frankly—walking in the streets, mumbling (probably about the film business) in an old coat with a tattered lining and all my possessions in a small cardboard suitcase that's falling apart. I can see that happening at any moment. So there was something about *Spider* that was very compelling and close to home."

Not all of Cronenberg's followers find it close to home as well. Usually sympathetic critics have been ambivalent about the movie—it was selected for the prestigious official competition at Cannes, but overlooked by the New York Film Festival, the most selective North American festival—and reviews have been mixed. If the filmmaker has taken these developments to heart, Cronenbergian effects and gore could rule the rest of his career. If not, he might feel encouraged to conduct further experiments along subtler, less cinematically explosive lines.

This would be a welcome development. I have long admired Cronenberg's pluck and audacity, but his films are often more interesting in conception than execution. While they're exciting to think and talk about, actually watching them can be dull by comparison—prime examples are *Naked Lunch* and *Crash*, as theoretically bold as any feature films in memory, yet so sluggishly paced and cinematically labored that it's not tempting to revisit them on-screen very often. The comparative restraint and inward-looking mood of *Spider* indicate a new willingness on Cronenberg's part to embrace elements of narrative nuance and psychological ambiguity that have eluded him in the past. Here's hoping he keeps deepening his cinema in this direction.

Fargo

THE MIDDLE OF NOWHERE?

"Out of respect for the dead. . . ."
—from the opening text of *Fargo*

"A lot can happen in the middle of nowhere." So asserts the well-received promotional tag for *Fargo*, which has accompanied the film's propitious commercial and critical career from its 1996 theatrical release through its later video incarnation.

But while *Fargo* indeed takes place in the middle of nowhere—if one accepts the notion that Minnesota and North Dakota are thus accurately described—it was clearly not conceptualized there. Joel and Ethan Coen had written, directed, and produced six feature films during the eleven preceding years, and as of 2001 they have completed three more. *Fargo* reflects, refracts, and refines a variety of thematic and stylistic ideas that have preoccupied the brothers throughout this period. To appreciate *Fargo* one must take into account the context in which it was made—a multifaceted context that encompasses not only the picture's production history but a set of social and cinematic notions deployed here by the Coens with a vigor and consistency that make this grim comedy one of their most fully realized achievements, even as it encapsulates other qualities that many critics rightly find problematic.

The comparatively small scale and proudly monochromatic look of *Fargo* have been described as outgrowths of the fact that this movie went into production at a ticklish time in the Coens' career. Their previous picture, *The Hudsucker Proxy* (1994), had fared disastrously at the box office, failing to recoup the then-imposing budget (reported at anywhere from $25 million to $40 million) that Warner Bros. had imprudently (and unnecessarily) poured into it.

This was not the first time the brothers had found themselves in such a position. Coen biographer Ronald Bergan calls *The Hudsucker Proxy* their "most expensive film and their only box-office disaster" (Bergan, 161), but the 1990 melodrama *Miller's Crossing* had also been a major disappointment, despite a high-profile premiere in the prestigious opening-night slot of the New York Film Festival and a major promotional push by Twentieth Century Fox intended to translate the art-theater momentum established at Lincoln Center into a wave of mass-audience appeal at neighborhood screens everywhere. Interestingly and perhaps perversely, the Coens' next picture was *Barton Fink* (1991), an aggressively surrealistic comedy for which the brothers themselves had appropriately skeptical commercial expectations. Shortly before *Barton Fink* debuted I asked the Coens what project they would proceed to after it was launched. "Something people will want to see," they simultaneously replied in slightly different words, indicating rueful awareness that *Barton* was not destined for ticket-window glory.

None of the previous Coen movies had been a walloping hit— *Blood Simple* (1985) did well and *Raising Arizona* (1987) did better, but neither was a blockbuster by Hollywood standards—and the lackluster returns of *Miller's Crossing* and *Barton Fink* were topped by the awful performance of *The Hudsucker Proxy*. The brothers' status in Hollywood's eyes at this time is crisply described by William Preston Robertson, a Coen commentator who speaks from his personal relationship with them: "The broad artistic license the movie industry had granted them for so many years in the hope that such patience might someday be rewarded with a box-office hit in addition to a merely critical one was, the Coen brothers believed, swiftly narrowing. The clock was ticking. The heat was on"

(Bergan, 166). Many another filmmaker would have recognized their plight—for example, Martin Scorsese, when he tried to recover from Paramount's cancellation of *The Last Temptation of Christ* in 1983 by turning to *After Hours*, which did not draw huge crowds when released in 1985 but reassured Hollywood that the serious-minded filmmaker of *Taxi Driver* (1976) and *Raging Bull* (1980) was perfectly willing to tell a quirky comic story with plenty of potential laughs. Feeling the heat and hearing the tick, the Coens did something similar when they moved from the relatively rarified world of *The Hudsucker Proxy*, with its top-heavy budget and film-referential glibness, to the leaner, meaner terrain of *Fargo*.

Not that anything connected with the Coens is likely to proceed quite so simply and straightforwardly.[1] They had expected to follow *The Hudsucker Proxy* with *The Big Lebowski*, which they had written before *Hudsucker* began its ill-starred theatrical run. But they wanted Jeff Bridges for the lead, and since he wasn't available at the time (although he did star in the picture when it was eventually made) they closeted themselves away and wrote the *Fargo* screenplay, exploring a subject and story that appealed to them for several reasons. Among these were the specificity of its setting in the part of the northern United States where they had grown up; their affection for plots that center on kidnapping (see *Blood Simple* and *Raising Arizona* for further evidence); and the opportunity it presented for them to shoot "a crime film with characters away from the stereotypes of the genre," as they later put it. They also liked the prospect of engaging with a "smaller crew and a much more intimate production" after the *Hudsucker* extravaganza (Bergan, 167).

In addition, they were plugging into a current filmmaking trend—the vogue for intertwining elements of crime and comedy in deliberately exaggerated ways—that had taken on considerable momentum thanks in part to their own previous work, most notably *Blood Simple* and *Raising Arizona*. Other such films released to American theaters in 1996 include Wes Anderson's *Bottle Rocket* and Benjamin Ross's *The*

FARGO: THE MIDDLE OF NOWHERE? [135]

Young Poisoner's Handbook, both of which show signs of influence by the Coen approach.

By and large, the principal photography for *Fargo* went as smoothly as the Coens had hoped. (In this they were more fortunate than, say, Francis Ford Coppola, who embarked on *Apocalypse Now* in 1976 with high-spirited expectations of a fun action-movie shoot that would contrast with the anxiety-filled intensity of making *The Conversation* and *The Godfather Part II,* only to be walloped by production woes ranging from star Martin Sheen's heart attack to a cataclysmic Philippines monsoon [Cowie, 7].) Athough anticipated support from Warner Bros. fell through, Eric Fellner and Tim Bevan of Working Title stayed committed to the project along with PolyGram and Gramercy Pictures, which held distribution rights for the North American market. All were attracted by the $6.5 million budget, a modest but realistic figure that was the Coens' lowest since *Raising Arizona,* still their most profitable picture.

Shooting started a brief three months after the screenplay was finished, with Roger Deakins behind the camera in his third consecutive stint with the brothers after replacing Barry Sonnenfeld as their regular cinematographer. Production designer Rick Heinrichs worked with Deakins and the Coens on the challenge of making the film's midwestern landscapes look simultaneously bleak, boring, fraught with dramatic possibilities, and worthy of Dante in their potential for immanent horror. Heinrichs also devised the Paul Bunyan statue that towers portentously over the town of Brainerd with its axe-murderer stance and mad, glaring eyes. Former assistant costumer Mary Zophres replaced her ailing employer Richard Hornung to design the characters' clothing. In the cast, Frances McDormand signed on to play Marge, working with her husband Joel in the first major role he'd given her since *Blood Simple.* (The couple reportedly stayed in adjoining but separate hotel rooms during the shoot to maintain domestic and professional harmony.) Also on board was previous Coen collaborator Steve Buscemi (*Miller's*

Crossing, Barton Fink) as Carl Showalter, the picture's talkative thug. Rounding out the ensemble were Peter Stormare as Gaear Grimsrud, the taciturn thug; William H. Macy as Jerry Lundegaard, the larcenous car salesman; Kristin Rudrüd in the thankless role of Lundegaard's kidnapped wife; and Harve Presnell as her father, a businessman whose soulless self-absorption is a wry complement to that of his pathetic son-in-law.

Together this group headed for Minneapolis in January 1995, looking forward to vistas of endless snow—which failed to materialize, ironically, since this proved to be a historically warm winter for the Twin Cities area. Snow machines sufficed for a while, but eventually the filmmakers trekked on to North Dakota's chilly Grand Forks region, where they found sufficient snow for the icy exterior shots that they considered essential for the story's frigid mood. Virtually all of the film was shot on actual locations rather than studio sets, and Deakins used natural light whenever possible, seeking a documentary look that would suit the film's distanced, insects-under-a-microscope tone. Many scenes were worked out in storyboards, but some were left to last-minute inspiration so as to take advantage of the flexibility allowed by a comparatively small cast and crew. Postproduction also went smoothly, with the brothers editing the film under their pseudonym, Roderick Jaynes, and Coen regular Carter Burwell composing the score. Burwell incorporated elements of Scandinavian dance and religious music along with jazz and popular hits from the story's 1987 time period, producing an eclecticism that echoes the film's comic-tragic complexities.

Looking at *Fargo* in the context of its production history, one finds that the Coens brought forth this chilly, sardonic, sometimes savage movie through a filmmaking process notable for its cozy, companionable nature. One might see this as evidence of the professionalism they had cultivated by this stage of their career, combining no-nonsense technical competence with easy-going creative capabilities.

Alternatively, one might see the efficiency of the production as evidence of facile tendencies in the Coens' aesthetic sensibility. Calling

their body of work "alarmingly coherent," critic Kent Jones attributes this quality to "their monotonous syntax, the sense that any given
film has been fed through some hitherto unknown image/sound
processor, with pre-sets for shot duration, centered framing, emotional
tone, and visual handsomeness." On this view, one might imagine the
Coens as amiable but soulless artisans presiding over a carefully calculated exercise that's as glib and mannered as it is meticulously
designed and cinematically self-congratulatory. "You can set your
watch by their remarkably uniform editing rhythm," Jones continues, "which features a percussive yet deadpan one-two combination:
probably intended to surprise, it's become as predictable as the rising
of the sun." So have "cartoonish play with scale" and "deliberately
freakish use of actors popping up around the edge of the movie like
paper cutouts on sticks" (Jones, 46).

These criticisms apply to *Fargo* as to other Coen films—one thinks
of the relentless Hollywood cleverness in *The Hudsucker Proxy* and the
strenuous gag-mongering in *O Brother, Where Are Thou?*, among other
examples—calling attention to the Coens' penchant for ingeniously
arranged but self-enclosed and self-limiting cinematics. To be sure,
Fargo embodies many of the best possibilities of Coen-style genre
revisionism, with its genuinely surprising plot (is there a more
jolting gambit in nineties film than the moment of Showalter's
abrupt demise?) and its imaginative juxtaposition of contrasting
characters, from Grimsrud the feral brute to Marge the articulate
earth mother. Yet the very exactness of its immaculately assembled
tropes has an undertone as chilly and detached as the icy snowscapes
captured with such clinical precision by Deakins's long-lens
camera.

Genre revisionism is, of course, a crucial aspect of the Coens' creative signature, and their films can easily be sketched in the short-
hand terms of this popular postmodernist game: *Blood Simple*
blends *film noir* with EC Comics visuals; *Raising Arizona* is a mixture
of crime comedy and live-action cartoon; *Miller's Crossing* is a

Dashiell Hammett spin-off; *Barton Fink* introduces Nathanael West and Clifford Odets to William Faulkner and Luis Buñuel; *The Hudsucker Proxy* inflates a screwball-comedy story with countless in-joke allusions; *The Big Lebowski* is a deliberate knock-off of Raymond Chandler's fiction; *O Brother, Where Art Thou?* bites off *The Odyssey* of Homer and *Sullivan's Travels* (1941) of Preston Sturges in one heedlessly ungainly gulp; and *The Man Who Wasn't There* (2001), heavily influenced by the work of James M. Cain, ends with the hero writing his bittersweet tale for the sort of forties men's magazine that the movie's tones and textures have evoked from the beginning.

Fargo is less specific and more subtle in its genre-parody characteristics than most other Coen films. Nevertheless, even casual spectators may easily detect the movie's roots in longtime traditions of small-town comedy, Grand Guignol grotesquerie, true-crime docudrama, and especially *film noir* edginess, however much the brothers' heavy irony may seem to reconfigure the contours of seminal forties and fifties *noir*, and even of the neo-*noir* cycle that was partly launched by *Blood Simple*. The failure of *The Hudsucker Proxy* may have taught the Coens that too much film-reflexive foolery can be off-putting to moviegoers who don't think of themselves as cineastes; but the sincerity of their own cinephilia shines through their inability to resist more of the same in their subsequent film. Still, they're careful this time to wrap genre horseplay in a mantle of humor, violence, sex, and suspense designed to satisfy mass-audience expectations even as film-savvy connoisseurs enjoy a steady stream of insider *frissons*.

Of the genre categories relevant to *Fargo*, the true-crime label has generated the most critical attention. This began when some early reviewers noticed the contradiction between the film's standard-issue disclaimer in the closing credits ("The persons and events portrayed in this production are fictitious. No similarity to actual persons, living or dead, is intended or should be inferred.") and the claim of docudrama reality made in its opening text: "This is a true story. The events depicted in this film took place in Minnesota in 1987. At the request of the survivors, the names have been changed. Out of respect for the dead, the rest has been told exactly as it occurred."

If casual moviegoers and careless critics tend to believe the first of these mutually canceling statements, it's for three reasons: First, the opening statement is foregrounded by its stark presentation in the film's first moments; second, there's no self-evident reason *not* to believe it; and third, the closing statement that contradicts it may not be heeded or even noticed by spectators accustomed to exiting the theater or hitting the fast-forward button long before the end credits are over.

People familiar with the Coens' work may be instantly skeptical about the "true story" assertion, however, since the brothers' imaginations have always inclined toward the surrealism of oneiric fantasy (e.g., *Barton Fink*) and psychological delirium (e.g., *The Big Lebowski*) rather than the realism of journalistic reportage or naturalistic docudrama. What's most compelling about the "true story" statement is the ingenuity with which the Coens have appropriated one of conventional cinema's most banal gestures to serve precisely the storytelling interests—oneiric fantasy and psychological delirium—that are their habitual stock in trade. Indeed, the bracketing of *Fargo* by paradoxical paratexts is one of the elements (along with bizarre plot twists like the woodchipper scene, hallucinatory images like the Paul Bunyan statue, and so on) that mark the movie as a quintessential Coen work.

Disorienting forms of duality and doubleness are integral to many facets of the brothers' *oeuvre,* from its mercurial moods (comic/tragic, menacing/reassuring, formulaic/innovative, etc.) to its penchant for parody. Parody is itself an inherently double-faced mode that reflects what literary theorist Mikhail Bakhtin calls the "laughing aspect" of the world. When deployed in contexts of carnivalesque irreverence (such as a darkly humorous entertainment film) it serves as a "system of crooked mirrors, elongating, diminishing,

distorting in various directions and to various degrees" (Bakhtin
1984a, 127). The opening text of *Fargo* is a parody in the root sense
of the term: It *parrots* the commonly made truth-claims of fact-
based narrative, only to be comically contradicted by an opposing
statement at the other end of the movie.

Its assertion of truth is negated not only by the disclaimer in the
closing credits, moreover—assuming that the *second* statement isn't
the false one, either a deliberate hoax or a technician's mistake. It's
also contradicted by producer and co-writer Ethan Coen, in his
introductory essay to the published version of the *Fargo* screenplay.
"The story that follows is about Minnesota," he writes. "It evokes the
abstract landscape of our childhood—a bleak, windswept tundra,
resembling Siberia except for its Ford dealerships and Hardee's
restaurants. It aims to be both homey and exotic, and pretends to
be true." The final clause grows out of that essay's brief discussion
of the ubiquity of narrative in human experience and the difficulty
of sorting out the factual from the false: "The stories that are not
credible will occasionally . . . turn out to be true, and stories that
are credible will conversely turn out to be false" (Coen and Coen,
ix–x). But it spills the beans about the veracity of *Fargo* even as it
begs us to complete its gesture of make-believe by surrendering
our good sense to the movie's aggressively ingratiating (and tantalizingly unstable) blend of hominess and exoticism.

Doubleness surges through Ethan's essay, which uses a long example of unverifiable family lore—the anecdote of "Grandma and the
Negress," endlessly told to him and Joel by an elderly relative when
they were children—to illustrate how even the simplest and folksi-
est truth claims are fraught with enough undecidability to gladden
Jacques Derrida's heart. Grandma's story is itself steeped in duali-
ties, from the contrasting traits of its title characters to its invocation of Jewish-Russian values in Jewish-American surroundings.
Ethan's discussion of it also has a dual structure, oscillating between
psychological-narratological inducements to *believe* the anecdote and practical-commonsensical reasons *not* to; between the
midwestern landscape imagined as white-screen abstraction and as

commerce-crowded Ford and Hardee habitat; and between the intricately imbricated pleasures of the homey and the exotic, the familiar and the uncanny, that which is purposefully pretended and that which is tantamount to truth.

In all of this, Ethan's essay makes an appropriate gateway to *Fargo* as both screenplay and movie. The bizarrely twinned figures of Grandma and the Negress subtly anticipate the film's own obsession with doubles and doppelgängers, which bring into bodily form the ambivalent attitudes toward bedrock existential constituents of the human condition—joy and sorrow, hope and despair, love and hate, life and death—that characterize the darkest, richest moments in *Fargo* and other Coen works. Bakhtin traces a fascination with grotesque bodies in general—and the trope of twinning in particular—through a centuries-old tradition of carnivalesque art and literature. "All the images of carnival are dualistic," he writes; "they unite within themselves both poles of change and crisis: birth and death (the image of pregnant death), blessing and curse . . . praise and abuse, youth and old age, top and bottom, face and backside, stupidity and wisdom." Also common in carnivalia are "paired images, chosen for their contrast (high/low, fat/thin, etc.) or for their similarity (doubles/twins)" (Bakhtin 1984a, 126). Coen movies have tapped into this tradition ever since *Blood Simple*, which intermingles love and death in a tangled horror-comic dance with such grotesque elements as (among many other examples) an all-but-murdered man who can't stay alive but refuses to rest in peace, and a bathroom finale that evokes the fascination with "the material bodily lower stratum" that Bakhtin points to as a recurring preoccupation of carnivalesque art.[2]

Carnivalism and grotesquerie work themselves into different Coen films in different ways, but certain of the brothers' strategies are tellingly consistent. One is their use of exaggerated speech patterns and distorted forms of body language to signal the inability of individuals to dwell harmoniously in the social world that surrounds and contains them. Another is their preoccupation with violence as not only a central factor in the American cultural ethos, but also a grimly efficacious conduit for social interactions perceived as necessary by their intellectually challenged characters. Still another is their sardonic view of business (i.e., capitalism) as a site not of mutually beneficial communication and cooperation, but of spasmodically destructive competition and exploitation. The brothers habitually explore these preoccupations through the social, cultural, economic, psychological, and discursive traits of particular American regions, which are rendered unfamiliar and grotesque via the brothers' distinctive tactics of overstatement, caricature, and parody. There is no Coen movie (even a comparatively "serious" one like *Miller's Crossing*) that does not etch a militantly parodic geographic and/or cultural chronotope, and in the years since *Fargo* this tendency has become even more conspicuous, culminating in the archly bizarre South of *O Brother, Where Art Thou?* and the somnolent California city of *The Man Who Wasn't There*.

Fargo marks a high point in the brothers' Bakhtinian habit of physicalizing—or desublimating, to use a psychoanalytic term—the complicated mixture of attraction and repulsion that characterizes their shared attitude toward cinema, toward storytelling, and apparently toward life itself. Every type of personality that figures in the story, for instance, is defamiliarized and destablized by the presence of what Bakhtin would call a "decrowning double" (Bakhtin 1984a, 127) that throws the personality's idiosyncrasies and mannerisms into high relief. The showily loquacious Showalter and the grimly taciturn Grimsrud are distorted mirror images of each other, up to and including the moments when Grimsrud finally imposes (eternal) silence on his counterpart by felling him with a Bunyanesque axe and feeding him into a woodchipping machine. The two of them are low-grade parodies of businessmen Wade Gustafson and Stan Grossman, themselves a twinned pair of narcissists. The arduously unctuous Lundegaard and his horrifically victimized wife are another distorted-mirror duo, as are Marge's husband Norm and the psychologically troubled Mike Yanagita, a school chum whom she meets for a bittersweet rendezvous.[3]

As an obvious heroine-figure for the filmmakers, Marge herself escapes the full decrowning treatment, finding her comparatively dignified double in the fetus that's growing inside her. This is sometimes a source of bodily grotesquerie, as when she lumbers clumsily through a snowfield or when she announces, "I think I'm gonna barf," to her policeman partner. Also grotesque is the proximity that *Fargo* produces between the pristine unworldliness of her fetus (one needn't be an antiabortion ideologue to find the fetus a signifier of life and innocence) and the existential horror represented by the physically decimated corpses and spiritually decayed psychopaths that her job regularly places in her path. (Bakhtin would have appreciated the dark irony of this motif, given his fondness for images that bring the opposite extremes of earthly existence, birth and death, into intimate dialogue.) Still, the fetus is fundamentally a symbol of Marge's human warmth and womanly stature, so much so that the story concludes with an image of her motherly anticipation: "I love you. . . . Two more months," the pregnant policewoman and her gentle husband identically say as the film prepares to fade to black.

In general, the prevalence of twinning in *Fargo* is one mark of this movie's refinement relative to the rest of the Coen canon. The brothers' other pictures are invariably populated with at least one fat man (played by such talented actors as M. Emmet Walsh, Charles Durning, John Goodman, and Jon Polito, to name the most prominent) whose very appearance contributes to the films' atmosphere of pervasive grotesquerie. (Or to the Coens' dubious habit of "turning actors into effects," if one shares Jones's intermittently skeptical assessment of their work [Jones, 46].) *Fargo* exchanges this visual motif for a more sophisticated tactic, however, replacing the comparatively crude humor of obesity with the subtler device of doubled character pairs. Amid this film's flat landscapes, the excessive body becomes an excess of bodies.

The parodic use of regional speech patterns, another key component of the brothers' carnivalizing technique, brings us to one of the most important factors in contextualizing their work: their darkly ambivalent attitude toward American culture and, more particularly, their view of Americana as an expression and embodiment of the human capacities for error, immorality, and evil. Here, as with other aspects of the Coen canon, *Fargo* provides a key text.

Ethics in Coen movies "tend to be situational at best," as Harvey Roy Greenberg has observed, adding that the violence produced by their characters' harebrained schemes "is likely to partake equally of low comedy and Grand Guignol horror" (Greenberg, 144). The penchant for depraved behaviors and baneful consequences is not a matter of individual predilections, moreover. It is part and parcel of the American sociocultural ethos, which the Coens view in terms that might be construed as almost paranoid if they didn't leaven their despairing vision with large doses of carnivalesque humor.

Perceptive critics like Greenberg and Mikita Brottman have noted the links between *Fargo* and the parade of grim grotesqueries—violence, dementia, paranoid persecutions, and the like—limned by Mark Lesy in *Wisconsin Death Trip*, a 1973 book that has subsequently been made into a semidocumentary film (Lesy).[4] It is interesting to observe that Lesy's volume didn't reach the motion-picture screen until 1999, a quarter-century after it was first published; and it is tempting to speculate that the cinema world's belated interest was sparked not only by slow-blooming respect for the book but also, more broadly, a growing perception of the American Midwest as a place very different from the idealistic haven of work-driven pastoral values that traditional depictions have long painted. In a similar spirit, one might wonder if the Coens' perennial fascination with boondocks and backwaters has similar roots—i.e., a sense that heartland America is unutterably darker, murkier, and scarier than American mythologies have commonly allowed—and whether the public responded to *Fargo* as readily as it did in 1996 because of escalating skepticism toward middle America prompted by Timothy McVeigh's cataclysmic Oklahoma City bombing the previous year.

Coen films often take place in "small towns or heartland urban locales inflected by backwater mores," as Greenberg puts it, and *Fargo* follows this pattern, "construing both its Minneapolis and surrounding small-town settings as resolutely provincial." Greenberg adds, however, that the "usual scabrous wit and cool detachment" of the brothers "are here leavened by unexpected sympathy," attributing this to their Twin Cities roots and their "evident abiding affection for Midwestern folkways" (Greenberg, 143). These are useful points, but one can't help noticing that the filmmakers' sympathy is reserved for a small number of characters: Marge, Norm, perhaps Mike Yanagita, and a handful of bit players whom we meet only for seconds at a stretch. For the rest, *Fargo* is home to people who are not like the Coens or you or me. If it is a home at all, for that matter, it's in the sense of home as "the place where when you have to go there it will take you in, but at an extremely high price and perhaps it will destroy you," in the words of critic Richard Gilmore, who compares the film's North Dakota city with the Chinatown of Roman Polanski's eponymous thriller (1974) and the Farolito of Malcolm Lowry's harrowing 1947 novel *Under the Volcano*, to wit, "the place of the forbidden, at the outskirts of society . . . a place where children are told not to play and [which] even adults tend to avoid unless to do things out of sight of the regular members of the town society" (Gilmore).

In short, it is a home where Paul Bunyan and his blue ox Babe would fit right in—not as these characters have evolved in American legend, but as they have been rethought and refigured by the Coen brothers. Fabled for his feats of strength and altruistic habits, the folkloric Bunyan of countless "tall tales" was forever clearing new farmland, accumulating needed water, and accomplishing other helpful tasks across great spans of the nineteenth-century American continent. Whether digging Puget Sound in the Pacific Northwest, scooping out the Great Lakes so Babe wouldn't go thirsty, or rendering the Dakotas fit for human habitation, he was an intrepid hero who embodied the lustiest fantasies of an agrarian society that venerated ideals of ambition, individualism, and sheer physical power. Clearly it takes only a small step of the imagination to transmute this paradigm of unimpeded might into an uncontrollable beast, freak, or fiend; and clearly this is the sort of step the Coens enjoy taking.

In their film Bunyan presides physically over Brainerd, the community alongside which his statue stands. (Note the grotesque-body connotations of the town's name, conjuring up subliminal associations with gray matter along with terms like "brained" and "brain dead.") Spiritually he presides over the entire narrative, however, as his recurrent presence indicates. Since he is in fact the monstrous twin of the movie itself, it's worth pondering the appearance he presents to those entering his domain. He is intimidating by virtue of his size alone; his eyes have the glassy gaze of a visionary, an obsessive, or a maniac; and as Brottman suggests, his mouth is twisted into a malignant smile more suited to a bizarre totem pole than to the welcoming icon of a friendly town. Beetling brows and a rough-hewn beard make his features largely inscrutable, and his body is similarly hidden by a tightly buttoned flannel shirt and dark-blue dungaree pants. Not hidden is the ominously tense-fingered hand swinging to his right or the lethal-looking axe slung over his left shoulder, one end bearing a dimly gleaming blade, the other resembling a cut-off stump that prefigures the Showalter leg we'll later view on its way into the woodchipper. Closest to the road he guards are his awful feet, arrested in mid-stride toward some mysterious and perhaps unthinkable destination. If the loyal Babe isn't with him, it's because Brainerd has borrowed the beast for a different kind of service, bestowing the name of its genus on the Blue Ox motel where Showalter and Grimsrud strenuously fuck the brain-free hookers they pick up during their errand in the area. (In a neat visual rhyme, the Coens have made Bunyan's trousers blue and bulging, subtly amplifying the film's implicit linkage of Bunyan's iconic image—and hence the American frontier myth as a whole—with the brute force of untrammeled sexual aggression.)

Bunyan is to the film's visual discourse what exaggerated speech patterns are to its use of language: a grotesque, incipiently paranoid critique of American origin myths. Storytellers who distort regional dialects as fulsomely and unapologetically as the Coens do in their movies are not engaging in innocent linguistic horseplay. They are revealing a spasmodic attraction-repulsion response to kinds of language (and behavior and thought) toward which they feel deeply ambivalent; and more broadly, they are expressing a deeply felt dread of associations evoked by those kinds of language (and behavior and thought) in their minds and ours. In *Fargo*, the overwrought Scandinavian vowel sounds (and the overexpressive facial expressions that accompany them, from Marge's reassuring nods to Grimsrud's menacing glare to the hookers' vacant smiles) are indefatigable remnants of America's immigrant past, and of the otherness—the quintessentially uncanny, incipiently terrifying, inexcusably *incomprehensible* otherness—embedded in those lingering remains.

This helps to explain the unexpected material that Ethan and Joel chose to introduce their published *Fargo* screenplay. They obviously loved the Grandma who fought so colorfully, memorably, and spuriously with the Negress in the anecdote (another Bakhtinian double-tale) that she enjoyed telling and they enjoyed hearing. But the exoticism of her Russian-immigrant mindset and the slipperiness of her Russian-inflected speech appear to have given the brothers a touch of uneasiness along with the entertainment value they provided.[5] While the *Fargo* screenplay introduction deals manifestly with the elusive nature of recounted truth, it also interjects the theme of immigrant experience—which we might not otherwise think of in relation to the film's narrative—and contributes a note of nervousness, even anxiety, with regard to the presence of alien elements in American life.[6]

Idiosyncrasies of language play an important role in the Coens' body of work, from the emotionally strained argot of *Blood Simple* to the self-absorbed ranting in *Barton Fink* to the country-and-western narration of *The Big Lebowski* to the pulp-magazine lingo in

The Man Who Wasn't There, for just a few examples.7 But the game is played with particular ferocity in the film that brings them closest to their own origins, roots, and memories. The bleak, windswept tundra upon which *Fargo* unfolds is a relentlessly focused manifestation of Grandma's conception of Earth as an elemental "great ball thinly crusted with oceans, soil, and snow" across which people "crawl . . . to arrive at some improbable place where they meet other crawling people" (Coen and Coen, ix). Not all the characters in *Fargo* crawl, but at some point almost everyone winds up in a conspicuously low position—physically, psychologically, morally, spiritually, or all of the above. The filmmakers' enthusiasm for treating these people's plights in savagely comic terms is partly a result of the TV-generation conde-scension that critic Jonathan Rosenbaum finds in their movies when he writes that "if one considers all the laughs found in *Blood Simple, Raising Arizona, Miller's Crossing, Barton Fink, The Hudsucker Proxy*, and *Fargo*, there are very few that aren't predicated on some version of the notion that people are idiots—the people on-screen, that is; those in the audience laughing at the idiots are hip aficiona-dos, just like the Coens" (Rosenbaum). But there's more at work in *Fargo* than the "peculiar posthumanist TV tradition" that Rosenbaum criticizes the Coens for embracing. On a deeper level, the brothers show signs of deriving a grim satisfaction from the act of humbling and at times humiliating these funny-talking remnants of an Old World otherness that they themselves have come to terms with no more fully than Grandma came to terms with the apocryphal Negress who engaged her in battle.

To humiliate is to punish, of course, and sure enough, whiffs of brimstone from Dante's indelible *Inferno* undergird this film's dark carnivalism. In some ways, *Fargo* could be called a decrowning double of *The Inferno*, mimicking Dante's icebound "bottom of the Universe" with Minnesota's bleak, windswept tundra and recruiting a grotesque Paul Bunyan to replace the Kong-like Lucifer anchored in Hell's deepest pit. This notion isn't as far-fetched as it may seem—the frenetic *O Brother, Where Art Thou?* is explicitly (if whimsically) modeled on *The Odyssey*, after all—and it produces an amusing variety of interpretive dividends, suggesting (for example) that one might explain Grimsrud's utter lack of human qualities by seeing him as a spiritual relative of Fra Alberigo, a damned sinner in the Ninth Circle who tells Dante that

. . . when a soul betrays as I did,
it falls from flesh, and a demon takes its place,

ruling the body till its time is spent. (Alighieri, 279)

Is there a more convincing way to understand Grimsrud than as a mortal so extravagantly rotten that Hell has whisked his soul away before his death, leaving his body to skulk around the Twin Cities area without a shred of sanity or humanity to call its own?

The point is not to cook up itemized connections between *Fargo* and *The Inferno*, but to stress the Coen film's broadly infernal underpinnings and to note the role these play in darkening and deepening its particular brand of carnivalesque narrative. In many respects, *Fargo* taps into a specific set of contemporary American anxieties related to pathologies of xenophobia, fantasies of race and gender purity, and a generalized fear of the ethnicized Other that has festered within this so-called nation of immigrants since its earliest days and lives murkily on in pop-culture petri dishes like the Coen brothers' canon. In other ways, *Fargo* reaches far beyond the American experience, evoking centuries-old images of existential dread and deploying a similarly venerable tradition of comic-grotesque parody as an antidote. Both strains of expression can be found in all of the Coens' films, twisted into a multitude of forms by psychodynamically driven mechanisms of cinematic condensation, displacement, and symbolization. Consider, for just one example, how the Dante-like trope of death-as-frozen-immobility so important to *Fargo* stretches all the way from *Blood Simple*, where an expanse of lumpish matter broods over the hapless detective's death, to *The*

Man Who Wasn't There, where the melancholy barber's story ends in the implacable grip of an electric chair's restraining belts.

Broadly speaking, the aesthetic and psychological spirit of the Coens' best work grows from two sources that are as vigorously at odds with each other as the contradictory truth/fiction claims in the opening and closing texts of *Fargo*. One is the genuineness and intimacy of the all-too-human fears and fantasies that the brothers are honest and audacious enough to let their narratives reveal. The other is the compulsive cleverness of the slickly artificial strategies they employ: their crisply streamlined compositions, their obsessively calculated montage, what Jones rightly calls the "machine-tooled perfection" and "tail-consuming circularity" (Jones, 49) of their narrative ideas.

Whatever additional attributes it may possess, *Fargo* unquestionably imparts the bare-bones truth about a key ingredient of the Coen sensibility. The brothers have a prodigious amount of respect for the dead, or at least for the symmetry, stability, and rigidity that death bestows on its beneficiaries. They venerate this so much that they're willing to rigor-mortis their own stories, characters, and themes in a stylistic deep-freeze that keeps them as audiovisually immaculate as they are conceptually and spiritually ossified. *Fargo* crystallizes the dead-alive duality that makes their most interesting work such an odd blend of fascination and frustration. Like the corpses who litter the brothers' narrative landscapes, *Fargo* and its Coen-spawned kin constitute a carnivalesque double of what habitually goes on in the bleak, windswept American psyche. The ultimate irony is that their work decrowns its own self-conscious shrewdness as ruthlessly as it parodies the mainstream cinema it seeks to surpass and transcend.

NOTES

1. The most helpful sources for the production history of *Fargo* are Bergan 2000 and Levine 2000. My account draws on both.

2. For extended discussion of the material bodily lower stratum, see Bakhtin 1984b, especially Chapter 6.

3. Asking himself whether the Coens generally feel affection toward their characters, Jones suggests that the answer is "yes, but in the same way that a hunter likes his trophies," and adds that their directorial stance suggests Albert Dekker in *Dr. Cyclops*, gazing down at his menagerie of shrunken humans with glee (never more so than in the supposedly warm-hearted *Fargo*). Jones captures the Coens' carnivalism when he says their attitude might be "less a question of cruelty than of bypassing respect altogether, creating a zoo-like enclosure of odd behaviors and eye-catching tics in which all characters are equal."

4. The film is *Wisconsin Death Trip* (1999), directed by Jamie Marsh from a screenplay by Marsh and Lesy. Mikita Brottman has noted that the American Midwest produced Ed Gein, the serial killer whose flamboyantly bizarre spirit hangs over films as different as Alfred Hitchcock's classic *Psycho* (1960) and Tobe Hooper's scruffy *The Texas Chain Saw Massacre* (1974).

5. The brothers share facts about her very selectively, and of the few they do throw out, the one they develop most thoroughly has to do with her unreliable grasp of language. Her old age brought a concurrent loss of memory and the ability to speak English, according to Ethan in his *Fargo* essay, and she spent the last year of her life speaking Russian for the first time in nearly eight decades. This certainly meant the end of her diverting (tall) tales, but she had already given at least two linguistic legacies to her two grandsons: the "Grandma and the Negress" yarn and, more unsettlingly, the phrase "Yayik do Kieva Dovedet," which she had encouraged them to memorize. Ethan translates this as, "By your tongue you will get to Kiev," and glosses it as, "If you don't know, just ask." He adds, "What use she thought we might find for that phrase in Minneapolis, we don't know." This is hardly a traumatic memory, but it's revealing that a screenplay set in an assertively Siberian version of the American Midwest should be prefaced by a childhood recollection of the uncanny overtones rung by an immigrant relative's unstable relationship with the English language. See Coen and Coen, ix, x.

6. More evidence of this nervousness appears as early as *Blood Simple*, where the detective says, "I don't care if you're the Pope of Rome, President of the United States or Man of the Year, something can all go wrong. But go ahead, complain, tell your problems to your neighbor, ask for help, and watch him fly. Now in Russia, they got it all mapped out so that everyone pulls for everyone else. That's the theory anyway. But what I know about is Texas, and down here . . . you're on your own." One suspects the Coens are more than a little skeptical of the specifically Russian "theory" their hard-boiled character cites.

7. They make similar play with ethnically marked names, some of which are amusingly allusive (the Snopeses in *Raising Arizona*), some assertively extravagant

(listen to characters experience the polysyllabic endlessness of uttering "Freddy Riedenschneider" in *The Man Who Wasn't There*), some flamboyantly inappropriate (the biblically dubbed pedophile Jesus Quintana in *The Big Lebowski*), and some indicative of inner attributes (the *Fargo* moniker Gaear Grimsrud progresses from an intimidatingly unfamiliar cornucopia of vowels to a word signaling his grim nature).

WORKS CITED

Alighieri, Dante. 1954. *The Inferno*, trans. John Ciardi. New York: A Mentor Book.

Bakhtin, Mikhail. 1984a. *Problems of Dostoevsky's Poetics*, trans. Caryl Emerson. Minneapolis: University of Minnesota Press.

Bakhtin, Mikhail. 1984b. *Rabelais and His World*, trans. Hélène Iswolsky. Bloomington: Indiana University Press.

Bergan, Ronald. 2000. *The Coen Brothers*. New York: Thunder's Mouth Press.

Brottman, Mikita. 2004. " 'Kinda Funny Lookin': Steve Buscemi's Disorderly Body," in *The Coen Brothers' Fargo*, ed. William Luhr, Cambridge: Cambridge University Press, 77–91.

Coen, Ethan, and Joel Coen. 1996. *Fargo*. London: Faber and Faber.

Cowie, Peter. 2001. *The Apocalypse Now Book*. New York: Da Capo Press.

Gilmore, Richard. 2001. "The American Sublime in *Fargo*," <<http://members.tripod.com/mcrae_tony/american_sublime_in_fargo.htm>>

Greenberg, Harvey Roy. 1996. "Prairie Home Death Trip." http://www.cyberpsych.org/filmforum, reprinted in *The Coen Brothers' Fargo*, ed. William Luhr, Cambridge: Cambridge University Press, 2004, 142–49.

Jones, Kent. 2000. "Airtight." *Film Comment* 36:6 (Nov.–Dec. 2000), 44–49.

Lesy, Michael. 1991 (1973). *Wisconsin Death Trip*. New York: Anchor.

Levine, Josh. 2000. *The Coen Brothers*. Toronto: ECW Press.

Rosenbaum, Jonathan. 1996. "The Human Touch." *Chicago Reader*. <<http://www.chireader.com/movies/archives/0396/03296.html>>

Coppola, Vietnam, and the Ambivalent 1970s

Francis Ford Coppola's most popular contribution to American screenwriting is surely Al Pacino's sardonic vow in the first *Godfather* film (1972): "I'll make him an offer he can't refuse."

There's a line in Coppola's equally massive *Apocalypse Now* (1979) that crystallizes far more of the last American century, however, with a wit so ferocious that audiences have never quite known whether to laugh, gasp, or shudder. It comes when surfboard-toting soldier Lt. Col. Bill Kilgore, played to the hilt by Robert Duvall, sniffs the warm Vietnamese air, flashes a contented smile, and expresses his satisfaction with the war he's so zealously fighting: "I love the smell of napalm in the morning!"

That line has been quoted countless more times since Coppola's epic returned to theaters in the form of *Apocalypse Now Redux*, a reedited director's cut with fifty-three minutes of footage that were left out of the original release. Its opening date (15 August 2001) was twenty-two years to the day after the movie's first American premiere.

Redux doesn't change the original *Apocalypse* story. Martin Sheen plays Willard, a soldier sent to hunt down and "terminate with extreme prejudice" the renegade Col. Kurtz (Marlon Brando), a brilliant American officer who has gone insane and established a jungle kingdom that answers to no law but his own megalomaniacal will. Meandering as unpredictably as the river bearing Willard's boat, the film etches an episodic portrait of the Vietnam war as historical farce, geopolitical tragedy, and psychological catastrophe.

Pundits started analyzing the formerly excised material the moment *Redux* arrived. It includes a longer look at Willard and company as they begin their upriver journey; a sexual encounter between Willard and *Playboy* playmates on a stranded helicopter; a scene where Kurtz dissects the lies in a *Time* article about the war; and a sequence on a French plantation hidden in the Vietnamese jungle, where Willard listens to a conversation about the history, morality, and futility of the war as seen by Vietnam's former colonial masters.

What has threatened to get lost as critics continue to probe this material is a broader perspective on Coppola as a quintessential voice of 1970s filmmaking. Like others of his generation—including director Michael Cimino, whose Vietnam epic *The Deer Hunter* debuted a year earlier—he spent the ambivalent '70s hovering between the flamboyant idealism of the radical '60s and the self-absorbed cynicism of the conservative '80s. *Apocalypse Now* mirrors this instability, oscillating between shock at the gut-churning horrors of war and pleasure with the spectacle war produces for the wide-screen Technicolor camera.

The ambivalence of *Apocalypse Now* grew partly from Coppola's collaborators, who channeled '70s sensibilities in wildly different ways. At one end of the spectrum was screenwriter John Milius, a military buff who had celebrated guns, guts, and glory in aggressively post-'60s movies like *Magnum Force* (1973) and *The Wind and the Lion* (1975). On the other end was actor Dennis Hopper, the hippie of *Easy Rider* (1969) whose on- and off-screen image had become an internationally known emblem of strung-out psychedelia. In a *Salon* review of the original film's DVD edition, Michael Sragow accurately summed up Hopper's portrayal of a drugged-up combat photographer who worships Kurtz's mad power: "He knows his brain has exploded even though he claims it has been enlarged. He catches himself up with a single word—'wrong'—that sounds out like his conscious mind's foghorn. Hopper may express more about the fallout of the '60s than anything else in the movie."

The heart of the film's ambivalence lies in Coppola's own creative personality, however. Coppola had revisionist impulses long before *Apocalypse Now* was launched. His early films plugged into traditional low-budget formats—the nudie (*Tonight for Sure*, 1961), the horror flick (*Dementia 13*, 1963)—but he soon started reworking genre conventions with a '60s sensibility: *You're a Big Boy Now* (1967) brought more sex to the teenpic, *Finian's Rainbow* (1968) was a race-conscious musical, and *The Rain People* (1969) had a proto-feminist tone. *The Godfather* brought forth both his nostalgic and progressive tendencies, exploring gangster-movie characters and milieus with unprecedented precision—and drawing out the genre's traditionally submerged violence with a savage enthusiasm that cleared a bloody path for the merciless gaze of *Apocalypse Now*. In the '70s he was an ambitious artist eager to tackle large-scale subjects and willing to court a reasonable degree of controversy. Yet he was also a savvy businessman, seeing mass-audience success as the key to his ongoing artistic freedom and the survival of American Zoetrope, the cinematic fiefdom he'd established as an alternative to Hollywood.

Many critics in 1972 hailed *The Godfather* as a brilliant meeting of artistry and commerce. To his credit, Coppola disagreed, seeing the movie's wide appeal as a missed chance to reach the public with ideas as well as entertainment. "What an opportunity that *could have been*," he said at the Cannes International Film Festival in 1974. And he meant it. Riding his *Godfather* success as exuberantly as Kilgore on a cresting wave, the Coppola of the mid-1970s was still enough of a '60s loyalist to want more social impact in his work. He proved this in *The Conversation* and *The Godfather Part II*, two 1974 releases with forthrightly sociopolitical themes: technological paranoia in the former, the hazy line between capitalism and criminality in the latter. Coppola the hitmaker was now Coppola the activist, bringing a taste of '60s rebelliousness to traditional genre-movie subjects.

Yet he was still pulling in enough box-office dollars to make him a New Hollywood hero. Even in his most audacious films of this period,

Coppola's businessman side remained strong, making sure that even his most high-minded projects took no more commercial risks than necessary. *The Conversation* placed well-liked Gene Hackman in an art-thriller plot heavily influenced by Michelangelo Antonioni's breakthrough hit *Blow-Up* (1966). The cast of *Godfather II* bristled with favorites like Duvall and Robert De Niro; its story moved at a compelling pace despite an unconventional flashback structure; and powerfully choreographed violence erupted frequently enough to keep crime-movie fans cheering whether or not they paid attention to the picture's deeper messages.

Given his sense of artistic and commercial security at this point, it was hardly surprising when Coppola revived an idea he'd been talking over with friends since the late 1960s: an adaptation of Joseph Conrad's 1902 novella *Heart of Darkness*, transplanted to Vietnam and drenched in the violence, madness, and escalating chaos of that awful conflict. Here was the ultimate genre-bending project, taking Hollywood's venerable bag of war-movie tricks—almost always twisted into reactionary shapes by cautious studios—and using them to condemn the sickness and senselessness of war itself. In addition, the enterprise suited Coppola's personal urges at the moment. After the intensity of *Godfather II*, he liked the notion of making an out-and-out action picture that would be fun for him to direct and bracing for audiences to watch.

While all of this had great appeal for Coppola and his colleagues, the project immediately ran up against Hollywood's uncertainty about how—and whether—to put Vietnam on screen. Studios had been dithering over the subject throughout the '70s, showing remarkable timidity even by film-industry standards. When a screenwriter proposed a Vietnam project in 1971, according to Peter Cowie's authoritative *Apocalypse Now Book*, one executive declared it five years too early and another proclaimed it five years too late. Coppola rushed into battle with his *Apocalypse* idea anyway, and felt even more confident that the time was right when a Paramount executive told him the public wasn't ready for it. In this respect as in many others, time proved Coppola right. The finished film attracted a wide following, if not a record-breaking one, and turned a profit despite a budget that ballooned due to inflated production costs (at one point a Philippines typhoon shut down shooting completely) and Brando's then-monumental salary of a cool $1 million.

Apocalypse Now opened new ground for Coppola—it was his first war film, and more important, his first foray into an unquestionably contentious topic. Yet it continued the *Godfather II* pattern by anchoring its serious themes in time-tested genre conventions. True, it refought the Vietnam conflict with an anguished ambiguity that couldn't be more different from the macho posturing ("Sir, do we get to win this time?") of *Rambo: First Blood Part Two* (1985) and its appalling ilk. It also paid obeisance to many Hollywood traditions, however, from its suspense-laden narrative—it's a road movie on a river—to its combat-film action scenes. Even as he hoped intellectuals would appreciate his ideas, Coppola's other priority was making everyday moviegoers line up at the ticket window.

The commercial aspects of *Apocalypse Now* underscore a side of Coppola's sensibility that would become increasingly visible in the less-adventurous '80s, when his projects ranged from the tame (*Gardens of Stone*, 1987) to the trifling (*The Outsiders*, 1983) to the woefully misbegotten (*The Godfather Part III*, released in 1990). These and other ventures seemed more interested in exploiting marketable material—how else to explain the half-baked mishmash of *Godfather III*?—than exploring ideas that genuinely engaged Coppola's intellect and imagination. Two qualities tie *Apocalypse Now* tightly to the Coppola of the disappointing '80s. One is his preference for making larger-than-life legend rather than in-the-moment argument about the recent political past. The other is his refusal to speak out too strongly on still-controversial issues so as not to jeopardize the financial success he needed to recoup the film's unexpectedly high costs. (The disaster he dreaded lay just ahead in *One From the Heart*, a 1982 romantic "valentine" that moviegoers found decidedly unlovable.) Balancing these attitudes—or, skeptics would argue, canceling them out—is the '6os bravado reflected in Coppola's willingness to revisit Vietnam on his own social and cinematic terms.

It's the historically generalizing, aesthetically operatic aspects of *Apocalypse Now* that ultimately cast the most light on Coppola's essentially conservative desire to treat momentous themes without unduly disturbing his audience. Despite the political ramifications of its story, *Apocalypse Now* has less to do with the history and morality of the Vietnam tragedy than with the possibilities for motion-picture mythmaking that Coppola saw there. The movie isn't about the Southeast Asian war in particular but about war in general, seen as a fundamental force of nature—no less inevitable than floods or famines, no less morbidly fascinating than the existential *Heart of Darkness* conjured up by Conrad in the novella that inspired Milius's screenplay. While the film can be read as a cry against the evils inflicted in and on Vietnam, it's more accurately seen as a humanitarian statement on the tragedy of war itself, as timeless and universal as the Homeric epic that some of its admirers likened it to.

There's a certain irony to the antiwar levels of *Apocalypse*, since Coppola had first reached Hollywood's big leagues in 1969 by co-writing (with Edmund H. North) the Academy Award-winning script for *Patton*, which President Richard Nixon viewed repeatedly during the Vietnam conflict. It's hard to think of a subject more freighted with political import than Gen. George S. Patton Jr.'s military mentality, especially in the Nixon era when warmongers and war protesters were at each other's throats.

Still, Coppola's wholehearted immersion in *Patton* doesn't mean he shared the general's views on war or anything else. Cowie asserts that Coppola was "never . . . a political animal," and Coppola's own comments on *Apocalypse Now* don't contradict this. Nor do the books and films that directly influenced the *Apocalypse* production. To be sure, tough-minded documentaries like Peter Davis's *Hearts and Minds* (1974) and Emile de Antonio's *In the Year of the Pig* (1969) were in the mix. But at least as many ideas and inspirations came from *Aguirre, the Wrath of God* (1972), the hallucinatory Werner Herzog mind-teaser about a demented river voyage in the sixteenth century. No wonder Eleanor Coppola told Cowie her husband's goal was less to analyze the Vietnam conflict than to weave "a kind of myth . . . an opera" around his larger-than-life subject.

As much as these qualities tie *Apocalypse Now* to the self-indulgent '80s era—its preference for myth over polemic, its hesitancy over hot-button commentary—the '60s links of the movie speak plainly too, through its antiauthoritarian spirit and its willingness (however mixed Coppola's motives may have been) to tackle Vietnam when conventional studio wisdom balked. Both sides of this chronological coin are captured in *Redux* by the restored scene showing Willard's visit to the French plantation. Coppola never explains how these French folks have managed to live undiscovered for years in the shadows of their country's lost colony. But their long conversation in Willard's presence says more about the specifics of Southeast Asian history than the rest of the movie's scenes put together. "We fight to keep what is ours," says the French patriarch played by Christian Marquand, summing up his argument that France has proprietary rights because it brought Vietnam into the modern economic world. "You Americans fight for the biggest nothing in history." Here we have Coppola in full '60s mode, diving into the murky depths of Vietnam's tormented past with depth and candor. Yet he excised this episode from the original cut, to shorten the picture and prevent too much dialogue from taxing Saturday-night moviegoers. This brings us back to Coppola the studio exec, ready to scrap his film's most bravely analytical sequence rather than risk offending audiences more interested in action and melodrama than talky historiographical interludes.

Caught though it is in '70s ambivalence, *Apocalypse Now Redux* looks fresher and healthier to my eyes than any other modern movie about American war. The competition is admittedly slim, with Steven Spielberg's strident *Saving Private Ryan* (1998) the reigning "classic" and Michael Bay's insufferable *Pearl Harbor* (2001) the worst debacle. These and most of their competitors deal in aggressive nostalgia, self-justifying spectacle, and a faux verisimilitude built on Hollywood clichés and the high-tech voyeurism exemplified by TV coverage of the first Persian Gulf conflict. All this makes a sorry contrast with the willingness of Coppola and company to enrich their audience-pleasing product with discursive elements ranging from literary allusion (citing Conrad and T. S. Eliot) to mass-culture critique (excoriating *Time* magazine) to apocalyptic mysticism (evoking the demonism of drug-dazed combat, the blood ritual of assassination, the ineffable "horror" whose invocation by Kurtz provides the film's indelible climax).

Coppola has his shortcomings as a filmmaker and a thinker, but there's no denying the energy and resourcefulness that surge through *Apocalypse Now* at its most powerful moments. While he found no magic key to unlock Vietnam's heart of darkness, Coppola's intuitive grasp of what may now seem an old-fashioned brand of cinema—there's not a computer-generated frame in sight—carries unique insights into one of the past century's most troubled historical moments.

Representing Atrocity

FROM THE HOLOCAUST TO SEPTEMBER 11

The attacks of September 11, 2001, unleashed waves of media representation that both recall and contrast with representations of the Holocaust and its horrors. Accounts of the Holocaust necessarily contain little authentic moving-image documentation, while the events of 9/11 became internationally visible while they were still unfolding. Conversely, the evils of the Holocaust have reached public awareness for decades through images of atrocity captured after the Nazi camps were liberated, whereas the physical containment of the damage inflicted on 9/11—facilitated by the nature of the attacks and the fact that the World Trade Center towers imploded instead of scattering their wreckage outward—rendered the death and destruction wrought there almost invisible to the eye.

The popular media have rushed to compensate for this with a blitz of belligerent journalism, hammering incessantly on aspects of the case that are readily turned into narrative (e.g., the hunt for Osama bin Laden) and seizing on a fitfully fought, nebulously defined "war against terrorism" as a durable support for commercially marketable "public affairs" coverage. In this context it is interesting to note the progression of Holocaust representation through several stages, beginning with the poetic evocations of *Night and Fog* in 1955, moving through more conventional documentaries and such widely disseminated narrative movies as *Exodus* (1960) and *Judgment at Nuremberg* (1961), and turning in more recent years to the intellectually sophisticated accounts of such cinematic historians as Marcel Ophuls and Claude Lanzmann, who have chosen to omit all "atrocity footage" from their works. On a representational level close to the experiences of ordinary people, it is also interesting to note parallels between homemade materials found at "makeshift memorials" near the World Trade Center site, the avoidance of direct atrocity images in films by Ophuls and Lanzmann, and the work of an artist like Christian Boltanski, who has skirted the twin pitfalls of sensationalism and sentimentality by exploring the Holocaust through ephemeral materials that achieve resonance through their very refusal of monumental form. These are the issues that I wish to explore in this essay.

Conventional wisdom on the events of September 11 is clear: Everything has changed since the terrorist attacks on New York and Washington, and nothing will be quite the same again.

We are still waiting to see what long-term forms this transformation will take. Responses by ordinary citizens during the first months after the attacks have run along traditional lines. As someone who lived one minute away from the World Trade Center at the time its towers fell, and walked past it several times each day in the weeks afterward, I have gotten a good look at the gestures made on the outskirts of Ground Zero—photos of lost loved ones, children's toys and stuffed animals placed as tributes to slaughtered or orphaned youngsters, countless American flags, and other items that one might expect to find at what newscasters like to call a "makeshift memorial."

As the film critic for a national newspaper, I have also taken a close look at how filmmakers—from Hollywood moguls to independent auteurs—have debated the propriety of retaining movie shots including the Twin Towers; and like them, I have wondered when the public would be ready to relive September 11 at the multiplex or on living-room video screens. My instinct was that films about September 11 would start flowing sooner rather than later, and that like the makeshift memorials at Ground Zero, they would take fairly conventional forms—newshour specials reprising the tragedy with retroactive commentary and recycled video, and docu-dramas recreating individual and collective traumas of the apoca-lyptic day. Full-fledged theatrical features would take a bit longer to arrive, given the lengthy turn-around time for feature-length narrative movies from initial conceptualization to the completion of final release prints, but they would surely reach the screen as soon as producers grew confident that they would not face charges of exploiting or capitalizing on the disaster; their likely focus would be on the terrors faced by victims, heroic acts performed by rescue teams, and (more ambitiously) reasons why the cataclysm was not prevented (or, according to some theories, why it was actually allowed to happen) by law-enforcement and national-security agen-cies. Sure enough, movies of this ilk are now positioned at various points along the production pipeline, preceded soon after 9/11 by a faltering parade of features that gained second-hand relevance to the event by virtue of shots depicting the Twin Towers them-selves (such as *Spider-Man*, which was reworked before its 2002 release to eliminate potentially distasteful World Trade Center action) or sequences with problematic images of urban disaster. The latter category included the Arnold Schwarzenegger epic *Collateral Damage*, which the Warner Bros. studio moved from an opening date of October 5, 2001, to February 8, 2002, because of nervousness over the premise of the story, which has an ordinary firefighter embarking on a vigilante-style hunt for the Colombian drug merchants who killed his wife and child when they bombed a Los Angeles building in order to assassinate a political enemy. Although it was widely reported that Warner Bros. delayed the film's release because the studio felt its depiction of fiery disaster in an urban building might be too disturbing for audiences in the immediate aftermath of 9/11, skeptics have suggested that its view of the fictional cataclysm, juiced up with standard-issue special effects, might have appeared not too troubling but too *tame* after ubiquitous television coverage of the real thing in New York City.

(Be this as it may, Warner Bros. did its best to protect its investment in the movie, prevailing on Schwarzenegger to preside over a Manhattan premiere accompanied by representatives of the Twin Towers Fund, a charitable organization. Ironically, the main controversy that greeted the release came from Colombian-Americans who complained that the movie was ethnically biased, citing the hero's hunt for Colombian bad guys in far-flung jungle villages. Few people seemed very exercised over the urban-disaster imagery.) The release of *The Sum of All Fears* on May 31, 2002, sparked widespread media speculation as to whether Americans were "ready" for an action-adventure melodrama in which nuclear bombs decimate Baltimore; they proved to be very ready indeed, making the picture an immediate box-office hit. One short week later, on June 7, 2002, the question returned with a different twist, asking whether Americans were "ready" for a rollicking comedy about a streetwise Central Intelligence Agency recruit racing to head off a nuclear device smuggled into Manhattan by terrorists. *Bad Company* fared less well financially than *The Sum of All Fears* did, but blame for its lackluster performance falls more on its dubious overall entertainment value than on its relationship to 9/11. In any case, one wonders whether the "readiness" debates had any relevance to a moviegoing public that was clearly ready for anything that provided a sufficient number of entertainment bangs for its ticket-window bucks.

As film and video representations of the September 11 tragedies multiply in time to come, I expect most critics will respond to them as they respond to other movies on "sensitive" issues: assessing the effectiveness with which they convey facts, elicit emotions, and accomplish the other audience-pleasing tasks traditionally associated with mainstream cinema. More thoughtful critics will also put strong emphasis on how earnest and responsible the representation appears to be—whether it seems motivated by a sincere desire to inform the living and memorialize the dead, or by the money-driven imperatives of Hollywood's neverending quest for cutting-edge subjects and stories. Anticipating this, producers will try to balance what they perceive as the requirements of entertainment against the special need for sensitivity and seriousness called for by such a topic. Examples of this highwire act arose immediately after 9/11, in network decisions about what to show and not to show in initial coverage of the catastrophe. One network played video of flaming victims leaping from the towers, for example, but withdrew the footage after a single late-night broadcast. Others chose not to display such material at all.

To show or not to show. This is one of the issues that lead my mind from the horrors of the World Trade Center disaster to the radically different horrors of the Holocaust, and to the ways in which filmmakers have struggled to come to terms with them over the past half century. A retrospective look at Holocaust representation in cinema provides revealing insights into paths that responsible film and video makers might choose to follow or to avoid with regard to the 9/11 cataclysm.

One reason why I find the comparison between historical representations of the Holocaust and present-day representations of September 11 so compelling is that, as already noted, the respective histories of these representations begin on such starkly opposite terms. In the case of the Holocaust, no imagery of any kind was publicly shown until the death camps had been liberated and the worst of the horrors were over; and even then most images necessarily depicted not the horrors themselves—aside from bits of footage shot by Nazis—but the appalling aftermath of these horrors as captured by Allied soldiers with sixteen-millimeter movie cameras. In the case of the World Trade Center, television video gave the entire world instant access to the traumatizing sight of hijacked planes crashing into the towers' walls and those walls crumbling under their own awesome weight as thousands struggled to escape and flee. Is it true, as Theodor W. Adorno resonantly wrote, that "after Auschwitz, writing poetry is barbaric"? As horrendous as they were, the events of September 11 were far less sweeping and staggering than the Holocaust's unimaginable evils. Yet the question of artistic representation vs. the pitfalls of vulgarizing barbarity remains an urgent one. Much light can be cast on it by observing how filmmakers have confronted it in the context of the Holocaust.

I will begin with two fundamental questions. On the level of content and technique, can images capture, reproduce, or convey the essence of events and situations more vast and horrifying than anything encountered in everyday life or the so-called normal world? And on the level of philosophy and ethics, is it decent or permissible to make the attempt in the first place? This issue has long prompted debate among film theorists and historians, with regard not only to documentaries but also to fiction films that incorporate documentary material, such as Stanley Kramer's prizewinning *Judgment at Nuremburg*, which incorporates film footage from the liberated camps, and the TV miniseries *Holocaust* (1978), which employs still photos from sites of the atrocities.

The question of whether displaying death-camp footage is appropriate did not trouble the makers of the first Holocaust documentary to become an enduring classic: *Night and Fog* (*Nuit et brouillard*), directed by Alain Resnais in 1955. Resnais was less concerned about the legitimacy of using authentic Holocaust images than about the equally basic question of whether he had a moral right to deal with the Holocaust at all, since he had not been personally involved with the camps in any way. He told film scholar Annette Insdorf that he decided to proceed with the project only on the condition that its voiceover commentary would be written by Jean Cayrol, a Holocaust survivor (Insdorf, 213). This pairing of narrator and imagemaker is a key to the distinctiveness and power of *Night and Fog*, since it juxtaposes the perspective of a witness with that of an artist working to make sense of the witness's survival and of the horrific circumstances that he overcame.

Later documentaries about the Holocaust have taken a wide variety of approaches—some relying heavily on archival film footage, others supplementing or partly displacing such images with didactic narrations, interviews with Holocaust survivors and participants, and the like. In positive or negative ways, all inevitably have some relationship with the issues I have mentioned above, which are also crucially relevant to present and future representations of the World Trade Center tragedy: whether filmed images can capture "truths" about sets of events so extraordinary, and what boundaries are established around representations of such events by compelling moral and ethical considerations. The mightiest of all Holocaust documentaries are implicitly addressed to these questions as well as to events of the Holocaust itself. I have in mind three films by American director Marcel Ophuls—*The Sorrow and the Pity* (1970), *The Memory of Justice* (1976), and *Hotel Terminus: The Life and Times of Klaus Barbie* (1988)—and two by Israeli director Claude Lanzmann, the 1985 epic *Shoah* and the more specifically focused 2001 work *Sobibor, October 14, 1943, 4 p.m.*

The Sorrow and the Pity was recognized as an unprecedented work from its first appearance, and its reputation has scarcely dimmed. Film historian Marc Ferro has called it "a kind of October Revolution" in documentary filmmaking, since it introduces a novel use for the time-tested device of the filmed interview (Ferro, 142). I second this view. Not only do the interviews in *The Sorrow and the Pity* serve to confront individuals with the past, and to challenge *versions* of the past that they would like to retain and promulgate; in addition, the interviews are so richly structured and artfully interwoven that Ophuls is able to substitute them for the voiceover commentary that had been a commonplace in previous Holocaust documentaries.

The most important element in this important film is therefore not a presence but an absence—the absence of anything corresponding to a "voice-of-God narration" in the traditional sense. In a 1988 interview with me, Ophuls explained his disdain for conventional narration in both practical and ethical terms (Sterritt). On one level, he said voiceovers are "too easy to do" and reduce films to "illustrated editorials." On a deeper level, he argued that narration "lends itself to propaganda [and] the legitimizing of all kinds of 'isms' [and] ideology." It seems to me that the implications of Ophuls's view are even larger than these statements indicate. For one thing, the omission of "voice-of-God" commentary puts the burden of expression on actual documentary materials, rather than on the guiding and explaining presence of the filmmaker; this heightens the authenticity of the film while enhancing the ability of verbal and visual montage to throw past and present into mutually illuminating relief. For another, as critic James Roy MacBean has suggested (MacBean, 478), it facilitates the collapsing of past and present in a depoeticized way—contrasting with the manner of a *Night and Fog*—by using a "window-on-the-world" approach to puncture time-honored myths about the film's primary topics, French resistance and collaboration during the Nazi era.

Ophuls carried his avoidance of conventional narration into two more Holocaust documentaries, where he also explored a new tendency in his work: a wish to project his own personality, opinions, and directorial problems visibly into the film. In *The Memory of Justice*, a massive work about the Nuremberg war-crimes inquiry, he includes conversation with his wife and daughter, and a remarkable sequence where songs on the sound track comment mischievously on the more commercial activities that his friends and colleagues might rather see him pursue. He escalates this personalized filmmaking even further in *Hotel Terminus*, with more ironic music and his own personal, sometimes fierce confrontations with interview subjects. Ophuls may have eliminated traditional narration, but commentary clearly enters his work, albeit in novel and increasingly personal ways.

In *Hotel Terminus*, Ophuls also confronts the main issue that concerns us here: that of when *utilization* becomes *exploitation* in the handling of actual Holocaust images. Lanzmann has come to grips with this issue as well, coming to even more radical—and radically effective—conclusions.

Critics and theorists have written extensively on this subject. Film
and art critic Fred Camper has suggested the possibility (Camper, 6)
that "the photographing of any cinema image of a part of the actual
world is an act of aggression," since the photographer "wrenches a
specific part of reality from the context with which it makes a whole,
places that fragment in a rectangular frame, and further delimits it in
time." Turning to the issue of proprietorship of the image, Camper
notes both the filmmaker's "need to exercise control over what is in
front of [the] camera" and the tendency of the passive spectator in
the darkened theater "to feel that the images are in some sense his
own." (This tendency might be even stronger in TV and video viewing, where the images are viewed at close proximity and can be
stopped, started, fast-forwarded, and replayed at will.) Such considerations must weigh heavily in the minds of Holocaust documentarists,
who do not wrench, place, delimit, and control just any "part of reality," but parts that are directly connected to this century's most over-
whelmingly horrific crime. If one grants film theorist André Bazin's
contention that photographic images are literal "tracings" of reality,
the moral ramifications are obviously profound (Bazin).

The situation is even more serious if, as Camper further argues,
film images viewed in big-screen splendor are "inevitably glorified
by the projector's beam" in such a way that they are "charged with
a certain aesthetic beauty, or at least a kind of energy [which] it is
hard to imagine . . . being utterly controlled by condemnation."
(Writing ten years earlier, Ferro also used the word "energy" to
locate the effectiveness of interview subjects in *The Sorrow and the
Pity* via their specific function in the film [Ferro, 143].) Again, this
must be carefully pondered by any filmmaker seeking to depict
an event as purely evil as the Holocaust—or the destruction of the
World Trade Center—without giving it any hint of aesthetic beauty
or artistic energy, however subtly, subliminally, or unwittingly.

Camper may overstate his case when he sees aggression as
inherent to the act of photography, regardless of the particular

object being photographed. In her book *On Photography*, critic Susan Sontag makes a similar suggestion that clarifies the issue by referring specifically to the photographing of human beings (Sontag 1990, 14–15). "To photograph people is to violate them," she writes, "by seeing them as they never see themselves, by having knowledge of them they can never have; it turns people into objects that can be symbolically possessed. . . . [T]o photograph someone is a sublimated murder. . . ." Judith Doneson (178) takes a somewhat more benign view, seeing the issue of who took the photographs, and under what circumstances, as deciding factors: Since some Jews documented life in the ghetto with photos, she says, "Using these testimonies today would . . . comply with the wishes of the Jews to have their history remembered." Be this as it may, to depict the Holocaust in any way and for any purpose is to depict an event that must be measured entirely on the scale of human anxiety, human suffering, human death. Photographs of human beings must necessarily be used, whether these are authentic Holocaust images or filmed statements by Holocaust survivors— which raises a moral conundrum if we see the photographed individuals as "violated" by being filmed as human beings and as objects in the material world.

One must add to this difficulty the even more profound problem of capturing the inhumanly vast magnitude of the Holocaust and its apparatuses of death. Holocaust film historian Ilan Avisar (Avisar, 1–2) cites Lawrence Langer's study of *The Holocaust and the Literary Imagination* on several points relevant to this issue: (a) that the Holocaust was "so fantastic and so extraordinary that it defies our basic notions of empirical reality, the raw material of every mimetic art"; (b) that "realistic accounts are limited by conventional patterns of thought and therefore cannot penetrate the darkest recess of human experience"; and (c) that literary "disfiguration" is preferable to realistic depiction because (in Avisar's phrase) it can "eliminate the possibility of aesthetic pleasure." Avisar takes issue with Langer's last point, noting (among other things) that modernism often returns to "the raw material of reality" in order to "seize and grasp its ontological dimension." It is worth stressing, however, that both Camper and Langer see the danger of "aesthetic pleasure" in realistic accounts of even the most hideous possible event. Writing on *Our Hitler, a Film From Germany*, Sontag strikes a similar note by suggesting that filmmaker Hans-Jürgen Syberberg could not "rely on documents to show how it 'really' was [since] the display of atrocity in the form of photographic evidence risks being tacitly pornographic" (Insdorf, 169)." Many assessments of Leni Riefenstahl's documentaries on Nazi subjects point up this danger, as well.

This is precisely the point addressed by Ophuls in *Hotel Terminus* and Lanzmann in *Shoah* and *Sobibor*, doing so by means of yet another absence—this one even more profound and far-reaching than the absence of spoken commentary discussed above. These documentaries make extensive use of interviews shot in diverse locations, but neither contains any trace of so-called atrocity footage from the Holocaust itself. Both films undertake to document the Holocaust entirely through the recollections of individuals who went through it. As with his dislike of voice-of-God narration, Ophuls tends to explain his avoidance of atrocity footage in simple and perhaps oversimplified terms. Such footage "doesn't get the job done anymore," he told me, indicating his feeling that audiences have become desensitized to it by seeing it in so many previous films. But his decision to make a four-and-a-half-hour film without a single minute of such material points to a deeper motivation, and clues to this may be found in *Shoah*, a film that Ophuls deeply admires.

I want to focus on one of the most memorable sequences in *Shoah*: the obsessive return to shots of the front gate of the Auschwitz camp, filmed by a camera moving along the railroad tracks that once carried trainloads of Jews to their deaths. Once it has reached the gate, the camera continues along its trajectory into the camp, but does so by switching to a zoom lens instead of moving physically ahead. "If camera movement tends to suggest movement through space, as of a human body," writes Camper, "the zoom tends to represent the movement of the mind, shifts in human perception." On this view, Lanzmann fulfills his film's obligation to take us into a concentration camp—yet by physically stopping his camera at the gate, he acknowledges the inability of present-day observers to *truly* enter such a place or *truly* understand what occurred there. He also tacitly acknowledges the "violation" that might take place if his camera *were* to penetrate the cursed space about which we hear so much from the witnesses he interviews. Lanzmann's refusal to use archival material of any kind, including film footage and still photos, may be understood in the same way: as a suggestion that to use *any* product of the death camps, for however well-meaning or enlightening a purpose, might be to participate, in however small a way, in the Nazis' enterprise.

The issues I have been exploring so far relate to the possibilities and pitfalls faced by documentary filmmakers seeking to convey unthinkable realities through cinematic images. The producers of forthcoming September 11 films will not all be practitioners of nonfiction, however. Some will be dramatic filmmakers, and their motives will vary widely, ranging from the responsible to the reprehensible. If we are fortunate, the responsible ones will emulate a creative and conscientious filmmaker like Israeli director Amos Gitaï, whose 2000 drama *Kippur* finds an extraordinary array of ways to depict the horrors of war as exactly what articulate veterans often tell us they are—an appallingly repetitive series of physical and psychological torments conspicuously lacking in the guts-and-glory heroics that war movies have fed us for decades.

Steven Spielberg tells us the same thing in the first twenty minutes of *Saving Private Ryan* (1998), then falls back on those very guts-and-glory clichés for another two hours or so. But the makers of future 9/11 films with theatrical and major-network ambitions are more likely to draw inspiration from *Schindler's List* (1993), and a thousand other Hollywood epics, than from the Ophuls and Lanzmann masterpieces I have been focusing on. The products of their labors may appall us at times, reinforcing Adorno's contention about the impossibility of civilized art in a world where civilization itself stands on shaky foundations. Adorno himself later modified his views, however, and the work of some principled artists has borne out the possibility that poetry after Auschwitz is possible, as it will surely remain after September 11. To suggest just one example, French artist Christian Boltanski has crafted his works from the most fugitive and transitory of materials—often visual materials like old photographs and newspaper pictures, sometimes more tactile kinds of ephemera like bits of clothing, clumsily strung lightbulbs, and candles casting shadows that are at once celebrations of life and dances of death. Through such materials he has evoked the most repellent and the most poignant aspects of modern Jewish history without ever, to my eye, crossing the slippery line between exploration and exploitation.

Looking at the less imaginative contributions to Ground Zero's makeshift memorial, I sometimes feel that they are inspired less by heartfelt grief than by reflexive reactions to the shallow patriotism being pushed by far too many TV pundits and radio talkers. One of countless examples is WABC radio's coverage of "Our War Against Terrorism" in the immediate aftermath of 9/11, complete with rock-style background music and crash-boom sound effects, shamelessly illustrating how our allegedly responsible media have turned what is supposed to be a holy war for democracy into an entertainment show of the crudest, crassest sort. Such embarrassments contrast vividly with the appearance on Ground Zero's fences of Xeroxed drawings, informally scrawled poems, and hastily assembled photo-collages that bear the mark not of knee-jerk jingoism but of deeply personal response to an ultimately incomprehensible event.

It is probably asking too much, but I hope professional chroniclers of September 11 will partake of their introspective spirit—which I take to be Boltanski's spirit as well—rather than the noisy extroversion that has hijacked most of the media so far. As artists like Ophuls and Lanzmann have discovered, the truest memorial may be built from the most unmonumental materials. And the image not shown may be the most telling image of all.

WORKS CITED

Avisar, Ilan. 1988. *Screening the Holocaust: Cinema's Images of the Unimaginable.* Bloomington: Indiana University Press.

Bazin, André. 1967. *What Is Cinema?*, trans. Hugh Gray. Berkeley: University of California Press.

Camper, Fred. 1987. *Shoah. Motion Picture* 1:3.

Doneson, Judith E. 1987. *The Holocaust in American Film.* Philadelphia: The Jewish Publication Society.

Insdorf, Annette. 1989. *Indelible Shadows: Film and the Holocaust.* Cambridge: Cambridge University Press.

Ferro, Marc. 1988. *Cinema and History*, trans. Naomi Greene. Detroit: Wayne State University Press.

MacBean, James Roy. 1988. "*The Sorrow and the Pity*: France and Her Political Myths," in Alan Rosenthal, ed., *New Challenges for Documentary*. Berkeley: University of California Press.

Sontag, Susan. 1980. "Eye of the Storm." *New York Review of Books* 27:2 (21 February 1980). Cited in Insdorf, 169.

Sontag, Susan. 1990. *On Photography.* New York: Anchor Books.

Sterritt, David. 1988. Interview with Marcel Ophuls in New York for *The Christian Science Monitor*, November 1988.

Thanatos ex Machina

GODARD CARESSES THE DEAD

Cars and car crashes are running themes in the cinema of Jean-Luc Godard, most notably during the sixties era that produced several of the classics upon which his reputation primarily rests. His first feature, the 1960 crime romance *Breathless*, begins with Jean-Paul Belmondo's anarchic antihero, Michel, stealing a car for a joyride during which he plays pop tunes on the radio, fiddles with a gun he finds in the glove compartment, chatters cheerfully to himself, and breaks the rules of commercial cinema by talking directly to the camera. His advice to us spectators is direct: We should go fuck ourselves if we don't appreciate the pleasures of the everyday world as much as he and Godard evidently do.

Moments later, Michel shoots a cop who chases him on the highway, initiating an association between automobiles and death that will continue in Godard films as different as *My Life to Live*, where the prostitute Nana dies alongside the car her psychopathic pimp has parked in front of the ironically named Restaurant des Studios; *Pierrot le fou*, where the protagonists use a car for their transition from incipient social misfits to full-scale cultural outlaws; and most famously *Weekend*, a crash-ridden extravaganza where the uproariously alienated main characters propel their battered convertible through a surrealistic traffic jam caused by a deadly accident complete with shattered corpses and blood-smeared pavement.

Godard depicts this *Weekend* episode in a heroically long track-ing shot whose leisurely rhythm provides a conspicuously lyrical contrast with the grotesquerie of the images on display. Attraction and repulsion vie for first place in his implicit attitude—attraction toward the gleaming techno-possibilities of a mechanized civiliza-tion that gives us horrific road accidents and exhilarating road movies with equal munificence; and repulsion toward the money-driven forces of materialism, dehumanization, and spiritual decay of which the automobile is the most obvious symbol and ubiqui-tous embodiment. Godard's political sensibility deplores the meta-physical degeneration induced by the ability of late-capitalist society to transform people into mind-numbed automatons. Yet his camera portrays its exanimate victims with the gentleness of one who understands and perhaps envies the escape they've made from a world that traps the mind in stultifying dead ends as readily as it frees the body for meaningless voyages to nowhere. Godard has been called a misanthrope and worse, and *Weekend* could be Exhibit A if he were prosecuted on this charge in a courtroom. Yet here as elsewhere in his work, he compassionately caresses the dead at the side of the road.

The uncanny mixture of *eros* and *thanatos* that courses through the car-conscious facet of Godard's career reaches one of its most expressive peaks in the 1963 masterpiece *Contempt*, made less than a decade after his mother was killed in a Swiss traffic accident that appears to have made a searing and lasting impression on her second-eldest child, then in his middle twenties. *Contempt* met with critical skepticism and general-audience bewilderment when first released in the United States, where its producers (including Carlo Ponti and Joseph E. Levine, no strangers to the mass-market exploita-tion of art-film cachet) had hoped to score a commercial success via the presences of Hollywood actor Jack Palance and French actress Brigitte Bardot, then at the peak of her international pop-ularity. No aspect of the film was more pointedly censured than Godard's decision to resolve its plot through an out-of-the-blue automobile accident that reviewers found at best an arbitrary trick, at worst a desperate act of narrative capriciousness by a lazy storyteller who had tired of his own tale and didn't particularly care how he extricated himself from it. The movie's reputation has skyrocketed since then—critic Colin MacCabe deemed it not just the finest film but "the greatest work of art produced in post-war Europe" when it was reissued in 1996—and the critical obtuseness of early commentators is hard to fathom today. This is especially true of the scorn that greeted its car-crash climax, an instance of profoundly inventive and deeply moving cinema that stands with the most inspired moments in all of Godard's work.

Contempt centers on Paul Javal, a French screenwriter (played by Michel Piccoli in one of his subtlest performances) who agrees to rewrite the screenplay of an Italian film production based on *The Odyssey* in order to pay for the Rome apartment where he and his wife (Bardot) want to settle down. Paul is troubled by taking a motion-picture assignment, since he sees himself as a serious writer more interested in high-flown theater than lowbrow movies. His intellectual side is soothed by the idea of working with legendary German filmmaker Fritz Lang, played in *Contempt* by Lang himself, one of Godard's longtime heroes. But he also has to work with Jerry Prokosch, a Hollywood producer (Palance) who is less interested in Homeric poetry than in the naked women he gets to ogle when viewing the daily rushes. Jerry is instantly smitten with Paul's wife, Camille, and flirts with her from their first moments together. When he invites the couple for a drink in his villa, Paul unhesitatingly agrees to let Camille ride in Jerry's two-passenger roadster while he finds a taxi for the trip. Camille takes this as a sign of Paul's decreasing commitment to their marriage—she gathers that he is indulging the producer's lust as a way of currying his favor—and begins revealing her own anxieties and insecurities about their future.

The situation grows more complicated as it proceeds, especially when the threesome move to an exotic villa on Capri, where the

Odyssey production is being filmed. Camille endures and even encourages Jerry's continuing flirtation; Paul shows a casual romantic interest in Jerry's attractive assistant; and Lang maintains a philosophical air while trying to keep his movie on a reasonably high plane despite Jerry's crassly commercial interventions. At one point Paul places a loaded pistol into his pocket, clearly intended for use on Jerry and/or Camille if her growing contempt for him (hence the film's title) erupts into a full-fledged refutation of their marriage. But fate intervenes before he can fire it, assuming that he could actually have brought himself to do so. Camille leaves Paul for a new life with Jerry; the producer's luxurious Alfa-Romeo is crushed in a crash that kills him and Camille instantly; and Paul prepares for his departure from Capri as Lang films a sweeping ocean-side shot that concludes *Contempt* on a note of intricately blended lyricism, melancholy, and resignation.

After constructing a narrative set-up that could compete with most Hollywood stories for conventional romance and suspense—will Camille stay with Jerry? will Paul chase after them? will he regain his errant wife or murder his ruthless rival?—why did Godard choose not to resolve it in a conventional manner, opting instead for a climax that seems to deliberately court accusations of arbitrariness and caprice? To understand this aspect of *Contempt* one must comprehend the film as a whole, with special attention to at least two related moments that come before and after the scene in question.

An early clue is given at the film's beginning, since *Contempt* starts with an evocation of movement—not a car traveling down a highway, but a camera traveling down a track, prefiguring the story's ultimate resolution in its very first shot. This opening scene takes place at Cinecittà, the fabled Italian studio. A camera track stretches into the distance, perpendicular to the camera that is filming the image we see, and a visible camera is gradually wheeling along this track toward our vantage point. In this moment we have one of Godard's most ingenious statements about the meaning(s) of movement in cinema. The tracking of the on-screen camera is steady in its course, carefully guided by the technicians at its controls, and imperturbably composed in its implicit attitude toward whatever vicissitudes of life may come within its purview. The cool, collected nature of this visible camera's motion is underscored further by the unseen camera that is providing the image to us, as it calmly reframes the shot, adjusting its angle until the gazes of the two cameras meet. Our camera looks upward at a slight angle while the on-screen camera looks imperiously down at our own lens, as if inviting our eyes to worship at an altar of cinema. Considered in retrospect, every aspect of this shot establishes a brilliant counterpoint with the deadly convulsion that will erupt at the film's climax.

An additional counterpoint comes from the voiceover narration that we hear during this scene: " 'The cinema,' André Bazin said, 'substitutes for our gaze a world that corresponds to our desires.' *Contempt* is the story of this world." Film critic Jonathan Rosenbaum has noted that Bazin is probably not the actual source of this quotation, which most likely comes from a writer less prominent and influential than the renowned theorist, and that the quotation itself is probably inaccurate. Rosenbaum also notes, quite rightly, that this doesn't matter. The idea expressed by the quote is perfectly in sync with the philosophy of *Contempt* in particular and Godardian cinema in general. We watch the spectacle of Paul the wanderer, Camille the not-quite-fathomable wife, and Jerry the self-absorbed suitor because it brings to us a concatenation of notions and emotions that conform to the world of our own desires; and one of humanity's most longstanding desires is to gain some shred of understanding vis-à-vis the deep-rooted tension between order and chaos in human experience.

Godard begins *Contempt* with a vision of *cinema* as *movement* as *order*, and he climaxes it with a vision of *life* as *stasis* as *disorder*. This may seem like an unhappy trajectory, yet the message underlying it is paradoxically reassuring, since the vision of Camille and Jerry in their wrecked automobile conveys a sense of calmness and restraint that counteracts the horror we might feel if we were watching the world that *is* rather than a world that *corresponds to our desires.* We never see the crash that kills them; we only hear it on the sound track (like the alleged Bazin quotation at the film's beginning) while the written word "adieu," penned by Camille in her farewell letter to Paul, fills the screen. When we do see the dead couple, they are in a state of peacefulness and repose. Their car stands motionless, crushed incongruously between the tail ends of two oil trucks that are as enormous as they are symbolic, suggesting that capitalism has taken a rage-filled revenge on Jerry for trying to choose the excitement of romance over the drone of money-spinning commerce. The lovers are equally still and silent, each lifeless head echoed by the empty hole it punched in the windshield during its catastrophic impact an instant earlier. The few traces of their scarlet-red blood are less jolting to our eyes than the matching orange-red of Jerry's sweater, the Alfa-Romeo's paint, and the fire extinguisher rudely protruding from one of the murderous trucks. Most tellingly, the couple's faces are turned in opposite directions, reaffirming in death the many forms of miscommunication and noncommunication— linguistic, social, spiritual—that marred their relationship and would surely have doomed it if they had lived. Their final nonembrace is auto/erotic in more than one sense, and the grotesquerie of this cinematic pun is well suited to the futility of the romantic fling they vainly tried to pursue.

Godard is not mocking this unhappy pair, however. He is mourning them. In his book *The Lives of a Cell,* biologist Lewis Thomas observes that although everything in the world dies, plants do it so gracefully that we hardly think of the process as death. Something similar happens with animals, he adds, since they have "an instinct for performing death alone, hidden," dying within the reach of human eyes so infrequently that we feel a "queer shock" when we pass a huddled piece of roadkill on a highway (Thomas 1978a, 97, 96). Human deaths are far more visible, in the movies at least, and Camille and Jerry are made quite a spectacle of, captured by a lens as imperious and implacable as that of the camera we saw in their story's opening shot. Yet here as in other films, Godard chooses to caress the vulnerable corpses, comforting their invisible souls and cushioning our queer spectatorial shock with the gentle motion of his camera, the soothing texture of Georges Delerue's rich musical refrain, and the calm precision of a mise-en-scène as eloquently arranged as a still life in a gradually shifting frame. Godard's serene depiction of this chthonic scene echoes another of Thomas's insights into the meanings and mechanisms of death: that dying "is not such a bad thing to do," notwithstanding the aversion to it that we acquire through our attachment to the "long habit" of living. Thomas cites the experience of a nineteenth-century explorer saved by a companion just as a lion's jaws had begun to crush his chest. Recalling the experience later, the near-victim was "amazed by the extraordinary sense of peace, calm, and total painlessness associated with being killed." He concluded that the coming of death is as benign as it is inevitable, marked not by agony and anxiety but by quietude, equanimity, and an easeful "haze of tranquillity" that envelopes consciousness as it gracefully glides into its opposite (Thomas 1978b, 50).

Godard agrees in *Contempt*, which culminates in imagery that indeed corresponds to our desires—our desires for untroubled sleep, peaceful death, and the termination of all tension, which psychoanalysis identifies as a fundamental human drive. The climax of *Contempt* has been attacked as a *deus ex machina* device, but how could that time-honored trope be considered offensive in a film whose narrative makes constant reference to the Homeric world and whose themes are animated by thoughts of fate, destiny, and the enigmatic actions of ancient and modern gods? This profoundly moving scene is precisely a *deus ex machina*, and its *deus* has been selected with exquisite care. It is *thanatos*, the urge toward a calming death that drowns all care, sorrow, useless striving, and bitter hopefulness.

Confirming this god's melancholy yet comforting message, Godard ends *Contempt* with a final scene at the Capri villa, where

Paul is bidding farewell to Lang and his *Odyssey* dreams. Lang is filming a valedictory shot on the roof of the ocean-bathed building, and again we see an on-screen camera in motion, this time not coming assertively toward us but sliding elusively to the side. The camera providing our image moves as well, outpacing both Lang's lens and the sword-wielding actor who is the ostensible focus of his shot. In mere moments the *Contempt* camera has found its true destination: the sea, blue and swelling beneath the sun, empty of detail yet teeming with significance as a deeply expressive symbol of the final, all-absorbing domain into which every road and river of life must flow.

"Silence!" cries Lang's assistant, played by Godard himself. Fittingly, this word (with an echoing Italian translation called into the air) is the last sound of the film that Lang is making and the film that Godard has made. The sea and the screen will now be as silent as the ill-starred lovers whom a thundering *thanatos ex cinema* has ushered into a quieter, calmer realm.

WORKS CITED

Thomas, Lewis. 1978 (1974). "Death in the Open," in *The Lives of a Cell: Notes of a Biology Watcher*. New York: Penguin Books, 96–99.

Thomas, Lewis. 1978 (1974). "The Long Habit," in *The Lives of a Cell: Notes of a Biology Watcher*. New York: Penguin Books, 47–52.

Noé Stands Alone

AN EXPERIMENT WITH TIME

Watching the shied core
Striking the basket, sliding across the floor
Shows less and less of luck, and more and more
Of failure spreading back up the arm
Earlier and earlier, the unraised hand calm,
The apple unbitten in the palm.

—PHILIP LARKIN, "As Bad as a Mile"

Beginning with a failed gesture—a missed attempt to land an apple core in a trashcan—the poet realizes this was no unlucky shot. He traces his failure back from the gesture, back up the arm itself, earlier and earlier—to when? To the moment the thought was formulated, or earlier? When does a failed action become determined? When do elements of personality become ingrained? When do the choices we make betray a pattern? These are among the philosophical and psychological issues explored by Gaspar Noé in *Irréversible*, which has sparked heated controversy since its 2002 premiere in competition at the Cannes International Film Festival.

Noé was born in Argentina in 1963 but has lived in France since the mid-seventies, when his father fled their native country for political reasons. He studied filmmaking during his late teens, then turned to philosophy, although he recalls being the opposite of a conscientious student. He entered the French film industry as an assistant director of short movies, then made his own directorial debut in 1991 with the forty-minute *Carne*, the brutal story of a misanthropic butcher who takes revenge on the wrong man for molesting his autistic daughter and goes to prison for it. Noé explored these characters further in his 1998 feature *Seul contre tous* (*I Stand Alone*), in which the butcher opens up a new shop in the suburbs with his mistress, then reunites with his daughter and contemplates the prospect of ending their bleak lives in a murder-suicide.

Both films caused a critical uproar, but *Irréversible* went a ferocious step farther, reportedly inducing physical illness among film-festival spectators and leading a normally unshockable *Village Voice* reviewer to denounce it for aiming to inflict "nausea, moral indignation, and . . . epilepsy" on its viewers (Hoberman). According to press accounts, the Cannes premiere of *Irréversible* provoked fainting and a walkout by an estimated 250 of the 2,400 audience members. People were supposedly nauseated not only by the film's scenes of explicit violence but also by the frenzied, restless camera work in the long opening shot. Audience members were also apparently upset by the film's frequent use of expletives directed at homosexuals and women, and by a several-minute scene in which the character played by Italian actress Monica Bellucci is anally raped.

Critics in general dismissed the film at Cannes, and many despised it, although it was better received at the Toronto International Film Festival a few months later. A prevailing view was summed up by Jonathan Rosenbaum in the *Chicago Reader*, where he called it "stupid, vicious, and pretentious, though you may find it worth checking out if you want to experiment with your own nervous system" (Rosenbaum). In sum, Noé's work got short shrift from critics too offended by the film to seriously consider its structural complexity.

Irréversible consists of about thirteen long, apparently unbroken shots,[1] beginning with a short prologue featuring Philippe Nahon as the violent, dissolute butcher who is the main character in *Carne* and *Seul contre tous*. Half naked and all repugnant, the butcher is rehashing his sordid past with an equally unappealing companion in his squalid Paris apartment. "Time destroys all things," he sighs, as police sirens wail beneath the window. Throughout the scene the camera constantly swirls and dives, providing us with only the most fleeting, temporary moments of clarity.

The camera then plunges into the street below and makes its way into the darkest bowels of an underground homosexual night-club called The Rectum, where two men are violently determined to commit murder. These men are Marcus (Vincent Cassel) and Pierre (Albert Dupontel), and they are hunting down a male prostitute known as Le Ténia—The Tapeworm (Jo Prestia)—who, we later learn, has just raped and tortured Alex (Bellucci), the current girlfriend of Marcus and former lover of his pal Pierre. The furious Marcus violently barges into room after room, disrupting scenes of anonymous sex and beating up the participants in a long display of unrelenting violence that momentarily pauses only when one of the aggrieved men breaks his arm. Thinking he's found Le Ténia, the hitherto hesitant Pierre then savagely and methodically smashes in his skull with a heavy fire extinguisher—only it isn't Le Ténia at all, but a hapless bystander who gets his brains bashed out while Le Ténia himself watches cheerfully from the sidelines. The camera never stops shaking, bobbing, weaving, bouncing off walls, turning upside down, moving in and out of focus—showing us nothing and showing us everything. Its movement mirrors the chaos and violence of the situation and the characters' wildly out-of-control state of mind.

Moving back in time, we next see Marcus harassing an Asian taxi-driver and a transvestite hooker as he searches for The Rectum, while Pierre—a philosophy professor—pleads with him not to be so violent. Moving back in time again, we see Alex walking into a dark subway underpass and getting brutally raped and beaten by Le Ténia. In this long scene of violence time seems to stand still, as Alex screams for help and reaches her hand toward the camera in a gesture of desperation and futility. We then see the situation preceding the rape—a party, at which Marcus takes dope and plays around with other girls, causing an irritated Alex to walk home on her own.

Gradually, moving through a reverse chronology, the film explains the reasons and motivations for the scene in The Rectum, as the frenzied camera slowly begins to relax and allow us to make sense of the plot. Eventually a more natural, unobtrusive directorial style comes into play, and we see Marcus and Pierre as calm, pleasant young men. We watch them joking around with Alex as the three of them take the subway to the party, and then we observe a long romantic sequence in which Marcus and Alex lie around in bed together, indulging in love-play and play-fights, laughing and kissing. The film ends with a scene in which Alex, newly pregnant—though she has yet to discover the fact—lies happily reading in a park surrounded by picnicking families and playful children. At this point the camera soars free of its moorings in a different way than earlier, flying into an overhead shot and thence into an exhilarating gyroscopic spin that turns the mise-en-scène into a swirling hallucination of dizzying, delirious intensity. This gives way to a strobo-scopic barrage of black-and-white frames assailing the eye with split-second speed, and thence to a printed repetition of the film's grim motto, first articulated by the miserable butcher in the opening sequence: "Time destroys all things." This was the film's original working title, gleaned by Noé from Ovid's *Metamorphoses,* and it recalls a key insight of Arthur Schopenhauer as well. "Time is that by virtue of which everything becomes nothingness in our hands," he wrote in 1851, "and loses all real value" (Schopenhauer, 51).

The numerous critics who readily dismissed *Irréversible* as racist, vacant, and homophobic seem to believe that the film's kinetic camera work, transgressive verbal and physical violence, and reverse chronology are merely tricks and gimmicks, rather than fundamental signifiers of its meaning. *Irréversible* is not, in fact, simply a story told backwards, but a complex study of the nature of time. Its director is less interested in cause and effect than in the form of time itself. (This is part of what distinguishes *Irréversible* from other "reverse chronology" narratives, such as Harold Pinter's 1983 *Betrayal* and Christopher Nolan's 2001 *Memento.*) Nor is *Irréversible* the mere nihilistic anti-romance that some have found it to be. In fact, Noé describes himself (perhaps a tad disingenuously) as "very sentimental," and *Irréversible* as an "intimate" film. "The structure is all funny and the camera work is full of energy," he says, "but it's really about losing someone you love" (Sterritt).[2]

It's also about a lot more, to be sure. Part of the significance of the film's structure is bodily. We begin in the realm of the anal (The Rectum)—a filthy, dark, destructive place—in search of Le Ténia (the tapeworm), whose violence turns out to be infectious. Alex is anally raped in an underground passageway, and the later conversation sequence in a rumbling subway continues the anal motif. As the film continues, however, we find ourselves progressing—as Freud might say—to a more mature realm, that of the vaginal. Alex and Marcus make love, and when Alex tests herself with a home pregnancy kit, she learns she is expecting Marcus's child. The final sequence, the rapid-fire explosion of pure black-and-white frames, may be seen as a vision of the symbolic uterus, evoking the moment of conception and perhaps the beginning of life itself. This journey also has a Dante-esque quality—starting in the pits of Hell, continuing along the tortuous slopes of Purgatory, and ending with an apparition too blazingly delirious for human perception to take in, much less grasp and comprehend.

Another clue to the film's meaning is the book Alex is seen with more than once in the movie, most notably at the end, when she relaxes in a sunny park surrounded by playing children. The book is J.W. Dunne's treatise *An Experiment with Time*, first published in 1927. Its appearance is not, as one critic complained, merely a glib allusion to the film's non-linear structure. Rather, it sheds a great deal of light on the movie's intricate and innovative composition.

Dunne's theories are too complicated to discuss at length here, but they hinge on the notion that there are multiple kinds of "time states," beginning with the most immediate ones that he calls Time 1 and Time 2. Time 1 is the kind of time we're accustomed to in daily life—linear time, moving steadily forward, with states of the external world experienced in succession. Time 2—which coexists with Time 1—is not linear but integrated in a kind of fourth dimension, where future, past, and present merge together. Dunne suggests that we experience most of our lives in Time 1—linear time—but we can access Time 2 in various ways, including through our dreams, when our cognitive faculties don't concentrate so intensely on the present moment. Dunne compares Time 2 to the "Everlasting Now" of Eastern philosophy, and asserts that our dreams always take place in Time 2, where future, present, and past are experienced as superimposed rather than separate and linear, as they appear in Time 1.

According to Dunne, states such as trances, dreams, and hypnosis give potential access to Time 2. Our perceptive faculties try to interpret a dream's events as a succession of views similar to those we experience in Time 1—so what we *experience* as our dream (and recount upon waking) is an attempt to make sense of Time 2 via the perceptual faculties we use to operate in Time 1. Dunne's account of the dreamer's experience closely resembles what the audience of *Irréversible* undergoes, as if Noé is recreating the chronological concatenation of Time 2 as experienced from the perspective of Time 1. In our dreams, as Dunne describes them,

. . . nothing stays to be looked at. Everything is in a state of flux. . . . And, because of the continual breaking down of your attempts at maintaining a concentrated focus, the dream story develops in a series of disconnected scenes. . . . You are always trying to keep attention moving steadily in the direction to which you are accustomed in your waking observation . . . but attention relaxes, and, when you recontract it, you find, as often as not, that it is focused on the wrong place. . . . You start on a journey, and find yourself abruptly at the end (Dunne, 104).

An Experiment with Time has been in and out of print sporadically since 1934, and Dunne's contributions to space-time metaphysics have not been embraced by the scientific community. Like that of renegade philosopher Charles Fort, his work has been taken up not by the academy but by dilettantes and dabblers, kitchen mystics and bedroom psychics—and an occasional artist like Noé, whose *Irréversible* enacts a similar kind of experiment. "You want to hypnotize with a movie," Noé says. "The hypnosis either takes you somewhere or it doesn't. You're in a trance or you're not. . . . If the hypnosis works well, the audience will get into your dream."

Looked at from another important perspective, the narrative of Noé's film seems characterized by a belief in human helplessness in the face of a future that is as unchangeable as it is unavoidable, since—as Dunne suggests—it is already present. *Irréversible* abounds in signs and omens of what is to come, although these always have an elusive quality. For example, certain moments in the film's first, more violent scenes are later replayed in a romantic, affectionate context, suggesting some of the many complicated connections between what we call "romantic love" and the brutality of rape and violence. Le Ténia's brutal treatment of Alex, including the way he spits disgustedly into her face after raping her, is echoed by the friendly play-fighting between Marcus and Alex, during which Marcus lightly sputters saliva into Alex's face as a joke.[3] When she first wakes up on the morning of the horrible events, moreover, Alex recalls having a strange nightmare about being trapped inside a red tunnel that then broke around her; although she pays little attention to her dream, it is a clear presentiment of what is to happen that night. Marcus, similarly, is unable to feel his arm when he wakes up—a premonition of his arm being violently broken in the Rectum nightclub. "I want to fuck you in the ass," he tells Alex teasingly a little later, a line clearly anticipating Alex's violent anal rape. The banter that Marcus, Pierre, and Alex engage in on the subway is all about Alex's sexuality, which again links up with the rape scene—and, in the conversation's emphasis on ways of bringing a sexual partner to orgasm, with instrumental, power-oriented approaches to sexuality in general. In the bleak narrative of *Irréversible*, banter, play-fighting, and real violence are all enmeshed with one another; all are continually present. Only human perception interprets one as distinct from another. A sense of imminent catastrophe, as well as the helplessness of humanity, pervades all the "romantic" scenes involving Marcus, Alex, and Pierre, however casually these are presented.

In some respects, these aspects of *Irréversible* reflect Noé's conception of the film as an exercise in the meanings and mechanisms of memory. "You experience things in a linear way," he explains, "but when you reconstruct them with your mind, they're not linear any more. Your remembrance of your own past is not linear. It's just emotions, and moments, and they're in a chronological disorder. If you want to write a diary of what you did—say, three years ago—it will take you a long time to remember in which order the events took place. You just remember faces, moments, doors, rooms."

On other levels—including its nonlinear ordering of single-take sequences that in themselves are linear—the movie is also an elaborate puzzle that spectators are invited to solve as they watch it. "It's linear, and it's not linear," Noé says. "There was an article in France where the writer said it was [like] a Rubik's Cube; you could take it to pieces and put it together [another] way. . . . It's like a game. I think that after the third scene, people understand the rules of the game, and they want to play with you and try to understand it. You could do something [even] more complex, but that would get people lost."

More profoundly, *Irréversible* is influenced by Dunne's sense of the past and future as states that are constantly with us in the present, and to this extent the movie is philosophically inflected as much by fatalism as by nihilism. Fatalism has been characterized as "the view that whatever happens must happen of necessity and whatever does not happen of necessity does not happen at all. . . . It is generally taken to be an obvious consequence of fatalism that nothing a man does is ever really up to him. What he has done he had to do; and what he will do he must do" (Adams and Kretzmann, 3–4). Noé's characters are powerless to control any aspect of their future; all are predestined from the outset to a fate from which they cannot escape—a fate that is irreversible.

Violent brutality and romantic affection are closely connected in *Irréversible*, but not in the sense that one causes or leads to the other. The connections simply exist: This hellish state is just the way things are. Humans, through their own efforts, cannot save themselves from their fate, which, in the case of Alex, Marcus, Pierre, and a number of other characters, including Alex's unborn child, is destruction and disaster. Any attempt to save oneself from this disaster is futile, and yet people like Alex and Marcus continue to delude themselves that the future is in their hands. This is a key reason for the reverse chronology of the film, which Noé sees as not a drama but a tragedy in the fullest sense of the term. "In a drama," he says, "dramatic things *happen*, and in a tragedy, they *unfold*. In a tragedy you cannot change events. In the way [*Irréversible*] is told, the characters cannot change their future, because you've already seen what's going to happen next. So all you can ask is, 'What happened before?'"

According to scholar Daniel Wojcik, fatalism, nihilism, and powerlessness are the trinity of secular apocalyptic thought (Wojcik, 201). The content and structure of *Irréversible* closely resemble those of the traditional apocalyptic narrative, in which perceived threats, social turmoil, and anomalous occurrences are interpreted as signs that foretell imminent worldly destruction. The effects of Noé's apocalypse may be limited to a small handful of characters, but its larger implications are inescapable—chief among them, that the social and cultural rituals human beings have developed to perpetuate the concept of "civilization" are meaningless acts of denial and repression. Noé describes *Irréversible* as a poignant drama about "losing someone you love," but the narrative clearly has ramifications far beyond what he idiosyncratically owns up to.[4]

The literal meaning of "apocalypse" is "an unveiling," usually in the sense of an unveiling of a state of affairs that has been present all along. Often, in apocalyptic narratives, what is unveiled is the future, which turns out to have its roots in the present moment. As philosopher and theologian Martin Buber notes, in apocalyptic thought "everything is pre-determined, all human decisions are only sham struggles" (Buber, 201). This is certainly true of *Irréversible*, which is inflected by a strong mood of secular eschatology, using scenes of apocalyptic violence as metaphors for contemporary *Angst*. In *Irréversible*, rituals and institutions like romantic love, marriage, the family, and friendship are revealed to be no more than vacant shams, and we are left with a resulting sense of anomie, disorientation, lawlessness, and chaos.

In this sense, the narrative of *Irréversible* can be regarded as a synecdoche for twentieth-century thought, which has been characterized by the breakdown of previous meaning systems and subsequent feelings of disillusionment, apathy, and anxiety. In the past century as in previous ages, tragedies, disasters, uncertainty, and threat have led people to attribute causality to external factors, whether God's will, the devil, fate, the government, one's parents, an Axis of Evil, or the configuration of the planets at birth.[5] In *Irréversible*, however, Noé instinctively suggests that in the twenty-first century we can no longer attribute violence and disaster to any cause outside the brutal nature of humanity itself. In his apocalyptic scenario, worldly destruction is considered immanent in human nature rather than externally prescribed, fulfilled by the actions and character of human beings rather than determined by outside forces. This is a chief reason for the film's unbridled eruptions of misogynistic and homophobic hate. Noé isn't merely toying with current cultural taboos. He's unmasking strains of inchoate revulsion and anarchic rage that surge through the allegedly civilized discourses of modernity with no less feral viciousness than they possess in the most lawless and barbaric instances of human existence. All that's different in modernity is the degree of repression and dissimulation with which rage and revulsion are disguised. And in Noé's view such camouflage is the worst enemy of all—concealing truths of human instinct and impulse that are as unshakeable as they are grim, and encouraging humanity's woeful urge to disavow its own realities by cowering within hard, hypocritical shells of numbness and denial. It's this existential deadness that *Irréversible* assails, using the most radical resources Noé can muster to distress, disorient, and alarm an audience accustomed to movies as a narcotizing pleasure, not a galvanizing journey into its own most desperately hidden truths.

The branch of apocalyptic thought most clearly evoked by *Irréversible* is "unconditional apocalypticism" (Wojcik, 209). This is the belief that history is predetermined and unalterable (or, as Dunne would describe it, perpetually present); the world is irredeemable by human effort, and its cataclysmic destruction is therefore inevitable. Some writers and scholars attribute the strand of unconditional apocalypticism in twentieth-century thought to the development of nuclear warheads and the bombing of Hiroshima and Nagasaki. After the invention of the bomb, there was a sense that humanity could not reverse its inevitable path to destruction, that scientists had created an uncontrollable weapon that would ultimately destroy the world. "The bomb," according to Alfred Kazin, "gave the shape of life, inner and outer, an irreversible change; a sense of fatefulness would now lie on all things" (Kazin). What the bomb symbolized to earlier writers and scholars is represented in *Irréversible* by human nature in and of itself. Noé's apocalyptic vision presents us with an infernal, chaotic society cursed by violence, fear, paranoia, and a sense of fatalism that time can only make worse. "For the world is Hell," as Schopenhauer articulated this grim insight a century and a half earlier, "and men are on the one hand the tormented souls and on the other the devils in it" (Schopenhauer, 48). The veil has been lifted. What it reveals is death-in-life, and life-in-death.

NOTES

1. In fact there are invisible cuts within some of these shots, and some visual details were digitally added in postproduction.
2. All quotes from Noé in this essay are taken from this interview.

3. Interestingly, Vincent Cassel and Monica Bellucci—who were married to each other during production of *Irréversible*—filed for divorce not long after the film's release, in summer 2002.
4. In discussing his film Noé tends to downplay its seriousness, describing it as "not that ambitious." He may think of the movie as a fairly straightforward story about love and loss, but the narrative has apocalyptic and eschatological implications that—as in the folk or fairy tale—go far beyond his putative intentions.
5. For more on this historical view see Leonard W. Doob, *Inevitability: Determinism, Fatalism, and Destiny* (New York: Greenwood Press, 1988), 20–29.

WORKS CITED

Adams, Marilyn McCord, and Norman Kretzmann. 1969. "Introduction" to William Ockham, *Predestination, God's Foreknowledge, and Future Contingents.* New York: Apple-Century-Crofts.

Buber, Martin. 1957. *Pointing the Way: Collected Essays,* trans. Maurice Freedman. Baltimore: The Johns Hopkins University Press.

Dunne, J. W. 2001 (1927). *An Experiment with Time.* Charlotteville: Hampton Roads Publishing.

Hoberman, J. 2002. "All or Nothing at the Cannes Film Festival," *Village Voice* (5–12 June). <http://www.villagevoice.com/issues/0223/hoberman2.php>

Kazin, Alfred. 1988. "Awaiting the Crack of Doom." *New York Times Book Review* (1 May), 1.

Rosenbaum, Jonathan. 2002. Quoted in *Metacritic.com*, "What the Critics Are Saying:" <http://www.metacritic.com/film/titles/irreversible/>

Schopenhauer, Arthur. 1970. *Essays and Aphorisms,* trans. R. J. Hollingdale. London: Penguin Books.

Sterritt, David. 2002. Interview with Gaspar Noé at the Toronto International Film Festival (12 September).

Wojcik, Daniel. 1997. *The End of the World as We Know It: Faith, Fatalism and Apocalypse in America.* New York: New York University Press.

Time Code

NARRATIVE FILM AND THE AVANT-GARDE

Mike Figgis has made a long list of movies, from the nightclub thriller *Stormy Monday* (1987) to the Oscar-honored hit *Leaving Las Vegas* (1995). But when he *goes* to the movies, he often feels more trapped and controlled than intrigued and excited.

Most films make you a "prisoner of the narrative," he says, because they use a simplistic "cartoon structure" to control the viewer's thoughts and emotions. "Character is far more interesting than plot," he adds, but since character traits are complex and multifaceted, filmmakers take the easy way out by submerging human nature in manipulative story events. "Film has become the slave of plot," he states with disappointment. "It's something like a drug."

Deciding to fight the system by revolutionizing it, Figgis made *Time Code,* one of the most offbeat theatrical releases in memory. Its story deals with the commercial filmmaking scene, and its high-powered cast includes Salma Hayek as a wannabe star, Jeanne Tripplehorn as her jealous lover, Stellan Skarsgård as a philandering executive, Richard Edson as a movie director with a drug problem, Leslie Mann as an unhappy actress, and Danny Huston as a dope-dealing security guard.

The driving force behind the production wasn't plot or dialogue, though, and it wasn't made through a conventional process of screenwriting and rehearsal. Deciding to create this unorthodox work in an unorthodox way, Figgis started with a brief treatment instead of a full-fledged screenplay, and asked his actors to improvise their parts as the cameras rolled. They performed the entire movie fifteen times during a ten-day period, with every performance shot in continuous ninety-three-minute takes by a team of videographers using four digital-video cameras. At the end of these sessions, Figgis chose his favorite set of four simultaneously shot versions and transferred them to film as a four-part mosaic, with four different pictures showing the action from different perspectives on a single screen.

Viewers are free to wander through the images—at any speed and in any order—loosely guided by the sound track, which moves from one quadrant to another as the story takes its course. Everyone watching *Time Code* sees a different movie, since no two people shift their eyes from picture to picture in the same way, or forge the same mental connections among the four images on view. The screen contains no editing at all, but the spectator's mind pulses with idiosyncratic "cuts" that mutate and multiply every moment.

The movie's first few minutes plunge us directly into this, providing a vivid example of what will follow for the rest of the story. In the upper left, Tripplehorn's character fiddles with a flat tire on a car; to the right of this image, a female patient speaks with her psychotherapist in a neatly furnished office; below this, a camera tracks through the long, narrow corridors of Red Mullet Productions, a fictional company that happens to have the same name as Figgis's real-life organization; and on the lower left we see a security guard's surveillance-video screen, which itself carries four different views of the building's interior. What we hear on the sound track is the conversation between the patient and therapist, cueing this image as the story's main focus at this particular moment. But alert viewers will take in all four quadrants, and this will pay off later—since the flat tire is the set-up for a fateful conversation, the security guard will become a pivotal character, and key moments of the plot will unfold in Red Mullet's rooms and hallways.

The crucial point is that *Time Code* allows our eyes and imaginations to wander wherever they want, just as a Figgis camera wanders through Red Mullet in search of whatever dramatic incident may turn up there. The overall effect is less like a cause-and-effect narrative than a modernist collage that invites us to combine the artist's creation with our own ideas and fantasies. If most movies make us prisoners of the linear plot, this one makes us explorers of the moving image. In this respect the *Time Code* aesthetic is closer to other video-linked experiences, like channel-surfing and Web-surfing, than to film-watching in a traditional sense. This goes double (or quadruple!) for the DVD version, which allows the viewer to shift and re-shift the sound track from image to image, creating a potentially infinite number of variations on the *Time Code* theme.

All of which is a brilliant technical feat—and a tremendously risky one. By using improvisational methods of acting and photography, Figgis has allowed huge amounts of chance into the film-making process; and by creating a four-part mosaic that nobody will view the same way twice, he has also brought spur-of-the-moment surprises into the film-*watching* process. Ordinary screen-writing and directing are based on a power-driven desire to "control the story, control the ending, control the audience," Figgis says. By contrast, the process of "observing several things at the same time" feeds the brain in completely different ways. "It's far more invigorating and stimulating," he argues, "and it releases far more of the subconscious." That's because the multiple-image format plays down story "specifics" in favor of artistic "abstractions" that are far more interesting and fun.

Such talk of abstractions doesn't mean *Time Code* is a mere aesthetic exercise, though. Just the opposite, many critics have praised it for carrying a strong emotional punch. Equally important, the film has a practical and even political dimension, since it combats the egotistical notion that human beings can control their destinies. "I love the idea of planning certain things very clinically,"

Figgis says, "and the rest is up to how the dice fall. That's far more interesting than any other way . . . to tell a story."

This opens up a brave new style that promises to break the chains of narrative for good, ushering in an era of liberated viewers and free-flowing cinema. Or does it? And would it be a good thing if Figgis's ideas did succeed at their subversive task? Narrative has a long and tenacious history, and it's hard to imagine a time when moviegoers won't want solid, coherent stories to sink their teeth into.

So it's important to emphasize that Figgis hasn't thrown out narrative entirely, he's just changed its outward appearance so it can surprise us in new ways. Consider a scene late in the movie, when Mía Maestro appears as a media-infatuated director pitching a project to Red Mullet that hilariously resembles a super-pretentious version of *Time Code* itself. She earnestly describes her ideas in the lower left as Skarsgård listens with laughter and derision in the lower right. This presents the same narrative and emotional information you'd receive from a conventional editing sequence—the characters appear in different shots, making us feel how mentally distant they are from each other—but the effect is enhanced by the fact that see them *simultaneously* as well as *separately*. This grows even stronger as Maestro reacts to Skarsgård's insults with shaky bravado; we see her face steadily in the lower left while the lower-right camera moves unsteadily around the conference table, acting as nervous and embarrassed as the people gathered there. Nothing happens in this scene that a normal movie couldn't convey, but Figgis's technique adds tremendous resonance, proving that his interest lies in renewing and refreshing the conventions of screenwriting, not evading or degrading them.

The same goes for his approach to spoken words. Despite the innovations *Time Code* brings to on-screen imagery, its dialogue contains enough conventional exposition to make a by-the-book screenwriter perfectly happy. Take the moment when a masseur (Julian Sands) arrives at the Red Mullet office to service some clients, beginning his visit by introducing himself at the reception desk. We learn his name, his nickname, his occupation, his reason for being here, and even the kind of massage he gives. When he finishes describing his professional technique with a flippant phrase—"Whatever makes you come!"—we also gain instant insight into his personality and the kind of customers he's used to dealing with. He may occupy only one of the screen's four segments, but he's a real and tantalizing character, and his first appearance is accompanied by enough background to make us feel we know him as clearly as we'd know a similar figure in a conventional movie.

Time Code strikes an artful balance between old-fashioned story-telling and new-fangled imagemaking, using a string of bold maneuvers that investigate, interrogate, and deconstruct the rules of screenwriting. We live at a time when best-selling books assure us that commercial movies should be undemanding beasts guided by well-understood conventions of content and style. *Time Code* is certainly a commercial movie, complete with stars, spectacle, and a plot spiced with suspense, romance, and violence. It even climaxes with a shootout, when the jealous lover (Tripplehorn) pulls a gun on the two-timing executive (Skarsgård) right in the Red Mullet office. But it spins sharply away from the philosophies of Syd Field and company, replacing the widely shared certainties of three-act structure and narrative arc with the unmoored excitements of improvisation, indeterminacy, and synchronicity.

Consider a moment about twenty minutes into the story, when the plot starts to thicken in surprising ways. In the upper left, Tripplehorn plants a listening device in the purse of Hayek, her lover. Directly below this, Edson prepares to videotape Mann's audition for a movie he's frantically trying to get off the ground. To the right, one of Figgis's cameras makes particularly kinetic pans around the Red Mullet conference room during a group discussion of the company's plans. And just above this, the psychotherapy scene keeps rambling on. At first glance, this appears like a motley collection of material linked by nothing but Figgis's need for four different images—until you realize that this four-part collage is also a super-bly unified portrait of the different ways people can watch, listen to, and spy on one another in our technology-saturated age.

Confirming this interpretation, Figgis then moves each frame into a closeup: Hayek in the car with Tripplehorn, the patient talk-ing with her shrink, Mann tightly framed on Edson's video moni-tor, and Holly Hunter pitching a project to the Red Mullet gang. We are all on display in one way or another, the scene suggests, every moment of our media-drenched lives. And in case this point escapes us, Figgis punctuates the movie with a recurring image painted on a wall across the street from the Red Mullet building: the outline of a large, gazing eye that sums up the idea of society-as-spectacle that *Time Code* simultaneously analyzes, celebrates, and cautions us to beware of.

The sort of storytelling Figgis gives us here—some parts explicitly on screen, other parts evoked by our own creative thoughts—are at once aggressively new and deeply rooted in experimental prac-tices that forward-looking artists have explored for ages. Figgis is happy to acknowledge this, peppering his comments on *Time Code* with references to performance art, avant-garde cinema, and the increasingly blurred boundaries among film, plays, and music. He loves theater as much as he loves movies, noting that the wide-angle layout of a proscenium stage causes the audience to scan it actively, bringing in "detail, irony, and parallel imagery . . . without this having to be the main point of what you're watching." Music has been another source of inspiration ever since he learned about jazz from his father, who taught him to appreciate "the phrasing of Lester Young, say, in relation to Billie Holiday's vocal line," and to be "aware of the function of a brilliant drummer who you couldn't hear unless you really strained your ears, and who was a profound drummer *because* you couldn't hear him." Lessons like these encouraged him to look for "the invisible factor that makes something work. . . . If you have a deep understanding of what an ensemble really should be, at its most spiritual level, then that knowledge can transfer to any structure you look at. It becomes your metaphor, your blueprint."

Figgis's fascination with the emotions of ensemble structure explains why *Time Code* packs so many strong feelings despite its mosaic-like appearance. Take a segment about a third of the way through the movie, when the four quadrants show Tripplehorn snooping on her lover Hayek through her secret listening bug; Hayek rehearsing audition lines while waiting for her second lover Skarsgård in an empty screening room; Skarsgård seducing another woman with sexy talk of an Italian vacation; and Sands leading the Red Mullet crew in a relaxation exercise (everyone in a circle, hands joined, rocking up and down) right after Edson's mentally addled character has jangled their nerves with a wild outburst. Again the images are very different—as different as the interwoven melodies in a complex jazz arrangement—but again there's a brilliantly unified theme: These people are all making emotional connections with others, and the connections have overtones and undertones as varied as the characters themselves. Details within this four-part scene make its feelings even richer—the fact that Tripplehorn and Hayek are the only characters who are physically alone, for instance, yet are more closely connected (through Tripplehorn's bugging device) than anyone else on screen. This is exactly the sort of detail, irony, and parallel imagery that excites Figgis in theater and performance art, brought to the screen with a verve and imagination that any screenwriter could be proud of.

Figgis's interest in multiple art forms is a key to understanding not only *Time Code* but the brave new world of narrative that's emerging from the marriage between new technologies and avant-garde sensibilities. Like other sharp-eyed observers, he is keenly aware that as innovative outlets for screen storytelling proliferate—from Web site to laptop DVD to living-room HDTV—experimental ideas will proliferate as well, expanding our notions of what stories are and what they ought to be. He also knows that the seemingly self-evident rules of cinematic storytelling are comparatively recent inventions, arising from years of trial and error. A look at their history helps us share his alertness to the many new forms they're starting to assume.

What we take for granted today as "narrative form" emerged in the silent-screen era, when visual stories had their first great blossoming as filmmakers realized they could cut from shot to shot whenever the logic of the tale demanded it. Think of D. W. Griffith leaping from the war-torn walls of ancient Babylon to the site of a twentieth-century hanging in *Intolerance* (1916), making his opinions about human cruelty as vivid as the fast-paced action captured by his hand-cranked cameras. Story conventions continued to evolve in the early sound era, when synchronized dialogue entered the picture. Think of Alfred Hitchcock conveying a young woman's psychological terror in *Blackmail* (1929) by distorting the voice of a neighbor who utters the fateful word "knife" over and over, not knowing her listener has killed a man with just such a weapon. Storytelling formulas crested in the post-studio era, when complicated market pressures spurred new approaches to everything from the shape of the screen to the "realism" of computer-generated imagery. Think of the move to rectangular aspect ratios (CinemaScope, Panavision) that use the screen less as a frame for tidy arrangements than a playground for movements and juxtapositions.

For decades, most critics saw these developments as a parade of progress, from clunky "primitive" cinema to our enlightened age of wide-screen, surround-sound extravaganzas. A new breed of historians has challenged this view, though, finding great artistic merit in very early works like the single-shot documentaries of the Lumière Brothers and the stagebound fantasies of Georges Méliès, dating from the end of the nineteenth century.

How can anyone compare these antiques with the elaborate feats we're accustomed to today? The key is to recognize that pioneers like Lumière and Méliès were not low-tech tinkerers groping in the dark, but sophisticated artists who recognized the quintessentially modern excitement of film's ability to surprise and stimulate us with moment-to-moment changes of picture and perspective. The fifty-two-second "actualities" shot in Paris by the Lumières may have been short and simple, but when they photographed a train pulling into a station they were careful to capture not only the documentary event but the beauty and efficiency of an exciting new world in which intricate machines (from locomotives to movie projectors) became the servants of ordinary people. Later masters like Sergei Eisenstein and Dziga Vertov picked up where their predecessors left off, cultivating the possibilities of high-energy montage based on contrast, conflict, and contradiction. Excited by new technologies that promised to eliminate both hunger and capitalism, Eisenstein depicted the humblest objects—check out the dairy-farm equipment in *Old and New*, his 1929 masterpiece—with dynamic editing that carries a potent visual charge to this day. In his first feature, *Strike* (1924), he even anticipated Figgis by breaking the screen into mini-segments at key moments in the story, illustrating his view of society as a collection of individuals who must unite if they're going to change the world. Eisenstein considered montage such a powerful tool that human performances could be completely bypassed at some points in the storytelling process. See the stirring moment in *The Battleship Potemkin* (1925) when a ship's explosive gunfire is followed by shots of three statues of lions—one reclining, one stirring to action, one ready to leap—that evoke the rising of the outraged masses as pungently as acting ever could.

These filmmakers helped create a chameleon-like "cinema of attractions," as historian Tom Gunning calls it, aimed at giving story material extra impact via the speed and variety of constantly changing visuals. But this went out of fashion when Griffith's followers realized they could sell more tickets with films of "narrative integration," modeling their scenarios on popular dramas and nineteenth-century novels. This began the age of seamlessly told stories, with each shot leading to the next as smoothly as Lillian Gish's innocent country girl leaps from one ice floe to another in the 1920 melodrama *Way Down East.* These emotion-grabbing yarns triumphed at the box office. Still, enterprising avant-gardists kept up the more poetic practice of celebrating each individual image, treating it as an expressive object in its own right as well as a link in a narrative chain—as Vertov did in *The Man With a Movie Camera* (1928), for instance, portraying Moscow in such a visually freewheeling way that we see the title character not just drinking from a beer mug but literally climbing out of one, cheerfully ignoring the laws of narrative logic and physical possibility alike.

Some early experimenters also fended off the influence of plays and novels by finding unexpected ways of dealing with words. In his 1924 drama *The Last Laugh,* director F. W. Murnau tells the psychologically complex tale of a lonely doorman through wholly visual means, without intertitles to provide dialogue or description. Taking a different track, Robert Wiene allows printed words to invade the image in his 1919 chiller *The Cabinet of Dr. Caligari,* as a character howls out the villain's name and we see it literally written across the surface of his mentally deranged world. Behind such ventures is the idea of making words serve images, rather than the other way around—a notion that was sorely tested when sync-sound movies barged into theaters in the late '20s, threatening to turn the art of motion pictures into what Hitchcock scornfully called "photographs of people talking."

Efforts to renew cinema's inventiveness have continued ever since. Some filmmakers have tossed out anything even vaguely related to the traditional screenplay. One is Stan Brakhage, who substitutes the camera for his own spontaneous eye, presenting a flow of images as quick and changeable as thought—as in *Mothlight,* a silent collage of twigs, sticks, and wings that conveys his impression of the world viewed through a fluttering insect's eyes. Another is Ken Jacobs, who recycles preexisting "found footage" in groundbreaking ways, such as his "Nervous System" method, which brings a slice-and-dice approach to narrative by showing identical filmstrips through two projectors one frame at a time. This wrenches characters and settings free of their stories and turns them into shuddering, shimmering explosions of pure cinematic texture, revealing hidden beauties crystallized within the celluloid strip itself.

While experimentalists like these dispense with storytelling altogether, others challenge the screenplay on its own ground, calling into question the basic relationship between written text and projected image. Scott Macdonald has collected intriguing examples in his valuable book *Screen Writing: Scripts and Texts by Independent Filmmakers*, illustrating a wide range of slyly subversive approaches. Some project their "screenplays" directly onto the screen in written form, like Michael Snow in *So Is This* (1982), where the script appears one word at a time, and Hollis Frampton in *Poetic Justice* (1972), where the viewer reads a growing pile of manuscript pages stacked on a table. ("#132. Middle Shot. Bedroom. Love making. Outside the window are rings of Saturn, looming. Dissolve to. . . . ") Yoko Ono's *Mini Film Scripts* of the 1960s are meant as brief conceptual "scores" that all interested filmmakers are invited to "play," anticipating Figgis's notion of cinema as a kind of music. ("Film Script 3: Ask audience to cut the part of the image on the screen that they don't like. Supply scissors.") Su Friedrich's *(Script) for a Film Without Images* (1984), a dialogue between two characters, is a movie for the mind's eye, meant to be read and imagined rather than acted and photographed. (Left column: "Does it make you happy? From what you've said, it appears to make you happy to be angry." Right column: "Of course not, but it doesn't make me unhappy. . . . ")

These and countless other examples—stretching back at least to Marcel Duchamp's 1926 *Anemic Cinema*, where punning words (starting with the anagrammatic title) fill the screen in slowly spinning spirals—foreground the many ways in which independent spirits have used screenwriting not as a blueprint for filming, but a tool for shaking up the very idea of cinematic language.

Within this cavalcade of experimental approaches, multiple-screen movies like *Time Code* make up an enticing subgenre. Its first major masterpiece was the 1927 epic *Napoléon* by French director Abel Gance, who used a process called Polyvision to synchronize multiple cameras and projectors so a triple-sized panorama could fill the screen in the story's last scenes—a grand finale if ever there was one. When the film was restored by archivist Kevin Brownlow and reissued to theaters in 1979, audiences cheered as three side-by-side images combined to form a unified wide-angle view, anticipating the remarkably similar *This Is Cinerama* (1952) by a quarter of a century. In other sequences that are still more adventurous, the three screen-segments present three different pictures, or flank a primary image in the center with twin echoes on the right and left—a dozen heavily armed horsemen galloping toward battle in the middle, say, and two or three of them galloping straight toward *us* on either side. Far from being a gratuitous visual thrill, Polyvision helps Gance convey the historical complexity of Napoleon's time and the logistical ingenuity of his political and military tactics. While the single-image moments encapsulate the sweep and breath of the general's career, the triple-image moments capture the boisterous hurly-burly of history itself.

It's a testament to the ingrained conservatism of commercial cinema that so few filmmakers have picked up on the multiple-image idea between Gance in the '20s and Figgis more than seventy years later. Brian De Palma and others have cooked up occasional split-screen shenanigans, but these are often fleeting "visual gimmicks," as Figgis calls them. Of the few who have experimented with full-fledged multiple images, Andy Warhol made the most resounding splash with his 1966 tragicomedy *The Chelsea Girls*, released in theaters during a brief '60s moment when distributors felt there was money to be made by pitching avant-garde movies at a growing "youth market" with countercultural tastes. The immediate fame of *The Chelsea Girls* owed less to its style than to its subject matter, as audiences lined up to watch sundry Warhol superstars—from the vivacious Viva to the self-absorbed Ondine—merge their real-life personalities with whimsical personas adopted for cinematographer Paul Morrissey's voyeuristic cameras.

But its most enduring artistic value lies in its brilliant use of double-screen aesthetics, with a pair of sixteen-millimeter reels projected side-by-side and the sound track alternating between them. The semi-improvised nature of the movie's acting is matched by the semi-improvised nature of its exhibition: The dual projectors are not carefully coordinated, as in Polyvision or Cinerama, but are simply switched on at approximately the same time. Which image has synchronized sound at any given moment depends pretty much on the projectionist's caprice. Since no particular showing can ever be precisely duplicated, screenings of *The Chelsea Girls* have as much in common with musical and theatrical performances as with ordinary film exhibitions. Add to this the element of viewer individuality that all multiple-picture movies encourage—as with *Time Code*, each spectator makes distinctive eye movements from one instant to the next—and you have an audiovisual experience that's drastically different from the point-by-point logic of a linear screenplay conveyed through traditional continuity editing.

The Chelsea Girls is just one of many experiments that made Warhol a legendary figure in avant-garde cinema. Others include fixed-camera silent films like *Eat* (1963) and *Haircut* (1963); fixed-camera talkies like *Vinyl* (1965) and *Poor Little Rich Girl* (1965); and more elaborately produced pictures like *Bike Boy* (1967) and *Lonesome Cowboys* (1968). His subjects seem uproariously random, apart from the photogenic fascination of their performers: Robert Indiana eating a mushroom, John Giorno sleeping for six hours, Edie Sedgwick powdering her nose while listening to an Everly Brothers album. But there's no denying the ingenuity of his stripped-down techniques—unmoving camera, single-shot cinematography, black-and-white film stock—as means of capturing raw-as-life reality complete with the accidents, blemishes, and dead time that conventional pictures leave on the cutting-room floor.

Warhol's confidence ran a tad wild when he got the notion that ticket-buying audiences would actually pay to see this stuff, but it's hard to imagine a more ego-free approach to cinema than the idea that a director's job is to put someone in front of the camera, turn it on, and then leave it alone until the film runs out. Doubling the imagery with two projectors was a logical extension of this concept, adding the spectator's spontaneous visual choices (and the projectionist's spontaneous sound manipulations) to the chance elements of the filmed material.

While it's true that Warhols's films didn't attract many mainstream moviegoers, they didn't imprison him in an avant-garde ghetto, either. Narrative and characterization crept into his work as his sound tracks took on more importance, and his protégé Morrissey picked up on these, combining them with his own determination to dissolve differences between acting, behaving, and simply being. Marching under the "Andy Warhol Presents" banner, Morrissey carried his mentor's radical aesthetic smack into commercial theaters—if only for the limited time that performers like Joe Dallesandro and Candy Darling, plots about impotent hustlers and horny transvestites, and titles like *Trash* (1970) and *Heat* (1972) could retain a hold on the public imagination.

Years later, *Time Code* lies squarely in this tradition, reinvigorating Warhol's interest in unedited reality and multiple imagery while using digital equipment to stretch the Warholian time frame far beyond its sixteen-millimeter limits. Not surprisingly, Figgis remembers being "blown away" by *The Chelsea Girls* in the '60s, and he experimented with multiple-projector film in some of his theater work. Watch the spur-of-the-moment pans used by the *Time Code* camera operators when the action takes them by surprise— when a sudden earthquake throws the Red Mullet conference into chaos, for instance, each character responding with a personalized panic that's echoed and reinforced by the cameras' wild swings. Notice the bits of extraneous noise on the sound track, as when Tripplehorn strains to hear Hayek's screening-room tryst while a sex-movie sound track strains the limits of her listening bug. Observe the offbeat tilt of performances being elaborated and refined while the cameras whir, as when a woman's crying in one quadrant is heightened by the fact that people are laughing in the other three. Then piece together the partly planned, partly spontaneous gestalt that these elements add up to—and you're experiencing semi-improvised cinema at its Warholian, warts-and-all best.

A key ambition of experimentally minded filmmakers from Warhol to Figgis is their desire to reduce the rigidity of preexisting formulas, opening the door for unplanned events and amazing accidents. This goes for radical filmmakers of other kinds as well, such as French-Swiss director Jean-Luc Godard, who takes an improvisational approach to every aspect of production, from conceptualizing a project through the final edit—strongly influencing Figgis, who wrote the treatment for *Time Code* after reading a collection of Godard interviews. Giving a major role to chance is uncommon in the movie world, but it happens so frequently in contemporary music that there's a word for it: "aleatory," often associated with John Cage and his followers. They changed the course of modern aesthetics by seeking ways to bypass the egos of individual creators— and consumers—of artistic works.

Named after a Latin word for dice-throwing, aleatory techniques are designed to loosen up artistic creation by diminishing the artist's control over the process. While this has a long history, it picked up steam in the early twentieth century when the Dada movement launched its tumultuous anti-art crusade, paving the way for Conceptual art—made for the mind rather than the eye— and the Surrealist fascination with dreams and the unconscious, as in Salvador Dalí's hallucinatory paintings of melted watches draped over the branches of impossible trees. The trend reached a pinnacle in the '40s and '50s when Jackson Pollock inaugurated "action painting," the Living Theatre broke down the proscenium between stage and spectator, and Cage started choosing musical notes according to the placement of stars on an astronomy chart or speckles on a piece of cardboard. Not all of these projects were aleatory in the strictest sense, but they shared a desire to open new realms of possibility by blasting away old habits and attacking Aesthetic Correctness of every kind. Among the best-known leaders of the trend were Beat Generation writers William S. Burroughs, whose "cut-up method" called for slicing a prose-written page with scissors and pasting the pieces into a new unpremeditated form, and Jack Kerouac, whose improvised "spontaneous bop prosody" created cascades of words as free-flowing as the notes unleashed by a wailing sax player in a smoke-filled jazz club.

Films like René Clair's hilarious *Entr'acte* (1924) and Man Ray's collage-like *Emak-Bakia* (1927) launched what might be thought of as the motion-picture branch of this enterprise, wildly different from one another in all respects except their disdain for the deftly planned scenarios of ordinary cinema. The 1928 shocker *Un Chien andalou*, directed by Luis Buñuel from a scenario he wrote with Dalí, is arguably the movement's greatest achievement, with images—a man watching ants crawl from a hole in his hand, a woman standing in trancelike indifference as a speeding car rushes to strike her dead, a barber slicing a woman's eye as a sliver of cloud passes across the moon—that obey the filmmakers' single rule of eliminating narrative sense in order to unveil the full anarchy of the unconscious. The enemy of such artists was Hollywood and all its works: Where everyday moviegoers saw crisp storytelling, these rebels saw lazy clichés, designed to be passively absorbed rather than actively explored. Artists are capable of subtler, smarter achievements, argued these (literal) iconoclasts, and so are viewers, listeners, and readers. The world of truth and beauty is too vast to be contained and conveyed by traditional works. The artist's ego needs to be shoved aside so greater forces can assert themselves in all their majesty and mystery.

Musical purists may reasonably argue that *Time Code* is too controlled and coordinated to have strong links with the near-anarchy of full-blown aleatory pieces like, say, Cage's celebrated *4′33″*, where the "music" consists of ambient sounds in the vicinity of an unplayed piano. It's true that Figgis believes less in unmediated chance than in artful mixtures of the planned and the unplanned, allowing their interplay to enrich the final result. But it's also true that his desire to unleash elements of chance stands at the center of his current artistic approach.

So does his involvement with jazz, and specifically bebop, which creates its effects (considered very avant-garde when they were new in the 1940s) by spinning improvised tunes over established chord structures. Like the leader of a bop combo, Figgis grounded *Time Code* in predetermined material—the bare-bones story he handed to his performers and technicians—and then asked his collaborators to weave their own creative ideas around it, allowing them total freedom as long as they followed the basic outline, watched the clock, and kept on blowing even if a muffed line or awkward move seemed to spoil the take. This has fascinating results in the finished film. The camera that photographed the screen's lower-right image appears to have gone through an intermittent focusing glitch, for instance, giving that quadrant a hazy blur at certain moments— when Hayek reacts to one of the earthquakes during her audition for Edson, for example, and when Skarsgård leaves the empty screening room after having sex with her. The latter image has additional impact since the lower-left camera shows Skarsgård in completely crisp focus at the same time, as if the two lower frames are evoking the contrasting moods inside (moody, melancholy) and outside (cool, confident) the chamber where his lover is being left behind. By allowing the emotions of his movie to be affected by the technical idiosyncrasies of different cameras, Figgis underscores his resemblance to a jazz musician who allows the quirks of individual instruments to affect the overall textures of his sound.

Figgis cheerfully acknowledges the jazz roots of *Time Code*, although when searching for comparisons he cites classical music as well—and also punk rock, which shares the minimalist and antiestablishment impulses that he sees as primary principles of the coming digital-cinema age. Figgis trained as a jazz musician from childhood, and approaches film in what he considers an inherently musical way. He diagrammed the string-quartet structure of *Time Code* on music paper, using bar lines to indicate minutes of time much as a music composer uses them to designate units of rhythm. Carrying this line of analysis further, you might compare *Time Code* with two different kinds of serious music. One is music in the classical or romantic style, which blends melody and harmony into a seamless unity; the other is music in the baroque or polyphonic style, which weaves multiple melodies into pleasing counterpoint while allowing each tune to keep its own distinctive identity. Figgis goes for polyphony, respecting the individuality of each "melodic line" while braiding all four into a harmonious, well-balanced whole. He's the Johann Sebastian Bach of modernist moviemaking.

Figgis also sees a strong musical side to the film's acting. Although there was no formal script, he let his performers know exactly how they should relate to one another throughout the ninety-three-minute takes. "I gave the actors very clear directions about their ensemble function," he told me when I queried him on this, "and also the places where they might solo—individually improvise, I mean, carrying the piece alone for a while. But even then they'd be part of an ensemble, since they always had to relate to the other three screens."

Within these guidelines, *Time Code* underwent a jazz-like evolution over the ten days and fifteen shooting sessions needed to produce the final version, beginning as what Figgis calls "a wild and anarchistic piece of performance art" and ending as what he considers "quite a sophisticated, structured film." His decision to rely on improvisation rather than scripting was crucial to the liveliness of the final result, he feels, since the need to follow a conventional screenplay would have bogged down the production in technical rehearsal. "It would have become like one of those dance pieces where you have much clinical admiration for the coordination and synchronicity of the dancers," he says, "but you think, how long did it take them to learn that? Here the structure was very sophisticated and technical, yet the performances are somehow very human because they're not rehearsed into the ground." His directing was entirely "pre or post," leaving room for plenty of unexpected events while the picture was actually being shot. This way, he says, "things are going to occur which you could never have anticipated. That's interesting enough on one screen, but if you compound it with four screens it's completely delicious."

As his comments on acting indicate, Figgis's commitment to spontaneity and synchronicity has roots in theater as well as music. Before starting his movie career he headed an experimental stage company for about fifteen years. Near the end of that time he became interested in what he calls parallel storytelling, dividing the stage into different areas so the performers couldn't always see one another—or the filmed material that frequently added to the mix.

He eventually left the stage—and set aside most of his unorthodox ideas—in order to learn conventional movie-production methods. But he continued to push the content envelope, most notably in *The Loss of Sexual Innocence*, a boldly disjunctive 1999 release that operates more as a thematic essay than a linear narrative. Worried that filmmaking had sidetracked him too long from his experimental interests, he took another step away from tradition in 1999 with *Miss Julie*, a screen adaptation of August Strindberg's tightly compressed play about a privileged woman caught in an emotionally turbulent relationship with a servant. Using the Super-16 format, he photographed the picture with two cameras shooting fifteen-minute takes, and then—in what started as a simple time-saving measure during the edit—he began reviewing the footage from both cameras simultaneously, using a split-screen playback apparatus.

This taught him two surprising lessons: that doubling the visual experience *more* than doubles the information you receive, and that different parts of the brain are called on to interpret this overload and make sense of its messages. One pay-off from this discovery is a key scene showing a sexual encounter between Julie and the servant in split-screen mode, heightening the intensity of their sensual contact—and our awareness of its dizzying intoxication—by doubling the imagery of their caresses, embraces, and intertwining bodies. Another pay-off was his reawakened desire to capture an entire story in a single take through video technology. He expected this to result in a performance-art piece for galleries and museums, but it turned into the commercially viable *Time Code* project when a conversation with Sony led to a substantial budget and mass-market distribution.

Figgis is not the only major storyteller to rearrange his artistic priorities in view of digital video and other new media possibilities. Another is Russell Banks, whose novels have inspired such first-rate films as *The Sweet Hereafter* and *Affliction*, directed in 1997 by Atom Egoyan and Paul Schrader, respectively.

Banks has written an adaptation of Kerouac's novel *On the Road*, still unproduced at this writing, although it was penned at the behest of Francis Ford Coppola, who has regarded a movie version of Kerouac's book—perhaps shot on inexpensive Super-16-millimeter film to allow for on-camera improvisation—as a pet project for years. *On the Road* did more than any other single work to place the Beat Generation on the cultural map during the 1950s era. It's also a book that vividly anticipates current revolutions in narrative form. Kerouac banged it out on a continuous roll of paper so he wouldn't have to interrupt his improvisational writing even to put blank sheets into his typewriter, and he packed its hyperactive paragraphs with an ever-shifting stream of images and impressions inspired by everything from jazz to drug-induced visions—captured so spontaneously that a friend described his writing process as "simply recording the 'movie' unreeling in his mind." Add actors and video cameras to this highly intuitive technique and it sounds amazingly like Figgis's approach to *Time Code*.

Describing himself as a traditional "wet clay and stylus" writer rather than a new-technology adventurer, Banks feels "it's not the artist's problem to worry about technology." But, he adds, "it's a foolish artist who doesn't open up to new technology and utilize it." He is convinced that digital media may soon change the art of screenwriting as drastically as the switchover from silent to sound cinema.

Speaking at the Lake Placid Film Forum in upstate New York on the subject of new technologies, Banks contrasted reading novels, which he considers a private and interactive experience, with watching movies, a public and passive activity where the filmmaker exerts ultimate control over how and when we perceive the story and characters. To read a novel is to allow the author to conduct a "controlled hallucination" in your mind, he says. New technologies are starting to edge cinema in this direction, by making film-viewing far more personalized and intimate than it used to be—allowing you to take a complex narrative, for instance, and choose which storyline you want to follow, just as you might choose which strand of a thick novel you want to give the most attention to.

During the thirty-two years that Coppola has owned the rights to *On the Road*, three previous writers have tried and failed to adapt it for the screen. In launching his own attempt, Banks has avoided the conventional approach of radically altering the novel. Instead he has returned to Kerouac's text in a direct and receptive way, seeking to reproduce its jazz-like qualities through media-mixing techniques.

His remarks on this are thoughtful and perceptive enough to deserve quoting at length. "The only way I could imagine returning to the novel," he says, "was through compositional means [that would allow me to] simultaneously present different layers of time, and different layers of consciousness and perception. . . . It's not the big screen I'm thinking of, it's the small screen. I'm thinking one-to-one: Kerouac to me, me to the viewer. I'm also mixing textures—newsreel footage, eight-millimeter home movies, thirty-five-millimeter '50s film with bleached-out color, thirty-five-millimeter

1999–2000 film, flattened-out digital, snapshots, silent movies. . . . I'm inspired simultaneously by [Kerouac's] novel, which is in many ways a collage, and by the technology that permits me to do this. And also by an audience that I know will be sophisticated enough— visually, intellectually, and in literary terms—to respond to it. . . . The new technology has allowed me to imagine an audience of the future that doesn't see going to a film as the same as going to church, but rather as something done at home, privately, by one-self. The way one reads a book."

Banks calls himself an old-fashioned "dinosaur" of the print era, so his open-minded embrace of new media may be as prophetic as it is enthusiastic. But since one person's Exciting Possibility is another person's Looming Menace, it's not surprising that voices are being raised against the changes made imminent by new screenwriting and production techniques. Most commonly heard is a fear that the storyteller's special talents will be drowned in a swamp of mass-market ignorance, as sensation-hungry spectators use interactive gizmos to filter out challenging or unconventional material in favor of the same old audience-pleasing pap. Another frequently expressed dread is that the ever-increasing ease and economy of media pro-duction will unleash an unstoppable flood of unwatchable works by untalented hacks.

These views present a daunting vision of our media-saturated future. On one side: Hollywood wannabes cranking out so much low-grade trash that nobody has time or energy to cull the awful from the slightly less awful. On the other side: impatient audiences sabotaging sophisticated work with the fast-forward and happy-ending buttons on their interactivity clickers. Surely this is the dark side of democratic art!

If anything rescues us from such a fate, it may well be the art of screenwriting—not clinging stubbornly to its past or present forms, but continually reshaping itself to profit from new production technologies and changing audience expectations. Throughout its history, avant-garde screenwriting has shown ways of bringing word, image, and narrative into endlessly productive series of new and surprising configurations.

Many of these have proved too esoteric or obscure to infiltrate the mainstream. But others have made their presence felt in commercial works as different as, say, *2001: A Space Odyssey* (1968), with its sparse dialogue and psychedelic montage; *Easy Rider* (1969), with its intuitive story and free-floating visuals; and *Natural Born Killers* (1994), with its savage sociology and eye-assaulting camera work. In these and other films with a subversive edge, words and pictures lose their literary and painterly baggage, merging into sustained eruptions of quintessentially cinematic power. Screenwriters who use this energy to dynamize the coming panoply of technological innovations will be driving forces of tomorrow's moving-image scene.

Time Code is just another step down this unpredictable road, but its success in blending minimalist scripting with other experimental techniques—improvisatory acting, aleatory shooting, multi-image viewing—makes it a milestone work that auteurs will mine for ideas and inspiration in years to come. Ultimately, its greatest contribution may be the sense of creative freedom and sheer imaginative energy it unleashes in the receptive spectator.

"I'm very interested in getting pieces done quickly," Figgis told me, "with a specific high energy I feel is lacking in most films. What one often sees is very dead art, because you can smell how long and expensive the processes are—big, top-heavy processes that have conspired to rob the life from an idea. I'm trying to move toward a more *spontaneous* form of cinema. Every time I watch *Time Code*, even though I made it, I see many things I've never seen before."

Renaldo & Clara Meet John Cage

ALEATORY CINEMA AND THE AESTHETICS OF INCOMPETENCE

"I need a dump truck mama to unload my head."
—BOB DYLAN, "From a Buick 6"

The evolution of rock music has been marked by an intermittent but generally expanding interest in the display of traditional music competencies, such as instrumental virtuosity and disciplined vocal technique. In the world of rock'n'roll cinema, this is echoed by the formal disparities between deliberately scruffy 1950s movies—e.g., Will Price's teenpic *Rock, Rock, Rock* (1957) and, on a more sophisticated level, Frank Tashlin's parody *The Girl Can't Help It* (1956)—and such meticulously planned, highly polished '70s and '80s productions as Martin Scorsese's elegant *The Last Waltz* (1978) and Jonathan Demme's inventive *Stop Making Sense* (1984), both directed by established auteurs who approach their concert-hall material (performances by The Band and Talking Heads, respectively) with a measure of "art film" seriousness.

Youth cultures tend to mutiny against whatever status quo happens to prevail at the time, however, so it's not surprising that the '70s saw a spate of resistance toward the increasingly well-schooled and well-behaved rock that was thought by some to be draining the subcultural scene of whatever vitality it had once possessed. The emergence of punk rock in the '70s, via such innovative young performers as The Sex Pistols and The Ramones, has been viewed by many critics as that period's most salutary return to the carnivalism and grotesquerie of early rock'n'roll. Yet certain older performers who had risen to prominence during the '60s shared the desire to rebel against rock's growing investment in professionalism and decorum. Launching a cheerfully atavistic campaign to recapture the improvisatory energy and self-inventing spontaneity of rock's formative years—but hesitant to pursue this agenda in the rock arena itself, now steeped in values of conventional virtuosity that they themselves had helped to introduce—some of them turned to cinema as a means of developing and disseminating their more aesthetically subversive ideas.

Among the key films in the subgenre that resulted are *200 Motels*, co-written and co-directed by Frank Zappa in 1971, and *Renaldo & Clara*, written and directed by Bob Dylan in 1978. In keeping with standard rock-film practice, both contain large amounts of concert footage, much of which is effectively and excitingly filmed. On their other levels of meaning, however—as fictional narrative, *cinéma vérité* documentary, and pop-star portraiture—both are characterized by a remarkable degree of structural tenuousness and semiotic indeterminacy. While the latter qualities may seem like liabilities in many respects, they serve the positive function of allowing us to see both films as exemplars of rock's most healthily anarchic possibilities, with tendencies toward conventionally construed "correctness" and "proficiency" neatly deflected by the technical amateurishness of their cinematically untrained filmmakers. Considered in the larger context of contemporary music as a whole, moreover, these unabashedly meandering works constitute filmic equivalents of the aleatory compositions associated with John Cage and his high-modernist disciples—David Tudor, Charlotte Moorman, et al—as the filmmakers' deliberate refusal of traditional competence allows copious amounts of cinematic and performative excess to contaminate, variegate, and invigorate their texts.

The desire to foreground such apparent formlessness and uncontainability points to the roots of these artists (Dylan and Zappa on one hand, Cage and his school on the other) in an implicitly nonrational sensibility that may broadly be called romanticist. Partaking of what Friedrich Nietzsche termed the Dionysian spirit, this sensibility is grounded in ideals of individuality, immediacy, unpredictability, and freedom from sociocultural norms. It has been shared by many artists who see spontaneity and extemporaneity as idealized routes to the authentic expression of a unique soul, spirit, or inner self. I have argued elsewhere (Sterritt 2004) that while improvisation has played a significant role in artistic creation for centuries—it flourished in European music during the baroque and classical periods, for instance—it has achieved a particularly high reputation in the modernist era as a result of twentieth-century anxieties, or at least uncertainties, regarding the authenticity of artistic works and practices themselves. Cultural philosopher Walter Benjamin helps us understand the origins of these uncertainties when he uses the word "aura" to identify certain characteristics of the traditional art work, including its existential connection with a particular time and place, and the quasi-mystical "phenomenon of a distance" that such a work presents to the beholder no matter how physically close it may be (Benjamin, 221, 223). Contemporary mass audiences wish to bring things "closer" in both spatial and human terms, Benjamin maintains, adding that this desire to overcome traditional values of "distance" and "uniqueness" has an anti-auratic effect insofar as it lends indiscriminate legitimacy to copies and reproductions at the expense of the original works upon which they are modeled. This tendency facilitates the "decay" of art's traditionally auratic nature and fosters an ascription of "universal equality" to the objects of our perception. This in turn militates against the "essentially distant" and "unapproachable" nature of the "unique" auratic work, and thereby threatens the prestige of art itself.

One way to combat all this is to cultivate an improvisatory aesthetic that evades the norms of mass-produced art by placing a romanticized emphasis on notions of spontaneity, authenticity, and individuality as pathways to artistic originality and uniqueness. Cage did this by developing aleatory techniques that allow chance and indeterminacy to play key roles in shaping musical results. Some of Cage's methods involve elaborate uses of high technology (e.g., mixing sounds into dense electronic collages); others turn to what might be called low technology (e.g., transforming household objects, office furnishings, etc., into "musical instruments"); others call on extramusical procedures for generating random series that can be transposed into musical terms (e.g., casting dice according to protocols derived from the *I Ching*); still others subordinate the performers to their environment (e.g., the famous *4'33"*, wherein the silence of an unplayed piano throws into relief the ambient sounds in its vicinity). In all cases, the composer seeks to bypass his own structuring ego and allow a larger system or set of systems (the ubiquity of sound, the processes of hearing and seeing, forces of synchronicity or "karma," and so forth) to take the foreground. As a highly desirable byproduct, dominant artistic practices and market forces are evaded and obviated at the same time.

In their primary field of music, Zappa and Dylan worked to achieve results very different from these. Zappa considered himself a high-art composer in the avant-garde tradition of Edgard Varèse, composing jauntily melodic chamber and orchestral pieces when he wasn't busy leading The Mothers of Invention, his resourceful pop group. Dylan made an epochal contribution to the poeticization of rock's verbal component—nobody did more to bring rock lyrics from their "doo-wop" period to a new set of sophisticated options in the '60s and after—while cultivating a performance style attuned to idioms as diverse as the American folksong tradition and the Sprechgesang of the Second Vienna School.

In sum, these were serious, ambitious musicians who used rock's more "primitive" qualities as a point of departure for their own explorations of increasingly refined and complex artistic territory. As such, they had good reasons not to wax overly nostalgic over rock's earlier investment in deliberately simple kinds of musical and verbal play, even though a deep affection for early rock styles had clearly drawn them to pop-music formats in the first place. It therefore made excellent sense for them to seek out a neighboring cultural arena in which they could reengage with instinctive and improvisatory creative processes on a more radical basis than their middlebrow status allowed for in the music world. Their choice of cinema (as opposed to, say, painting or dance) also made sense, given the then-recent precedents set by such artists-turned-filmmakers as novelist Norman Mailer (e.g., *Wild 90* and *Beyond the Law*, both 1968) and John Lennon (various films, some made with Yoko Ono). All were attracted to film as an aesthetically malleable medium whose habitual adherence to Hollywood norms could readily be ignored by well-known culture heroes whose celebrity guaranteed access to financial and technical resources.

All of which helps to explain why the feature films of Zappa and Dylan stand out for their buoyant indifference to the sorts of discipline and competency that did concern these artists in the music field. Their movies are openly experimental and drastically heedless of contemporaneous standards regarding content, style, and coherence, as I noted when reviewing them at the time of their release. "Unusual cinematic and musical techniques were obviously brought to bear on this obviously unusual project," I wrote of *200 Motels*, the Zappa film (Sterritt 1971). "[It] is the first major feature-length movie to be shot entirely on video-tape (which was later transferred to film); both the fluidity and the versatility of the tape medium have left a definite mark on the final product. . . . Equally important is composer-arranger-scenarist Zappa's idea that all sounds and sights in the movie are part of its 'score,' no matter how gratuitous or careless—perhaps the word should be 'aleatory'—they happen to be. Cageian aesthetics via a rock'n'roll movie."

Co-directed by Zappa, who took charge of "characterizations," and Tony Palmer, who is credited with the "visuals" of the film, *200 Motels* was intended as an impressionistic portrait of a rock group on tour, evoking the "grueling hours, the seeming sameness of cities hurriedly visited, the banal plasticity of . . . motel rooms," to quote my 1971 description. Among the film's gratuitous and/or careless elements are long episodes of pointless horsing around by Mothers of Invention members (Mark Volman and Howard Kaylan, late of The Turtles, are among the most conspicuous) and equally long episodes of surrealistic-psychedelic showing off (rapid-fire montage, multiple superimpositions, and so on) introduced via editing and optical printing. Palmer's efforts can be seen as an attempt to impose a measure of cinematic order on Zappa's more drastically undisciplined antics; the images, as I wrote in 1971, are "spectacular and have been assembled with obvious care" so as to look "now like a color version of Stan Brakhage's *Desistfilm*, now like a nightmare parody of Hollywood musicals." It might be argued that the degree of cinematic control provided by Palmer cancels my claim that the film as a whole has an aleatory aesthetic, but Cage's own practice was based on a dialectic between indeterminacy (vis-à-vis pitch, sequence, duration, etc.) and rigorously structured means of producing that indeterminacy (throwing dice according to a carefully work-out protocol, choosing specific objects or instruments to produce specific sonic qualities, and so on). I don't suggest that the practices of Zappa and Palmer represent an exact parallel with Cage's techniques, but their blending of visual sophistication with flamboyantly extemporaneous material reflects a sensibility that I find quite close to some aspects of Cage's ideal.

If a dreamlike condensation is at the heart of *200 Motels*, a metonymic sprawl characterizes *Renaldo & Clara*, the Dylan epic made seven years later. Again the ostensible subject is a rock entourage on tour—the famous Rolling Thunder Revue this time—and again synopsis is difficult. "Dylan plays Renaldo, sort of," I wrote in 1978 (Sterritt 1978). "Ronnie Hawkins plays Bob Dylan. Sara

Dylan, Bob's ex-wife, plays Clara. Also on hand are Joan Baez (the Woman in White), Ronee Blakely (of *Nashville* fame, here playing Mrs. Dylan), the grand old singer Ramblin' Jack Elliott, poet Allen Ginsberg (who reads movingly from his great work *Kaddish*), and . . . Harry Dean Stanton, plus others too numerous to mention." Material in the film ranges from improvised dialogue scenes to *cinéma vérité* footage of the Rubin "Hurricane" Carter case, then in the news. As for the thematic center of all this, I wrote, "Dylan says it's about 'alienation of the inner self against the outer self . . . integrity . . . knowing yourself.' Indeed, the eerie shots of him singing through a transparent mask start the picture with questions about the 'identity' of the public personality and the private man. . . ." Dylan's predilection for long takes (and a long movie, clocking in at 232 minutes in the version originally released) reflects his statement that he and his collaborators "can cut fast when we want, but the power comes in the . . . faith that [a shot] is . . . meaningful" and should therefore be allowed to continue at length. My review also quotes Dylan's statement to *Rolling Stone* that about a third of the movie "is improvised, about a third is determined, and about a third is blind luck."

By and large, the portions that appear to be "determined" display little more conventional filmmaking competence than the episodes that flaunt an affinity with randomness and unalloyed spontaneity. As a whole, however, the deliberately shapeless mass of *Renaldo & Clara* spills over with what I called at the time "a dreamish logic and a generous, playful spirit" that lend an inspired and occasionally transcendent lilt to the film's surrealistic juxtapositions and polymorphous longueurs. Its length, ambition, and diversity place it at an opposite pole from the folk songs and '50s rock'n'roll numbers that Dylan's early career was grounded in; but as with Zappa's film, the very gap separating the artistic aspirations of its text from the cinematic proficiencies of its maker lend it an extra level of indeterminacy that places it into the same aesthetic arena explored by Cage and his colleagues from a different set of starting points and perspectives. The incoherence of *200 Motels* and *Renaldo & Clara* makes them intransigent texts that seekers of conventional cinematic pleasure have mostly avoided. But the chasm that yawns between these movies and the average moviegoer can be seen as an idiosyncratic reappearance of the "unique distance" that Benjamin found missing in mechanically reproduced culture at large. If cultists were the natural allies of traditionally auratic works, fans of cult movies may be among their heirs in our own time.

WORKS CITED

Benjamin, Walter. 1985. "The Work of Art in the Age of Mechanical Reproduction," in *Illuminations*, trans. Harry Zohn. New York: Schocken Books.

Sterritt, David. 1971. ". . . And Zappa's Surreal Look at Rock'n'Touring." *The Christian Science Monitor* (December 1, 1971), 16.

Sterritt, David. 1978. "Dylan's First Film—Unconventional: Fascinating Mosaic of Real Life, Fantasy and Music Demands Effort from Viewer." *The Christian Science Monitor* (26 January 1978), 19.

Sterritt, David. 2004. *Screening the Beats: Media Culture and the Beat Sensibility.* Carbondale: Southern Illinois University Press. Essay originally published as "Revision, Prevision, and the Aura of Improvisatory Art," in *The Journal of Aesthetics and Art Criticism* 58:2 (Spring 2000).

Challenging the Eye

THREE AVANT-GARDE IMAGEMAKERS

There is a very long list of avant-garde filmmakers I have happily (and in occasional cases not so happily) written about over the years. I'm also a longtime teacher of the history and theory of avant-garde cinema, most frequently in the School of the Arts at Columbia University, and student responses have given me a pretty good idea of what experimental films and filmmakers retain their bite and surprise for new generations of viewers. Ken Jacobs continues to amaze and amuse via classics like *Little Stabs at Happiness* and *Blonde Cobra*, both of which benefit from the great Jack Smith's manic acting as well as Jacobs's own antic stylistics. Stan Brakhage continues to challenge and flummox via everything from the epic *Dog Star Man* to the exquisite *Garden of Earthly Delights* to the sculptural . . . (*ellipsis*) series, although he's a lot harder to teach, for all sorts of reasons that will be obvious to anyone who's seen his work. I would use Robert Wilson as a classroom mainstay if his work were easier to get hold of, but while he's still a stage director first and foremost, I'm convinced that his best video work stands with some of the finest moving-image artistry of our time.

If space allowed, I'd love to include essays on the hugely talented contingent of younger film avant-gardists such as Lewis Klahr and his gifted wife Janie Geiser, and on video purists like Bill Viola and Gary Hill and Sadie Benning, and on more of the giants who paved the way for them, from Maya Deren and Kenneth Anger to Ed Emshwiller and George Kuchar and Bruce Conner . . . the list goes on and on. The essays that follow amount to a mere synecdoche, these three parts standing for a much grander whole that's as hard to pin down as a label for the enterprise itself. Avant-garde? A terrible term, meaning "advance guard," as if Steven Spielberg could ever see himself as lagging behind and needing to "catch up" with, say, R. Bruce Elder or the Quay brothers. Experimental? Just as bad, implying that such filmmakers don't have eloquently defined aesthetic philosophies but just fiddle around with their materials to find out what might happen. Underground filmmaking? Poetic filmmaking? The new cinema? It's hard to figure out what such phrases are meant to mean at all, even though they've been used by many a polemicist, sometimes with very different definitions in mind. (Manny Farber's conception of the "underground" diverges hugely from Jonas Mekas's, for instance.)

I'm using "avant-garde" here because it seems to be the term that gives the least amount of annoyance to the greatest number of practitioners. But call it what you will, and if you haven't experimented with viewing some of it yourself, bear in mind that literal armies of young visual artists are turning to nonnarrative expression through the moving image—when I started as a New York Film Festival programmer in 1988 we were proud to institute an annual evening of "Avant-Garde Visions," and these days there's an entire weekend every year—and that independent-minded screening venues, coupled with ever-improving DVD technology, is making their work ever more accessible for study and pleasure.

KEN JACOBS

Staying with the matter of terminology for just a moment longer, the word "experimental" is often tossed about in film circles as a synonym for or "unorthodox," meaning the work in question is somehow out of the mainstream. This obscures the fact that some filmmakers really are experimental in their outlook—not in the fiddling-around way, but in the way of continually tinkering with the fundamental meanings, methods, and even raw material of cinema. Ken Jacobs is one of these not-so-mad scientists. He regards challenging the mainstream as one of his primary purposes, as a writer, university teacher, and fiercely independent filmmaker.

What does a Jacobs film look like? It's hard to characterize his work, except to say that he rarely deals in storytelling. He believes in films that open up the world for their audience, instead of closing it off by wrapping plots and characters in tidy, carefully mapped-out packages. Instead of "actors acting" he likes to fill his movies with friends and family members "caught between who they are and their fantasy aspirations." Beyond this, his movies and occasional videos are extremely varied. They range from four minutes to about six hours in length, and make use of pre-existing "found footage" as well as material shot by Jacobs himself. He has also probed extensively into 3-D cinema, most notably by means of his self-invented Nervous System, which projects two film strips onto a single screen space one frame at a time while a sort of propeller spins between the projector lamps, blocking them alternately at very high speeds. His other 3-D devices include a method whereby one views a flat image with a piece of darkened celluloid covering one eye, and one that requires you to view side-by-side images with your eyes crossed. The first of these works very well, the second even better.

Visiting him in his lower Manhattan loft, one enters a crowded workspace overflowing with books, records, artifacts, and equipment. Yet it clearly makes a warm and comfortable home for him, his wife and helpmate Flo Jacobs, and in earlier times their two children, as well as a combination studio, library, and laboratory. Almost anything can happen there, as I was reminded when I ran into him on the street (we live fairly near each other) and he started enthusing about "3-D poems," whatever those might be. Later that day my fax machine coughed up a few pages of exactly those, dispatched by

Ken posthaste. Look at the identical side-by-side stanzas with your eyes crossed to just the right degree, and sure enough, they pop out at you as three-dimensionally as can be.

"I definitely am inquiring," Jacobs said when I asked him once about the energy behind his work. "I'm interested in a number of fronts. Some of them have to do with history, and an understanding of how [people] work. . . . I've invested in kids, and I want them to live. I've invested my feelings in the world, and I want it to continue." His other interests include "time and movement," and the discoveries that can be made by examining "strange caricatures of the past" in old movies. He calls these "eternalisms," and he can ferret them out of all sorts of footage, sometimes by rephotographing it, as in his 1969 classic *Tom, Tom, the Piper's Son*, and sometimes by simply presenting it the way he found it, as in *Urban Peasants*, an unaltered collation of home movies, and *Perfect Film*, a reel he literally discovered in a trash bin. He's fascinated by the possibility of finding truth and beauty in outmoded film images— or if not truth and beauty, at least "some kind of genuine commotion going on, something happening." In other words, this is not a stony-faced quest for solemn verities. "I'm amused by this," Jacobs says. "Everything tickles me. I get a big kick out of it."

Early influences on Jacobs included such great movies as *City Lights*, by Charles Chaplin, and *The Bicycle Thief*, by Vittorio De Sica, as well as Herman Melville and Miguel de Cervantes novels. When still a teenager he was also deeply impressed by an "art photograph" he saw in *Life* magazine, showing people whimsically draped in sheets but with ordinary trouser legs, shoes, and socks visible down below. Jacobs was fascinated by this "contradiction between fantasy and reality," and by what it suggested about "where the mind can go while the body remains." His life was never the same after this vision of what it might be like "to be [living] in the seedy reality of the '40s and '50s, and yet to have a head full of dreams." Jacobs decided to express his ideas in an ambitious movie, but soon realized that Hollywood wasn't about to knock on his door. So he filmed a more modest project called *Star Spangled to Death*, starring actor/filmmaker Jack Smith and shot "for pennies, with leftover [film] scraps." The result became an "experimental" classic that is still revived and admired—and surfaced in 2004 in a radically revised six-hour video version that will probably stand as its definitive edition.

Although he once hoped for a large mainstream audience, Jacobs decided as early as the late 1950s that he had been "dreaming and idealizing 'the People' in a kind of '30s left-wing way," as he later put it, and that mass audiences would probably not take an interest in his offbeat sensibility. Resigning himself to the fact that such spectators will always prefer Hollywood-type films, he followed his own nonconforming path—reaching a small number of viewers, but putting a special value on them since they share his disdain for mass-produced "art" that cares more about packaging than content. Jacobs feels mass-marketed films do a lot of harm to people who mindlessly and continuously feed on them, since such films cancel out the ideals and dreams their audience might otherwise have. "It could well be that romance is in people until it's beaten out of them . . . or bored out of them," he says. He feels that the roots of today's mass–audience culture are in the 1950s, a time when "you were supposed to adjust and conform to 'reality' . . . and you were 'sick' and 'out of it' unless you acknowledged and adapted to this." Jacobs warns that "the coercive pressure to 'adapt to reality' means to give up and fall in line. Maturity is defined as acquiescence. . . . It's the same value orientation as the . . . yuppies have."

To counter this mentality, Jacobs asks his audience to participate in the creative process—by thinking actively about what's on-screen, instead of letting it simply wash over them. "This is keeping the mind alive," he says. "Otherwise we just have habits; we're mechanistic." Using cinema to its fullest potential, according to Jacobs, means concentrating on the act of discovery rather than churning out polished productions. Asked to define the aesthetic "gold" he's digging for in his work, he answers, "Pleasure. Amusement. Pain. Realization. . . . To see where [my mind] will take me, and where this technology will take me. . . . And to exercise this power in a way that doesn't mean enslavement or subjugation to others."

STAN BRAKHAGE

For the sadly limited number of viewers who took the time and trouble to appreciate his work, the late filmmaker Stan Brakhage wasn't just an artist, he was a force of nature. Writing, teaching, lecturing, corresponding—and generating a staggering number of films—he strode across the cinema scene like a colossus, from his directorial debut with *Interim* in 1952 until his death from cancer in 2003 at the age of seventy-two. Through it all, his message was the same: that film is an art, with a much higher purpose than conveying the flashy entertainments and "illustrated stories" of Hollywood.

This was obviously a controversial idea. Most viewers like their movies neat and easy, decked out with familiar faces and comfortable ideas. Brakhage took the opposite tack. For him, a work of art began not with a plan or an outline, but with a "quirk" of the mind or heart. If you can manage to capture a trace or record of that quirk, he felt, other people can relate to it, and the human community will be just a little bit closer.

That's why Brakhage films tend to be deeply personal—or Romantic, as he usually put it—expressions, based on his own experiences and visions. Yet his "quirks" were rarely as simple as that whimsical word makes them sound. Translating them to celluloid, Brakhage brought enormous emotional, intellectual, and even scholarly weight into the balance. During one of numerous appearances at the Museum of Modern Art in New York, he was introduced as "the Picasso of cinema"—an overblown description, but not entirely off the mark.

Brakhage had failings, to be sure. I knew him for more than a quarter of a century and admired him greatly, yet I always wished he would use sound more often—most of his films are silent, and wasn't ungifted in the sound-track department—and I felt he acted too radically on his deep-down suspicion of lingering images. Quick rhythms are at the heart of his work: rhythms of shape, color, light, and dark, even the grain of the photographic stock. As great as most of his films are, I feel they would be vastly more accessible if they weren't so relentlessly dense, and so fearful of pictorial values that might distract viewers from editing, textural, and other values of the work as a whole. I think Brakhage underestimated the fact that alluring images can be gateways rather than impediments to broader understanding of complex works of art.

Some observers had (and have) deeper objections to Brakhage, to be sure. One mainstream critic chided him for not telling stories or developing characters. A feminist critic castigated him for making intimate works that didn't jibe with her politics. Even supporters of Brakhage have acknowledged the many attacks against him by leftist critics who faulted him for using the intricacies of the nuclear family as his most basic and enduring theme.

For viewers like me, though, this was part of Brakhage's charm. Unlike many radical artists, he generally avoided big cities, living for years in the Colorado mountains with his wife Jane and five children, all of whom were frequent "actors" in his films. Jane later (and understandably) divorced her mercurial mate, whereupon he moved to Boulder—a big city by his standards—and admitted in Jim Shedden's biographical film about him that he'd never really liked the country all that much. (Too many ticks, for one thing.) He promptly remarried and had additional children, though. The concepts of marriage, family, and domesticity were as central to his work and thought as his extreme aesthetic ideas. "They call me an underground filmmaker," he said to one audience, "but I'm more of a living room man."

When he left that living room and surfaced to unveil and discuss a new batch of films, Brakhage reminded the world what a prodigiously prolific worker he was. During one New York visit in 1981, when I dropped everything else to dog his trail, he made six public appearances in about a week, providing a good overview of that central phase in his career and leading a stimulating chase through New York's major showplaces for independent cinema.

The first two evenings took place at the Collective for Living Cinema, which closed its doors a few years later, in lower Manhattan's then-bleak Tribeca neighborhood. Here, before a large crowd of fans, Bakhage presided over the first complete screening of his enormously ambitious *Sincerity & Duplicity* series—a four-hour "autobiography" compiled from old footage that had been gathering dust in his workroom.

Brakhage didn't think much of written autobiography: Most of it is "lies," he felt. In telling his own story through film, he wondered if images could be more truthful than words, cutting through the usual poses and getting at the essence of life. Along the way, he decided it wasn't working as he'd hoped –after all, he reasoned, "sincerity" is a sort of pose, too—so in the spirit of honesty he added "Duplicity" to the original one-word title. The work itself continued, emerging as a massive act of self-examination, single-mindedly avoiding the pretty, clever shots most of us strive for when we film ourselves and our families. "It's what home movies could be if they were stripped of sentimentality," Brakhage said—a worthy goal, artfully realized.

Next stop was the Museum of Modern Art, for *The Roman Numeral Series*. In his classic book *Metaphors on Vision*, published in 1963, Brakhage had wondered how many colors might appear in a "green" field to a baby who hasn't yet learned the socially constructed concept of what "green" is supposed to be. The nine films in the *Roman Numeral* series push this line of exploration to new extremes, trying to catch visual essences devoid of all preconceptions, prejudices, and acquired ideas. It's a search for the "original vision" or *ur*-perception we are born with, and can still recapture if we keep "looking" when we close our eyes or go to sleep.

Briefly described, the films are exercises in pure color, motion, and shape. Many would call them "abstract" or "nonrepresentational," although Brakhage didn't tolerate those words, which pin his "quirks" into neat art-historical cubbyholes. He was nothing if not a rebel. In some cases, he proudly revealed, he couldn't even remember what he had photographed to achieve these rarified poems in unadulterated light.

The next morning, Brakhage gave a benefit for Anthology Film Archives, a venerable institution that was raising money to establish a major film museum—now long completed and surviving, by hook or by crook, under Jonas Mekas's idiosyncratic administration at the corner of Second Avenue and Second Street in the East Village district. Here he unveiled his magnificent *Song 23 (23rd Psalm Branch)* in a new sixteen-millimeter version that gives more "monumentality" to what also exists as an eight-millimeter work in Brakhage's multipart "Songs" series. A hugely complex "war film," it's intended to put that alarming subject right under our noses for our thoughtful consideration and (Brakhage hopes) total rejection. It's also a textbook example of Brakhage's methods, with its quick rhythms, sharp images, and fierce visual density.

This particular 1981 visit ended with two evenings at the Millenium Film Workshop in Greenwich Village, where Brakhage screened a selection of movies that are rarely shown even by the libraries, schools, and museums that collect and disseminate his work. More important, he introduced still more new films: entries in the *Arabic Numeral Series*, which continue his exploration into the essence of sight; a couple of less memorable efforts; and a pair of apparent masterpieces called *Aftermath* and *Murder Psalm*.

Here was the distillation of Brakhage's art. Discussing the bold *Aftermath*, he repeated his frequent admission to being an "image freak" with a weakness for watching television, not to mention the commercial movies he so often berated in his polemical speeches and writings. *Aftermath* is a frontal repulsion-attraction attack on insidiously seductive TV pictures that reached out and "clutched" even him, an artist who mercilessly stripped his own work of all that's easy and soothing and false.

The resulting film is only secondarily an attack on TV, though. First and foremost, it's a triumph of color and rhythms on Brakhage's own terms. As for *Murder Psalm*, it represents the filmmaker's search for material "that would have interested Dostoevsky," as he put it. It is a harrowing excursion into the untamed places of what is preeminently a gentle and civilized mind, expressed largely through stock footage—even animated cartoons—that have an ominous new meaning here.

I hope this account of a single string of Brakhage events is enough to give some idea of what encounters with his artistry and public personality were often like. Brakhage was one of a kind, a singular talent who continues to inspire new generations of independent movie-lovers.

ROBERT WILSON

"They have a mysterious logic to them," says director-designer-playwright-videomaker Robert Wilson, speaking of the grand but elusive productions that have made him a leading figure in the world of modernist/postmodernist aesthetics. Some observers fault his offerings as having too much mystery and too little meaning. Others applaud his style, finding both beauty and wit in the plotless, immaculately composed, gradually shifting pictures that make up his "theater of images," as some critics have dubbed it. Other artists, from director Elizabeth LeCompte to choreographer Lucinda Childs, have also drawn from his ideas in the course of evolving their distinctive approaches. Although he's best known as a director of plays, operas, and theater pieces, Wilson has also made a solid mark as a designer and director of videos, such as the surrealistically brilliant *Deafman Glance* and the deftly dreamlike *Stations*, among others. As a director he likes video because, he once told me, "you see what you're getting"—a standpoint harder to achieve in stage work, where every performance is bound to be different from every other, and where the director can occupy only one point in a space at a time while preparing the precise look of the work, while audience members occupy many different spaces and don't share the single perspective provided by an image on a screen.

After years of working mostly in Europe, where his productions were more readily welcomed than in the United States, he was able to start producing more and more pieces in his own country starting in the early to middle 1980s—even though this native of Waco, Texas, has at times sharply attacked what he sees as American resistance to new artistic experiences. Especially his. Deliberately, the pace of a typical Wilson work is glacial. Deliberately, the dialogue is often a series of non sequiturs with no clear relation to the visual action. Deliberately, the show has no conscious "meaning," and no purpose but to generate a flow of dreamlike images. With different particulars, this description of Wilson's characteristic stage productions would suit his videos as well. Sometimes different media overlap in his work, as in the video *Deafman Glance*, with is based on the prelude to Act 4 of his eight-hour theatrical work, *Deafman Glance*, sometimes presented as a stage piece on its own, running anywhere from about thirty to about one hundred minutes. The action—involving a black woman, a white child, a glass of milk, and a stabbing with a large knife—takes place in ultraslow motion, except for a single instant of ultrafast gesture. It is equally indelible on stage and screen.

Long fascinated with the odd resonances of Wilson's work, I've interviewed and conversed with him many times, and a recurring question has been why he's so attracted to a "mysterious" brand of logic, or rather, illogic. "I think mystery . . . allows us time to dream," the lanky director replied on one such occasion, peering dreamily through his horn-rimmed spectacles. "It allows for the knowledge within us to come forth. Socrates said we were born with knowledge within us—it's just the *uncovering* of the knowledge

[that] we need. It's through the mysteries we do this. That's why I don't like [realistic] theater. It kills the mysteries for me.

Wilson's disdain for "normal" theater is legendary. "In a Broadway theater," he says in a biting tone, "they almost always tell you at the end what it's about. I haven't seen that many Broadway shows, but I did see *Death of a Salesman,* and at the end [actress] Kate Reid was very upset when Willy Loman died. I felt like saying, 'Relax, lady! We knew it was gonna happen! When I bought my ticket, it said: *Death of a Salesman!'* It's all tied up in a little box with a string on it."

Wilson prefers an experience that's harder to pin down. But this doesn't mean he cuts himself off from tradition. Just the opposite: He has worked with many classic texts, such as *Medea* and *King Lear,* respecting their "richness" while bringing his own touch to them. Nor does Wilson indulge his visual ideas willy-nilly. He molds them rigorously—consciously shaping every detail of every image, down to the smallest nuance of light and shadow. In doing so, he tames the "mysteries" he loves without losing their haunted moods and haunting atmospheres. He likens the rules and structures of his work to the banks of a river, channeling and containing what might otherwise be chaotic and out of control. "They are the boundaries," he says. "And inside them you have a flow." In dealing with actors, Wilson asks them to "leave your ideas in a little black box at the side of the stage . . . so . . . you're like the audience, you're a reflection of them. We don't tell them what to think. We invite them to get an exchange of ideas. We don't say, 'This is it.' Instead we say, 'What is it?' And people will have many different interpretations." As for critics, Wilson wishes they would have the same "open-ended" attitude he has, instead of searching for meaning all the time. "If a critic says, 'This is what it is,' then there's no reason for people to go see it," he complains. "That narrows and limits the experience of the audience. Only philosophers—over a period of time—can say, 'OK, this is this and that's that.'

"That's why I usually work [on a piece] over a long period of time . . . so there's time to live with it," Wilson adds. "That's the only way I know whether I like it or I think it works." He admits that even he must "stay on guard" against imposing narrow, limited interpretations on his essentially mysterious texts and images. But it's worth the effort, in his view. "I'm not a philosopher," he says, "or an intellectual. I'm an artist. Most artists don't understand what they do, and I don't think we have to. Other people do that better. They understand what I do better than I do."

Many Selves

PARADOX AND POETRY IN THE CINEMA OF WILLIE VARELA

"I live, therefore I appropriate."

Willie Varela appends that whimsical variation on the Cartesian *cogito* to the end of his 2000 film *Real Mental Furniture*, and like many aspects of his extraordinary oeuvre, it's at once deceptively modest in tone and highly suggestive of key factors underlying his aesthetic sensibility. A close look at those five straightforward words is a useful way of approaching Varela's importance as an artist who simultaneously *sees and comprehends* the worldly realities around him; *captures and interprets* these through expressive cinematic techniques; and above all *transforms* them by reconfiguring the ways we perceive them in our everyday lives.

Transformation of the familiar is the heart and soul of Varela's unique vision, and this fascination with metamorphosis and transmutation is what lends his work much of its drama and distinctiveness. This is partly because of the excitement generated by the sheer dynamism of his visual style. More importantly, it is because his underlying intellectual rigor—along with aspects of his personal background, including his status as a Chicano artist who stands both inside and on the margins of mainstream American discourse—prevents him from seeing the world in either/or terms. He does not transmute "this" into "that" in the manner of avant-garde artists who base their art on metaphoric sleight-of-hand or eye-catching visual poetry. Rather, he sees the brute existence of material reality and the privileged insights of aesthetic intuition as equally true, equally significant, and ultimately inextricable from one another. He is an artist of ambivalence and ambiguity in the very best sense, savoring the paradoxical interplay of the physical and the metaphysical without feeling any obligation to resolve their indeterminacies through artifices of artistic structure or narrative design. The world as he sees it, interprets it, conceptualizes it, and fantasizes it is one great edifice of imaginative thought, conveyed through cinema with its beauties, terrors, mysteries, and enigmas exhilaratingly intact. To encounter this world is a pleasure, a puzzlement, and an adventure.

The verb "appropriate" provides the central irony in Varela's semi-playful credo. All cinema is appropriation, in a sense, since all cinema (except animations, *sui generis* works like Stan Brakhage's hand-painted films, and computer graphics, all of which are special cases) entails confronting and recording waves of light and sound that flow to us from objects in the world. Varela is referring to a particular kind of appropriation vis-à-vis *Real Mental Furniture*, of course, whereby images from preexisting films and videos are recycled in terms of his own voice and vision. These images take on so many new meanings from their new contexts, however, that the viewer's impression is one of a wholly new expression arising out of materials in which only an inspired artist could have seen such transcendent possibilities.

For an example, consider such image-clusters in *Real Mental Furniture* as the close juxtapositions of advertising material, news footage from the John F. Kennedy assassination, hard-core pornography, and a scene from Jean-Luc Godard's great 1962 film *Vivre sa vie*, itself a masterpiece of appropriation that combines shots from Carl Dreyer's silent classic *The Passion of Joan of Arc* with fictional shots made by Godard in an improvisational style he called *théatre-vérité*. It would take a full-length essay on *Real Mental Furniture* alone to interpret the multiple meanings of (a) each image Varela brings to us; (b) the manner in which he mixes and matches them for maximum cinematic effectiveness; and (c) the ways in which their denotations and connotations affect and inflect one another within individual segments of the film and over the course of its overall development. To choose just one way of regarding these clusters, however, they can be seen as a multilayered meditation on the monstrous in contemporary life—using "monstrous" in its commonplace sense of "horrible" and "unnatural," as embodied by the film's images of chaotic violence and loveless sex; and also in its Latin root sense of *monere*, to "admonish" or "warn" in the manner of a divine portent or manifestation, as embodied by the film's demonstration of how incorrigibly we humans allow suffering, sorrow, and callousness to persist in our allegedly civilized world.

Characteristically for Varela, the film makes its case not through a photojournalistic argument (flaunting unpleasant images with a didactic edge) but through a phenomenological argument, suggesting that the sensory impressions we generate and gather in the course of our quotidian lives—the day-to-day "furniture" that shapes our conceptions of reality, much of it derived from the media discourse that continually bombards us—are neither "real" on the one hand nor "mental" on the other, but are wholly both at the same time. In the film's content and even its title, we find a prime example of Varela's insistence on replacing our common "either/or" views with a "both/and" mentality that is far more productive and profound. He may "appropriate" as naturally and easily as he breathes, but the results are far too original and creative for that term to encompass them.

To identify Varela as a "both/and" thinker is not to label him a standard-issue dualist or dialectician, however. His complex and mercurial worldview is better characterized as "dialogic," to borrow literary theorist Mikhail Bakhtin's useful term for an artistic or philosophical approach rooted in an awareness and appreciation of the multitudinous, ultimately ungraspable nature of human experience. Bakhtin was as fascinated as Varela by the importance of interplay and interaction in artistic expression; this stands at the core of his writing on dialogism, and it also underpins his theory of the carnivalesque, which celebrates the expansiveness and uncontainability found in liberating forms of art. Like his Russian predecessor, Varela is a poet of liminality, steadily drawn to the borders, boundaries, and margins of human experience in a continual quest for meanings that evade the confines of unified definitions and explanations.

Many of Varela's works would serve as illustrations of this, and one of the best is the Super-eight feature *Making Is Choosing*, made between 1985 and 1989. Indeed, it calls attention to the dialogue between "creation" and "appropriation" in (once again) its very title. And then there's the subtitle, or rather the subtitles, wherein Varela reconfirms his refusal to see existential, psychological, and aesthetic issues in linear or schematic terms. "A Fragmented Life," reads one. "A Broken Line," says another. "A Series of Observations," announces the third. Following this lead, the film as a whole is divided into two parts, and each of them is divided into many separate sections, each with its own identifying sub-subtitle. To chart its development is to encounter Varela's bold brand of "both/and" artistry in a stimulating variety of forms. Hence, a survey of this film's segments (each identified by its introductory title) provides a helpful paradigm for much of his oeuvre as a whole.

"He Forgot to Duck." The film begins with news footage of then-president Ronald Reagan and his wife at an official function, at one point listening with (ostensibly) rapt attention to the recitation of a prayer. We then see Reagan taking his oath of office—a moment of solemnity slyly undermined by Varela's intermittent removal of film frames, giving the shots a hectic and incomplete look—and later we see the too-frequent results of uncritical American patriotism, in the form of guns, warfare, and combat footage. Varela is setting the scene for a film of personal reflection, not social or political commentary; but he needs to locate his introspection within its sociopolitical context, since he is acutely aware of his environment on all of its many levels. A final indication of his attitude toward Reagan arrives when we see the President speaking but hear the voice of a media commentator on the sound track. This suggests that even a popular Chief Executive is less significant as an individual figure than as a cog in the all-embracing machinery of mass-media manipulation and cajolery. Add all of this up and it's clear that Varela's dialogic sensibility is already in full sway during the opening moments of the film. "Politics" and "religion" have been established not as separate categories but as twin faces of a sociological coin; and the concepts of "outer/public" life (as in the ceremonies we've seen) and "inner/private" life (as in the personal perspective from which Varela is obviously addressing us) have been posited as intimately intertwined with each other.

"Thursday Night." We get our first glimpses of a dancing disc of light that will be a leitmotif of the film, recalling (among other works) the lovely "Moondance" shorts that Varela made in 1976. We also see fragmented, initially unreadable footage that resolves into TV imagery of sports-related violence, complete with extreme closeups of a man's battered face. This material adds an additional dialogue that will pervade the movie—between film and video as material substances (visible to the eye even when indecipherable by the mind) and, alternatively, as texts charged with coherent meaning. Note also how the initially inscrutable imagery does a violence to the spectator's comprehension that parallels the violence we eventually (and perhaps reluctantly) make out within that imagery. Again we find Varela exploring a liminal zone, this one between film/video as communication and film/video as sheer noise.

"Joe Gibbons." The eponymous Super-eight artiste delivers a wry (and fictional) monologue into Varela's camera, speaking about his awful childhood in Prussia, his vision of the United States as a land of happiness, and other unlikely stuff. On one level this is an amusing extension of other Varela films providing camera-eye encounters with fellow filmmakers such as James Broughton and George Kuchar, also shot in the mid-1980s. On a deeper level, however, it further invigorates this movie's increasingly complex network of paradoxes and oppositions, here focused on contradictions not only between happiness and unhappiness but also between appropriation (is Varela just co-opting Gibbon's readymade persona?) and creation; between the filmmaker as artist and the filmmaker as performer (since both filmmakers are clearly operating in both modes throughout this segment); and between the competing claims of performance and reality in their many, ever-shifting forms.

"The Untold Story." The camera (held by Varela, who is occasionally visible within the frame) wanders through an apartment until it settles on a pregnant woman (Varela's wife at the time) who speaks of her pregnancy as an experience of being "two people" at once. The camera stays on her, but we remain aware of Varela behind it. The birth and growth of Varela's daughter will be a primary focus of this film, so this is a key scene in its quasi-narrative development. In formal terms, however, we see the film's dialogic structure growing in more directions, now taking on the multiple resonances of pregnancy and birth, a pair of liminal experiences if ever there were any; parenthood and childhood; the notion of "two people" in one corporeal body; and the intricate interplay of sexuality as eroticism and sexuality as reproductive mechanism, poetically evoked at the beginning of this segment by the subtle disparity between the camera's sensuous wanderings and the state of conspicuous pregnancy upon which it comes to rest.

"Sunday Afternoon." Varela's daughter is born, and we see her first moments of life. Then we visit at home with her mother, her grandmother, and her father, who speaks from behind the camera. Again the lines separating observer, participant, artist, and performer are problematized and blurred.

"White Light, White Heat." We see white clay-like sculptures of bodies lying dead or standing behind barbed wire. We also see real flowers from time to time, contrasting vividly with the dominant images in terms of color and aliveness. Ambivalence abounds in the visual and subtextual relationships between the sculptures and the living bodies they represent; the stasis of the sculptures and the dynamism of Varela's interruptive montage and vigorous camera movement; and larger issues of presentation and representation, art and actuality, life and death.

"At Home." Views of the new baby include shots of her eyes in closeup, intercut with TV imagery, among which is footage of the perenially weird evangelist Rev. Eugene Scott asking his teleflock for money; bits from cheesy entertainment shows; and other images recorded at such close range that they're almost abstract. Varela's attention shifts here between a baby's eye and the TV tube that assails it; between the aggressive push of the mass media and the hand-made movie he himself is crafting; between the visible as art and the visible as noise; and perhaps most poignantly, between the formation of a new human personality and the banality of so much of the input that will inevitably be part of that formation-process in our media-drenched age.

"FDIC Insured." We see people in a cityscape, but emphasis is placed on the cityscape itself. A shot of a man's suit in a display window tellingly cuts to a sign reading "industrial." The freedom of Varela's camera here confronts many of the things that control us in our everyday lives—machines, traffic signals, advertising, architecture.

"Creative Thinking." TV static resolves into washed-out images of surf filmed off the TV set. The camera then wanders to the baby, her face beaming as her mother dresses her. The mood changes abruptly when the TV tube fills with an old movie whose content can be guessed at from portentous dialogue about "the raising of the dead," and from imagery of a man screaming as a coffin lid is lowered over his body, followed by "The End" as the awful-looking film mercifully ends—whereupon Varela zooms to his daughter's alert, attentive face. The segment concludes with more romantic and/or violent movie footage (some of it by Godard, a strong Varela influence) and then a return to the TV surf, accompanied by the voice of a "relaxation therapy"-type guru. Nature and media clash boisterously here, and Varela's critique of TV culture is impossible to miss.

"Colma CA." Images: Stained-glass church windows; a cemetery with photograph-decorated headstones; intermittent closeups of real flowers amid the headstones, and glass flowers within the window designs. Dialogues: Stone/flowers/sky; death/life; the ineluctable pull of materiality/the haunting possibility of transcendence.

"On the Road to Nowhere." The film's first portion ends with a brilliant lesson in how cinema mediates and interprets everything it is made to encounter, via (a) views of a city refracted through rippled glass and (b) views of the sea refracted through the quick montage and vital camera movements of Varela's visual style.

"October." The film's second portion begins with the dancing disc of light and the baby in a swing. The cosmic and the quotidian are as inseparable here as anywhere in Varela's work.

"The New Year." An expressionistic sensibility inflects views of a house, the great outdoors that surrounds it, and the TV imagery that pervades it.

"Seven." Prism-like nature shots give way to fragmented TV footage of Reagan and others at a memorial service for "seven brave Americans," where calls for solemnity are spontaneously undermined by the social, religious, and political/patriotic hypocrisy that Varela expertly exposes once again.

"February." A flame flickers in darkness; nature and TV footage vie for attention; sheets sway on a clothesline like the window curtains in *The Wind Variations*, the classic avant-garde film by Andrew Noren; and the camera peers curiously at what appears to be an artificial skeleton made of metal parts. This is a dance of the genuine and the artificial, the beautiful and the banal, the animate and the inanimate.

"In the Spring." We see the natural world, translated and punctuated by Varela's wild cuts and hectic camera movements. More important, we delve deeper into the spiritual dimension that tacitly underlies much of Varela's work; here he touches obliquely on the often-contentious dialogue between true mysticism and mere magical thinking, as the baby's ears take in the absurd narration of

Grave Robbers From Outer Space while we watch a snake and a skull in a cage.

"Hooray for Hollywood." We view a reprise of the film's religious iconography, stained-glass windows, cemetery statues, stones, and flowers. We also visit an elderly Hispanic woman as she tells a Hollywood-studio anecdote in what appears to be a cemetery vault. Hooray for Hollywood?

"Los Angeles." Does cinema free our thoughts and visions, or does it confine them within the limits of the camera and screen, not to mention the imperatives of mass-audience entertainment to which so many filmmakers sell their souls? Ambiguous answers to this conundrum are suggested by shots of a bird in a cage and aquatic mammals in amusement-park pools.

"Jake the Snake." He's still in his cage with the skull, but now we know his name and we see his handlers. We also see the baby in her bath, watching a TV screen within which the Muppets are confined like Jake behind his walls. Lest we doubt the metaphorical violence of such entrapments, the TV imagery turns to brutal pro-wrestling footage.

"The DDT." More wrestling, as fierce as it is fraudulent.

"At Home Yet Again." The baby is learning to talk! But the world remains a difficult place to embrace and understand, as we're reminded by the fragmented structure of the nature shots inserted here.

"September." The camera's mediating function is reasserted as we see Varela in silhouette while he shoots, and as we observe the highly diffused look of the nature shots he's taking, (Some shots in this segment recall the radically abstract visions of *Text of Light*, in which Brakhage transforms a household object into a quasi-cubist montage of line, form, and color.) This highlights a central theme of *Making Is Choosing* and other key Varela works: the complex dialogue between (a) reality as a scene to be represented and (b) as raw material for the artist's impulse to create a personal, internalized world that may or may not correspond to the actualities around us.

"Let Us Give Thanks." The baby is happy, the house and yard are in good shape, and football fills the TV screen. This is the very embodiment of domesticity. It is also the mediated, transmogrified, and artfully arranged vision of a profoundly personal artist who *both* preserves *and* transmutes the realities he records.

"Good Friday." Crucifixions. Are the bloodiest preoccupations of Christianity a route to transcendence or a fixation on apocalyptic morbidity? Or both, mesmerizing the popular imagination precisely because of the irresolvable nature of their millennia-old dance?

"He Is Risen." As if to emphasize the irresolvable nature of the multifaceted paradoxes, contradictions, and conundrums that he has been exploring throughout the film, Varela approaches its conclusion by evoking religious mysticism more strongly than at any earlier point. The baby, the artificial skeleton, and the TV set are overborne by the indelible image of Charlton Heston as Moses, parting the Red Sea before our very eyes. O spirituality! O humanity! Hooray for Hollywood!

"The Merry Month of May." The dancing disc of light. Expressionistic household views. The baby and the TV set, now showing Senator Orrin Hatch, surely the Charlton Heston of Washington politicians. And most important, the sound of a monologue about boredom, accompanied by a suggestively dark screen. Among the speaker's statements is a straightforward clue to an ultimate paradox that must trouble any artist with a self-critical sensibility: "I don't have anything to say, but I have to say it anyway."

"Kuchar in Sun City." Varela and his gifted colleague shoot their cameras at and with each other. This foregrounds another puzzle: Is a successful artist an individual creator, or merely one member of a stylistic or generic school that thrives on shared ideas and influences? Or . . . both?

"Alone/Fall 1988." An empty street, a pop song, a bent body, a praying man in silhouette. And subtitles: "Lamb of God/that taketh away/the sins of the world." The conclusion of *Making Is Choosing* is as mysterious, as melancholy, as comforting, and as ineffable as

the images and juxtapositions that we have encountered throughout it. There are no answers here, just a series of questions and
conundrums too all-embracing to solve but too urgent and immanent to ignore.

It is no wonder that Varela is drawn to cemeteries and churches
so often in this and other works. They are dancing grounds of
liminality—places where the living and the dead, the earthly and
the sublime, the static and the dynamic, the physical and the meta-
physical blend into one another with discomfiting ease.

Varela's refusal to conceptualize the world in limiting "either/
or" terms is reflected in a message he sent to me when I inquired
about the personal circumstances that surrounded the period
when *Making Is Choosing* was filmed and edited. It reads in part: " . . .
there is danger in getting too comfortable and yet there is also
danger in being too detached, too much for yourself . . . and not
being able to forge a relationship that isn't boring or confining but
that is still secure and warm and trusting. I haven't found that
yet . . . but looking back on this film, there are many clues as to my
state of mind, especially since I 'should' have been happy and content, instead I was like a caged animal just waiting to get some
breathing room. A fragmented life, indeed. Many selves. . . ."

Admirers of serious cinema are fortunate that Varela has chosen
to probe and explore his "many selves" through sensitively conceived,
meticulously crafted cinematic meditations. A poet of the liminal,
the dialogic, the carnivalesque, and the unfathomable, he has
brought a unique blend of philosophical insight, political seriousness, and aesthetic imagination to avant-garde film and video.

INDEX

Bakhtin, Mikhail, 120, 139–40, 141, 142, 143, 241; Bakhtinian, 142, 147; "material bodily lower stratum," 151n2

Ballard, J. G., 125

ballet, 107n5

Balzac (Honoré de), 71

Bamboozled. See Lee, Spike

Band, The, 218. See also *Last Waltz, The*

Banks, Russell, xxii, 214, 215–16; *Affliction,* 214; *Sweet Hereafter, The,* 214

Barbie (doll), 114

Bardot, Brigitte, xxvii, 176, 177

Barker, L., *Quest for Earthlight* series, 78

Battleship Potemkin, The. See Eisenstein, Sergei

Bay, Michael, *Pearl Harbor,* 160

Bazin, André, 169, 179, 180

BBC (British Broadcasting Corporation), xxiv, 83, 85, 100, 109, 111, 112, 114, 116

Beat Generation, 35, 210, 214. *See also* Burroughs, William S.; Ginsberg, Allen; Kerouac, Jack

Beatles, The, 113. See also *Yellow Submarine*

Beatty, Warren, 43; codirector and actor in *Heaven Can Wait,* 42

beauty, inner, 80

bebop, bop, 211; "spontaneous bop prosody" (*see* Kerouac, Jack)

Beckett, Samuel, 43, 102, 129; *Waiting for Godot,* 43

Belmondo, Jean-Paul, 175

Bellucci, Monica, 184, 194n3

Benjamin, Walter, 220, 225

Bennett, Alan, 113

Benning, Sadie, 226

Bergen, Ronald, 133

Bergman, Ingmar, xvii

Betrayal. See Pinter, Harold

Bettelheim, Bruno, *Uses of Enchantment, The,* 80

Bevan, Tim, 135

Beyond the Fringe, 113

Beyond the Law. See Mailer, Norman

Bicycle Thief, The. See De Sica, Vittorio

Big Lebowski, The. See Coen, Joel

Big Trail, The, 55

Bike Boy. See Warhol, Andy

Bin Laden, Osama, xxvi, 161

Bird. See Eastwood, Clint

Birth of a Nation, The. See Griffith, D. W.

blackface, 120

Blackmail. See Hitchcock, Alfred

Blair, Tony, 91

Blakely, Ronee, 224

Bleak Moments. See Leigh, Mike

blockbuster, 76, 133

Blonde Cobra. See Jacobs, Ken; Smith, Jack

Blood Simple. See Coen, Joel

Blood Work. See Eastwood, Clint

Blow-Up. See Antonioni, Michelangelo

body language, 101, 141

Boltanski, Christian, 162, 173

Book of Daniel, The. See Doctorow, E. L.

bop. *See* bebop, bop

boredom, 90

Boston University, xv

Bottle Rocket. See Anderson, Wes

bourgeois, 95, 97, 115, 126; values, 94, 99; *hautes bourgeoises,* 98

Box Play, The. See Leigh, Mike

Brakhage, Jane, 232

Brakhage, Stan, xxix, xxx, 204, 223, 226, 231–35, 240, 247
   Book: *Metaphors on Vision,* 233
   Films: *Aftermath,* 234; *Arabic Numeral Series,* 234; *Desistfilm,* 223; *Dog Star Man,* xiv, 226; *ellipsis* (. . .), 226; *Garden of Earthly Delights,* 226; *Interim,* 231; *Mothlight,* 294; *Murder*

Hayek, Salma, 195, 199–201, 208, 211
Hayworth, Rita, 28
HDTV, 201
Heart of Darkness. See Conrad, Joseph
Hearts and Minds. See Davis, Peter
Heat. See Warhol, Andy
Heaven Can Wait. See Beatty, Warren
Heaven's Gate. See Cimino, Michael
Heidbreder, Bill, 26, 29, 30. See also
    Cinemania
Heinrichs, Rick, 135
Helgeland, Brian, 36, 39. *See also*
    Eastwood, Clint, *Mystic River*
Hell, 148, 149, 187, 193
Help! (magazine). *See* Gilliam, Terry;
    Kurtzman, Harvey
hermeneutics, 118
Herzog, Werner, *Aguirre, the Wrath of
    God,* 159
Heston, Charlton, 248
Hi, Mom! See De Palma, Brian
High Hopes. See Leigh, Mike
High Noon, 74
Hill, Gary, 226
Hill, John, 94, 95
Hill, Roberta, 26, 27, 30. See also
    Cinemania
Hiroshima, mon amour. See Resnais, Alain
Hispanic, 247
historian, 51, 94, 161, 166, 167, 170,
    202, 203; historiography, 50
history, historical, 51, 56, 57, 58, 71,
    72, 77, 106, 109, 112, 117, 121,
    153, 154, 158, 159, 160, 165,
    170, 173, 192, 194n5, 198, 202,
    206, 209, 217, 226, 229, 234;
    consciousness, 50; film, 30;
    production, 132, 136, 150n1
Hitchcock, Alfred, 151n4 204;
    Blackmail, 202; *Psycho,* 23, 151n4;
    Vertigo, 23
Hitler (Adolf), 71, 120

hoax, 140
Hobbes, Thomas, 14
Hobbit, The. See Tolkien, J. R. R.
Hoffman, Dustin, 49
Holden, Anthony, 79
Holliday, Billie, 200
Hollywood, xv, xvi, xxi, xxix, 4, 5, 6, 8,
    9, 10, 20, 24, 25, 30, 31, 33, 36,
    39, 42, 43, 44, 50, 53, 54, 57, 58,
    72, 117, 121, 125, 133, 134,
    137, 155, 156, 157, 158, 160,
    162, 164, 173, 176, 177, 178,
    210, 216, 222, 223, 229, 230,
    231, 247, 248
Holocaust, xxv–xxvi, 161, 162, 165,
    166, 167, 168, 169, 170, 171
Holocaust (miniseries), 166
*Holocaust and the Literary Imagination,
    The. See* Langer, Lawrence
Holy Fool, xxiv
home movies, 215, 229, 233
Homer, *Odyssey, The,* 138, 149, 177,
    178, 182; Homeric, 158, 177, 181
Home Sweet Home. See Leigh, Mike
homophobe, homophobic, 120,
    186, 192
homosexual, 184, 185
Hornung, Richard, 135
Hook. See Spielberg, Steven
Hooper, Tobe, *Texas Chain Saw
    Massacre, The,* 151n4
Hopper, Dennis, *Easy Rider,* 48,
    154, 217
horror (film), 4, 53, 55, 124, 125,
    126, 129, 155
horror(s), 135, 144, 154, 160, 161,
    165, 172, 179
horror-comic, 141
Hotel New Hampshire, The. See Irving,
    John
*Hotel Terminus: The Life and Times of
    Klaus Barbie. See* Ophuls, Marcel

Paik, Nam June, xiv
painterly, 217; painting(s), 25, 85, 222
Palance, Jack, xxvii, 176, 177. *See also*
    Godard, Jean-Luc, *Contempt*
Palin, Michael, 110, 111, 114, 115,
    118–19, 120, 123. *See also* Monty
    Python
Palmer, Tony, 223
Panavision, 202
panning-and-scanning, 25
paradox, paradoxically, xxix, 71, 104,
    121, 179, 244, 248; paradoxical,
    139, 240
Paramount (Pictures), 134, 156
paranoia, 155, 193; paranoid, 126,
    144, 147
paratexts, 139
Parker, Charlie, xxi, 38
parodic, parody, 115, 118, 120, 121,
    122, 139, 140, 142, 143, 149,
    150, 218, 223; genre, 138
Passion of Joan of Arc, The. See Dreyer,
    Carl
Passion of the Christ, The, xiv
passivity, 94
pastiche, 113
Patch Adams, 23
pathology, 28
patriotic, 246; patriotism, 173, 242
patronize, 93
Patton, George S., Jr., 158
Patton. See Coppola, Francis Ford;
    North, Edmund H.
Payne, Alexander, *About Schmidt,*
    xxi, 46
Pearl Harbor. See Bay, Michael
Peckinpah, Sam, 57, 121; *Ride the High
    Country,* 57
pedophile, 152
Peña, Richard, xxxi
Pennies From Heaven. See Potter, Dennis
Perfect Film. See Jacobs, Ken

performance art, xxi, 54, 65, 109, 200,
    201, 212, 214
performance studies, xxii
permissive (society), 94
phenomenological, 241
Philip Glass Ensemble, The, xvii
philistine, 83
philosopher, philosophical,
    philosophy(ies), 17, 27, 28, 32,
    34, 39, 80, 101, 102, 123, 166,
    178, 179, 183, 185, 188, 189,
    190, 192, 199, 220, 227, 237,
    238, 241, 249
Picasso, Pablo, 231
Picasso at the Lapin Agile. See Martin,
    Steve
Piccoli, Michel, 177
Pierrot le fou. See Godard, Jean-Luc
Pilate, Pontius, 117
Pink Flamingos. See Waters, John
Pinter, Harold, 103, 187; *Betrayal,* 187
platitudes, 94, 98, 103
play(s), 20, 84, 100, 104, 124, 200,
    204, 213, 235; playwright, 235
Playboy (magazine), 154
Play for Today (BBC-TV), 100
poem(s), 173, 234; 3-D (*see* Jacobs,
    Ken, writer, 3-D poems)
poet, poetic, poetry, xxix, 20, 71, 86,
    161, 165, 173, 177, 183, 204, 224,
    242, 249; poetically, 244; film-
    making, 227; poeticization, 221
Poetic Justice. See Frampton, Hollis
Poitier, Sidney, *Let's Do It Again,* 5
Polanski, Roman, 145; *Chinatown,* 48;
    Rosemary's Baby, 33
polemic, 100, 159; polemical, 234;
    polemicist, 227
political, politics, xxiii, xxv, 13, 14, 24,
    29, 71, 73, 83, 84, 87, 88–89, 92,
    93, 94, 95, 96, 97, 99, 101, 102,
    105, 116, 117, 118, 119, 121,